The Formation of Critical Realism

D1617570

This series of interviews, conducted in the form of exchanges between Roy Bhaskar and Mervyn Hartwig, tells a riveting story of the formation and development of critical realism.

Three intersecting and interweaving narratives unfold in the course of this unfinished story: the personal narrative of Roy Bhaskar, born of an Indian father and English mother, a child of post-war Britain and Indian partition and Independence; the intellectual narrative of the emergence and growth of critical realism; and a world-historical story, itself theorised by critical realism in its discussion of the development of modernity.

This book gives an invaluable account of the development of critical realism, and its consolidation as a leading philosophy of our times. It takes us through the major moments of its formation, the principal objections to and controversies within critical realism, the establishment of its institutions, and considers its limits and future development. Special features of the book include discussion of the genesis of critical realism, and the origins and nature of the so-called dialectical and spiritual turns.

The informal dialogical style of *The Formation of Critical Realism* makes it compelling reading and an invaluable source for students of critical realism as well as all those interested in the intellectual story of our times.

Roy Bhaskar is the originator of the philosophy of critical realism and the author of many acclaimed and influential works, including *A Realist Theory of Science*, *The Possibility of Naturalism*, *Scientific Realism and Human Emancipation*, *Reclaiming Reality*, *Philosophy and the Idea of Freedom*, *Dialectic: The Pulse of Freedom*, *Plato Etc.*, *Reflections on meta-Reality* and *From Science to Emancipation*. He is an editor of *Critical Realism: Essential Readings* and was the founding chair of the Centre for Critical Realism. Currently he is a World Scholar at the University of London Institute of Education.

Mervyn Hartwig is a leading commentator on critical realism, and the editor of and principal contributor to the recently published *Dictionary of Critical Realism*.

Ontological explorations
Other titles in this series:

The Formation of Critical Realism

A personal perspective

Roy Bhaskar with Mervyn Hartwig

Routledge
Taylor & Francis Group

LONDON AND NEW YORK

First edition published 2010
by Routledge
2 Park Square, Milton Park, Abingdon, Oxon, OX14 4RN

Simultaneously published in the USA and Canada
by Routledge
711 Third Avenue, New York, NY 10017

Routledge is an imprint of the Taylor & Francis Group,
an informa business

© 2010 Roy Bhaskar and Mervyn Hartwig

Typeset in Goudy by Swales & Willis Ltd, Exeter, Devon

British Library Cataloguing in Publication Data
A catalogue record for this book is available from the British Library

Library of Congress Cataloging-in-Publication Data
   The formation of critical realism : a personal perspective /
   Roy Bhaskar with Mervyn Hartwig. — 1st ed.
   p. cm.
   Includes bibliographical references (p.) and index.
   1. Bhaskar, Roy, 1944-—Interviews. 2. Philosophers—
   Great Britain—Interviews. 3. Critical realism—History.
   I. Hartwig, Mervyn. II. Title.
   B1618.B474A5 2010
   149'.2—dc22
   2009040911

ISBN 10: 0-415-45502-2 (hbk)
ISBN 10: 0-415-45503-0 (pbk)
ISBN 10: 0-203-87808-6 (ebk)

ISBN 13: 978-0-415-45502-2 (hbk)
ISBN 13: 978-0-415-45503-9 (pbk)
ISBN 13: 978-0-203-87808-8 (ebk)

Contents

Preface

The interviews contained in this book were done over a period between August 2007 and March 2008. By August 2008 they were very largely edited, but this process was not completed until over a year later owing mainly to illness on Roy's part (see p. 200).

They tell the story of the *philosophical* formation of critical realism from the inside by its chief architect. This was a dialectical, and at times dramatic, process involving both what Roy calls a continuing struggle to be 'in his dharma', to do what he is best at doing, and successive critiques, and auto-critiques, of his pre-existing thought, in the course of which lacunae were identified and remedied. This process took critical realism philosophically through several distinct phases and levels of development, the main ones of which are original or basic critical realism, dialectical critical realism and the philosophy of meta-Reality. The struggles involved in this process took place in the context, and against the background, of struggles and upheavals in the wider society in which Roy lived, developments which form an essential part of the narrative of the book.

It is important to stress that this story is only of the *philosophical* formation of critical realism, and it is even then a personal perspective, because we would argue that critical realism has been practised in science and social science for centuries, and it is precisely the rationality of this practice that Roy's work has attempted to bring out. But it has not been self-conscious, and we would argue that it is explicit ex ante, philosophically self-conscious metatheory that is needed now, especially in the human sciences, precisely insofar as their practitioners are besieged by warring methodologies and philosophical standpoints, between which they are asked to choose (or make the choice of abstaining from choice). There is a sense in which we are all philosophers now. In this context the task that critical realism sets itself of 'philosophical underlabouring' has never been more urgent.

At the same time, Roy held in his work that philosophy only gets its importance and interest from engaging with the sciences and other human practices, especially practices oriented to human emancipation, and although much of his work has been done in relative isolation, it could not have been accomplished without the nourishment and support he has received from friends and colleagues in other disciplines. In the 1970s this involved relatively clandestine meetings with other self-conscious critical realists, then in the 1980s and early 1990s through annual

Realism and the Human Sciences conferences and cognate events such as the Chesterfield conferences through to the formation of the Centre for Critical Realism in 1995 and subsequently the formation of the International Association for Critical Realism in 1997. These have indeed sustained him.

These interviews have also been conversations; for if Roy has been the chief philosophical architect of critical realism, they have been conducted by one who arguably knows more about his work (and a fortiori philosophical critical realism) than he does! The questions contribute much to the dialogical process, which we believe will be genuinely informative about the formation of critical realism both for critical realists and for those who are just interested in its story or what it has to say. These conversations were also enjoyable encounters for the participants, and we hope some of this will pass over to its readers.

Unless Roy is explicitly indicated as the author, the notes to the text are by Mervyn. Their main purpose is to supply references for material in the questions.

We are very grateful to Jenny Cobner for typing the transcript of the interviews and to Cheryl Frank for expertly recording them.

Roy Bhaskar with Mervyn Hartwig
September 2009

Abbreviations

Note: square brackets indicate planned books that evolved into others or remain unpublished.

CCR	Centre for Critical Realism
CN	critical naturalism
DCR	dialectical critical realism
[DM]	[*Dialectic and Materialism*] (evolved into [DMHE])
[DMHE]	[*Dialectics, Materialism and Human Emancipation*] (evolved into *DPF*)
DPF	*Dialectic: The Pulse of Freedom*
[DST]	[*Dialectical Social Theory*]
EC	the theory and practice of explanatory critique
[EMS]	[*Empiricism and the Metatheory of the Social Sciences*] (evolved into *RTS, PN, SRHE*)
FSE	*From Science to Emancipation*
[HKHM]	[*Hume, Kant, Hegel, Marx*]
[HWP]	[*Critical History of Western Philosophy*]
IACR	International Association for Critical Realism
MELD	1M–2E–3L–4D (the ontological–axiological chain [DCR])
MELDARA	1M–2E–3L–4D–5A–6R–7A (the ontological–axiological chain [PMR])
MR	*The Philosophy of meta-Reality, Volume I*
PE	*Plato Etc.* (originally entitled *Philosophy and the Dialectic of Emancipation*)
[PES]	[*Some Problems about Explanation in the Social Sciences*] (evolved into [EMS])
[PI]	[*Philosophical Ideologies*]
PIF	*Philosophy and the Idea of Freedom*
[PM]	[*The Philosophy of Money*]
PMR	the philosophy of meta-Reality
PN	*The Possibility of Naturalism*
[PU]	[*Philosophical Underlabouring*]
RR	*Reclaiming Reality*

RTS	*A Realist Theory of Science*
SEPM	synchronic emergent powers materialism
SRHE	*Scientific Realism and Human Emancipation*
TDCR	transcendental dialectical critical realism
TMSA	transformational model of social activity
TR	transcendental realism

1 Childhood and adolescence

Dialectic of alienation and
wholeness (1944–1963)

MH: In this interview I would like you to delineate and reflect on the processes of formation of your identity and dharma in childhood and adolescence: the story of how, to use the terms of your dialectical philosophy, your core universal human nature came together with the rhythmics of your world-line and complex social mediations to constitute the concretely singular person Ram Roy Bhaskar – the self who is yourself, fundamental to which I take it is your mission in life as a philosopher of emancipation. The concept of personal identity will be familiar enough to most readers, pertaining in your scheme of things to the actual embodied person and their stratified personality as it develops. In its structural aspect it corresponds to 1M in the ontological–axiological chain (MELD), as does the concept of dharma. Can you begin by unpacking the concept of dharma a little, which you formally introduced into your philosophy in I think *From East to West*?[1]

RB: As I understand and use it, the concept of dharma refers to what could be called the unique genius of every person. If you look for synonyms you might think of 'vocation' or 'calling'. What is pretty close to it is the Greek term *ergon*, which is often translated as 'function'. It is basically what a person is good at, what comes easily to them. If you want an analogy, you could say the sun's dharma is to shine; it is what comes easily to it, it is its nature. Of course, people have many other aspects to their identity and personality. In the early Vedic use of the term a banal sense of dharma might have been an identification of the caste system, for instance, the notion that it is your dharma to be a Brahmin. In a lot of Indian philosophy it would often be translated into English as 'duty' but, in the sense in which I use it, it is only your duty in the way in which it is natural to do it. And everyone has a dharma, everyone has a set of things that they are best at doing. Of course, what your dharma is you might not know, it might take a long quest to actually discover what it is. And what it is will depend on a whole lot of social conditions and will change. If a person has a dharma to be, say, a mathematician or a musician, in general the fulfilment of that dharma will depend on being born into a family and living in a society that has mathematics and music among its practices and the instruments and other material means for engaging in them. And since a person's dharma is socially nurtured and developed, it will also be changing in the course of their life.

I think one of the dangers is for people to think that they have to give a description, or complete description, of their dharma or vocational calling. Thus to describe me as a philosopher might be pretty obvious, but in the context of a discussion, say, of globalisation with a group of economists, if one of them describes Roy as a philosopher that can have the connotation that Roy is only a philosopher and cannot therefore contribute in a meaningful way to the discussion. In contemporary Indian philosophy there is a reaction against this tendency always to define dharma. It is like the tendency to define what you might get at in prayer or meditation. Actually, what you can say more easily is what prayer or meditation is not; this is what is called the negative way. And most people perhaps have a greater sense of what they cannot do, or do not want to do, or what does not come easily to them, than of something positive that they can readily do. And when they do have something positive that they feel is their dharma they might not be able to verbalise it.

Finally, one can make a contrast between dharma and karma. Dharma is what comes most naturally to you, what is your element in life, and karma is a set of circumstances that you have to accept, the presence of the past, the nature of the context under which you operate, the conditions you inherit. For the moment that is all I want to say about dharma.

MH: Am I right in thinking that it aligns with your meta-Reality concepts of the transcendentally real self and ground-state?

RB: Absolutely. We will talk about that when we come to meta-Reality.

MH: Could you now indicate a few basic parameters of your childhood and adolescence – when and where you were born, your father, your mother, the schools you went to and so on?

RB: I was born in London in Hampton Court in 1944, towards the end of the Second World War. I was the first child of a family of two boys. My father was a doctor who met my mother in Brighton. My mother had been acting as a nurse, but by the time I was born she was performing all the functions that a GP's wife at that time characteristically performed, keeping the books, acting as a part-time secretary, and generally making things tick. I was given the name Ram Roy Bhaskar. Until I went up to Oxford in 1963 I was basically living with my parents and a younger brother, Krishan, first in Teddington in south-west London then at Weybridge in Surrey. As for my schooling, I was at what was called a prep school – Gate House, Kingston – until the age of thirteen. Then at St Paul's public school in Hammersmith, west London.

MH: Not everyone gets to be born in Hampton Court Palace. How did that come about?

RB: It had been commandeered as a hospital during the war.

MH: Tell us a little bit about your mode of being as a child in phenomenological terms. How do you remember those times, what were your leading themes and experiences?

RB: I think, perhaps, I could best put this in the context of a social conflict centring on my father's desire that I should become a doctor and my own reception, reaction and resistance to it. Calling it my father's desire is to put it a bit mildly; it was more or less a presumption that I would be a doctor.

MH: He knew your dharma already, right from the outset?

RB: That was it. I was to be made in his own image. He told my brother and me early on that we would have to be self-made men like himself, he was not going to leave us an inheritance. I should explain that my father had come from India just before the Second World War. His family were local Brahmins in the town of Gujranwala[2] near Lahore. The second son of a family of five, his own father (my grandfather) was an engineer in the Indian Railways, but when the eldest son became family head my father was cut off. My father, who had trained as a doctor, came penniless to England to do his FRCS (Fellowship of the Royal College of Surgeons) in 1939 – which as it turned out he was unable to do because of the war. However, ably assisted by my mother, he soon built up a thriving medical practice, first in Brighton and then in south-west London. Although he characteristically voted Tory, he had identified with Mahatma Gandhi, Jawaharlal Nehru and the Congress Party in the struggle for Indian Independence and became a great supporter of the National Health Service when it was introduced. My mother was English. She lost her father at birth during the First World War and was taken by her mother to South Africa. She returned to England just before World War Two and worked as a nurse in Brighton, where she met and married my father. There was strong opposition to the marriage on both sides of the family; one aunt from my mother's side attended the wedding and that was about it. After her marriage, my mother assumed an Indian identity; her maiden name was Marjorie and she now took the name Kamla. She and my father became adherents of Theosophy – basically Hinduism for westernised Indians – and remained such for the rest of their lives. The whole family was essentially an Indian family. My mother accepted this very willingly and happily I should say. But there weren't many Indian families in London at the time, not the number there are now. We were somewhat isolated. We lived in a house where the next Indian family was miles away, but even so there were Indian families that we were in regular contact with; it was almost like a big extended family. Much of my childhood when I wasn't at school was spent accompanying my parents on visits to these other Indian families or to the various societies and functions my parents attended, especially the Theosophical Society. My father was prominent in all the main societies he joined: at one stage he was president of the Punjabi Society, the Hindu Society, another Indian Society, and the Rotary Club. And my mother was equally prominent in these societies, and in, for instance, the Inner Wheel (the female equivalent of Rotary). My father was also a Freemason; on Saturdays I would see him packing up a little bag and taking it off for his various ceremonies. I think he was a member of several lodges and again he rose to the fore in institutional terms. My parents led quite busy lives.

And then of course my father was a very busy doctor, and he used to like to take me with him in the car on his rounds. So I spent a great deal of my childhood just accompanying my parents, not really doing what I might have wanted to do as a child, but just being with them. And this meant that I had to try to compensate for what I perceived to be the poverty of the activities in which I was forced to engage. I developed quite an active fantasy world, more generally a kind of inner reflectedness, and I found myself very much leading a double life: the life of the imagination and the life I could find in play and in books (which I read avidly), as contrasted with the overt behaviour I had to display in the social world. This was compliant of me. Actually, perhaps it was only that it seemed compliant to me, because my parents told me when I was about eight or nine that from a very early age I was continually questioning them. So they had started calling me Tumoori, which is Punjabi for Bumble-Bee, because I was always busy and running around questioning. Another nickname they had for me was Why-Because. I would be so insistent on getting an answer to my question, an explanation, that as soon as I said 'why' I would come out with 'because', trying to prompt them, to get them to actually provide an explanation. I think I took up this style of questioning, this outer questioning, because of the disparity I experienced between, on the one hand, who I was in my inner life and what I really wanted to do or would do if unconstrained, and, on the other, the outer compliance I had to show in my overt behaviour. So in an inward way I was questioning, and continually questioning, as it were, both the world and myself.

From quite an early age I felt that I could not understand the presumption that I should be a doctor, and that indeed it was unacceptable to me; I knew I wouldn't make a good doctor, but there the presumption was, and it would not go away. This was in fact the central conflict of my youth, and I was very aware of it from an early age. Partly because of the amount of time I had to spend with my father, I was very aware of what he was doing as a doctor and so of the fate that awaited me. In this phase of my youth there was thus a split between my inner reflectedness, my inner being, and my outer activity. What I started to do was not just question my parents and other authorities but to fight, in Gramscian terms, a war of position. I tried to out-manoeuvre them gradually, and then to seize an opportunity to have an engagement on favourable terrain. For example, I overheard my father telling some other Indian in London that he was quite wrong to stop his daughter marrying who she wanted to. I put it to him that, just as there are false/forced marriages, particularly strongly imposed on girls, so there are false/forced careers, particularly strongly imposed on boys. I seized the opportunity of my father's principled defence of free marriages to put in a point about careers.

MH: You caught him out in a theory–practice inconsistency.

RB: Really, the hypocrisy of parental positions was very apparent to me, and it led me at quite an early stage to develop criteria of what it was to be a good person. I thought at the time there were two criteria. The most important was theory and practice consistency. A good person is one who walks their talk. But closely following on from that there was universalisability, and this was something that struck me quite early. For example, when I was in India (my father took us there twice in our childhood) I would see beggars who were clearly not enjoying the privileges or rights that my family and people with whom they associated enjoyed, and I would want to know why. (There were of course beggars in London, but I did not get to see many of them.) Or again my parents were very disapproving of a boy who was my best friend because he was the son of a publican. To them he was a kind of outcaste. The questioning part of me wanted to know, well, what is the difference? When I saw differences all around me I wanted a ground for the difference.

This whole issue was closely connected to two concerns. One was a concern with freedom, and the root of that was a concern for my own freedom. The concept of dharma, I think, goes particularly well with such a conception of freedom, in which freedom is as much about who you are and what you can become as it is about what you do or what you have. The other concern was for social justice, because where there is a difference that cannot be grounded this is a form of injustice. As Thomas Hobbes I think put it, it is a moral absurdity. If the sort of life I was leading, certainly from the age of seven or eight, was a split life, what then was the contrast? Well, it was a life of wholeness or unity. I understood that being aware of possibilities meant that I could play. I could be whole in fantasy. But the notion of being whole in physical actuality was also of course very important. I spent a tremendous amount of time playing games, especially cricket. I felt whole when I played cricket, and I felt whole when I read or when my parents were talking to me (rather than at me) about their experiences, such as my father's involvement in the struggle of the Congress Party for Indian Independence, or my mother's experience as a school girl in South Africa. But obviously I had a notion that one could be whole all the time and not just in play and occasional moments of fulfilling activity. So, alongside the criteria for what it is to be a good person, there was a criterion of integrity, of wholeness. This was what I really wanted. I wanted to be not just a good person but to be whole, and that meant that I had to fulfil my dharma, I had to be doing what came naturally to me, what I was best at doing, what I had a bent for.

MH: So what you had going, really – we can see in retrospect – was a dialectic of alienation (split) and wholeness, the interplay of negative and positive conditions, as you struggled to come into your dharma.

RB: That's right. If one goes back to the period before I was about eleven, if I had been asked what I really wanted to do then, I would probably have said I wanted to be a sportsman. I would do anything to be involved in a game of cricket. I always wanted to be a cricketer with a slight difference though. From about the age of nine I wanted to edit a cricketing annual. I wrote to famous cricketers of the day, such as Len Hutton and Peter May, asking them to contribute to my annual, and a surprising number said they would. I remember Peter May saying, well, you have told me you are meant to be a doctor, but you want to be a cricketer; I can just see you as a captain of England! But by the age of eleven I started getting very bad hay fever and that more or less put paid to my cricketing aspirations. I developed other interests and obsessions. Music was a way of escaping. I could get lost in music, particularly classical music; later I found that possibility also there in pop music, especially in dance. I probably most enjoyed getting lost in books, and this was a recurring pleasure, not a phase-specific one like cricket. It became a symbol or badge of my identity. When I had to accompany my father, say, on his shopping trips to Harrods or something like that, I would always try to secrete a book about my person, even if I knew that there was no possibility of reading it. Whenever my parents took me to the Theosophical Society I used to really enjoy that, not so much for the content of the lectures and so on – I didn't attend many of them – but for the time I would spend in the library (if I didn't have to look after the younger children), where I got lost in a world outside my life and existence.

MH: What did you read? Did you read indiscriminately?

RB: No, I wouldn't say indiscriminately; I would have a particular interest.

MH: Not just fiction?

RB: No, these were mainly factual books, books about American history, psychoanalysis, and so on. I felt I knew quite a lot about Theosophy as there were many Theosophical books in my parents' house, and also many books about religion, and about medicine. So when I went to the Theosophical Society library, which was a good one, I picked on the things that Theosophy did not talk about, and I also avoided religion in general and medicine. As for my attitude to Theosophy in those days, when I was in my early teens or younger, I felt it was OK as far as it went, but there were many questions that it did not address, or did not seem to address, and I was equally interested in them. And in so far as I was interested in Theosophy, it was a this-worldly interest, my concern was with how it could alter situations in the here and now. For, being subject at school to bullying and being on a life-path that I knew was not for me, I was very aware of what you might call permitted or officially sanctioned (or authorised) injustice – the kind of injustice that people come in for when they are born into a situation or a context in which they have very limited opportunities for fulfilment. I was already quite concerned about such issues, and I knew all the standard arguments, and the pros and cons on questions such as freewill and determinism and so on. This was one thing I certainly had to thank my parents for: they had a home full of books where I could read about such things.

MH: What specifically was OK about Theosophy, and how did it relate to your concern about 'permitted injustice'? Did it command your intellectual assent? Some of the ideas of the spiritual turn are also central to Theosophy; for example, the notion that all religions are attempts to approach the absolute, so each offers a perspective on the same underlying reality. Indeed, if you substitute 'norm' for 'religion', the motto of the Theosophical Society could serve as a motto informing all your work: 'There is no religion higher than truth.' And the 'three objects' of the original Theosophical Society founded by Helena Blavatsky and others in 1875 seem entirely compatible with your mature outlook: 'To form a nucleus of the universal brotherhood of humanity, without distinction of race, creed, sex, caste or colour; to encourage the study of comparative religion, philosophy and science; and to investigate the unexplained laws of nature and the powers latent in man.'[3]

RB: Well, the ethic of universal brotherhood and sisterhood and the commitment to systematic enquiry are certainly things I approved of. I wasn't really indoctrinated in these three objects, but it would certainly have been the case that I had come to some sort of awareness of their necessity or desirability independently. Because of my experiences of racial intolerance, and finding myself to be very much an outsider in most of the contexts in which I was involved, I came to question anything other than, say, the universal brotherhood and sisterhood of humanity or what it was supposed to connote. So I might have been happy to discover that these were the objects. But I think what attracted me about Theosophy most, abstracting from my parents' involvement in it, was an idea that you also find in some theological critical realists, funnily enough. (Of course I didn't know anything about them at the time.) This was the idea you mentioned that the different religions are different paths to essentially the same goal, which is knowledge of, or identification with, or bringing about, the absolute. To put it in theological critical realist terms, the different main teachings of these world religions are different conceptions of the absolute.

Actually this marks out a distinctive tradition of interpretation within all the great world religions, with the possible exception of Christianity save in more recent times. In Islam you have the Sufis, in Judaism you have Kabbalah; both groups consciously learned from other religious traditions. In Hinduism you have this as a specific doctrine, at least in Vedic or, you could say, esoteric

Hinduism. What all these positions did is formulate a contrast between the higher truth, which was known to the esoteric, and the ordinary truth. The higher truth said of some particular religion that this is *one* path (or sometimes this is the best path). Very often, of course, this is one path means merely in effect this is the path you have been introduced to, or that you should follow in a certain kind of society; it is *one* of the paths to the absolute. However the ordinary, common truth said this is the *only* path, the only way to the absolute. This split between refined and tolerant religion, on the one hand, and a religion that asserts a monopoly of truth, on the other, was very clear to me in my teens. This idea appeared in a popular form in esoteric Hinduism and Buddhism: that Rama, Krishna, and so on, were followed by Buddha, by Jesus, and perhaps Muhammad; so that these were all equally but differently avatars[4] or, as it were, messengers of God. This is one of the features of Theosophy that I particularly liked. The idea that there are different paths to the absolute is a very important feature, particularly for anyone who is going to profess a religion.

I myself was not really religious. I did quite enjoy religious ceremonial in small doses. I was somewhat indifferent as to what sort of ceremony it was: I was mainly interested in the experience. I had childhood experiences of transcendence in a Christian service or mass as much as I ever remember having them in a Hindu *puja*.

MH: How did you come to go to Christian services? Your parents surely didn't take you?

RB: Well, there is no reason why they should not have taken me. But they did not. For some of my childhood there was a live-in helper to my mother who was a Catholic, from Ireland. Her name was Tessie, and her bedroom was full of crucifixes, as you often find with Irish Catholics. She was extremely devout.

MH: Was she your nanny?

RB: No, I would say a generalised helper.

MH: You were very fond of her? I've heard tell that you attended her funeral in Ireland much later.

RB: Yes. My brother and I helped to bury her, and I visited her on several occasions after her retirement at the time of my mother's death.

Returning to the theme of religion, since I went to schools where religion was taught, there were many occasions on which I had to go into a church. At St Paul's you did not have to attend the morning ceremonies, you could do something else because there were many Jewish boys there, but in general in England at that time attending public schools involved going to church. Although I could sometimes enjoy the experience and the religious ceremonial, I wasn't particularly interested in religion for its own sake. I was interested rather in the great injustices that afflicted me and most, perhaps all, of humanity. My cast of mind was always this-worldly. Even when I got into the spiritual turn there were secular motives. I did not affiliate with any particular form of religion or substitute religion.

MH: The fact that you had a really rich childhood in terms of religious and spiritual experience was probably important for the spiritual turn. Most people are brought up just in the one tradition, you experienced a whole variety.

RB: Yes. Theosophy is in many ways a westernised version of Hinduism, and also Buddhism (it is a moot point exactly what the differences between Buddhism and Hinduism are). I think it is interesting, and something I would perhaps like to follow up, that while I was growing up some self-styled theological critical realists within the Christian tradition were starting to formulate a similar view to the Theosophical notion that all religions are different paths to essentially the same goal. I had no knowledge of this school, or its name, until well into the spiritual turn of the late 1990s.

MH: Did you go to Theosophical rituals or services of any kind?

RB: There was a youth section of the Society that they called the Round Table, which my parents enrolled me in. Its ceremonies were very much like the services of the Liberal Catholic Church that the prominent Theosophist Charles Webster Leadbeater founded in the early twentieth century within the Theosophical movement, which offered completely open communion involving the breaking of bread and the drinking of juice. My parents were very interested in what was called the Esoteric Section of the Theosophy Society, but I never had access to that, just as I did not have access to the secrets of Freemasonry. They did not break the rules in that sort of way.

MH: How did the fact that you had a Theosophical and Indian background pan out for you at school?

RB: One sees everywhere a kind of absurdity, the oppressive nature of the ordinary truth as distinct from the higher truth. These terms by the way are the terms that Shankara, an Indian sage of the eighth century CE, formulated. I remember my first day at my prep school. My very first lesson was a class on religious studies and the teacher who was taking it started proceedings by asking everyone who was Church of England to put up their hand, and then everyone who was Catholic, and then those who were Methodist or some other denomination of Christianity. Finally she asked for anyone who had not put up their hand to do so, and so I put up my hand. Then she asked me what my religion was, and I said, 'Well, I am not really sure. I believe there is good in all religions.' That was the vulgar form of the higher truth, the Theosophy that my parents had instilled in me. And the teacher said, 'You mean you're a heathen!'[5] I was mortified. What a different place the world would be if the critical realist form of Christianity in a theological sense was more prevalent, and of course if the Sufi attitude was more prevalent in Islam.

Shall we go back to the question of my central conflict?

MH: This is related to it. Your teacher was denying you your freedom in the same authoritarian way your father did, with a goodly dose of ethnocentrism and racism thrown in.

RB: Indeed, at my first school I was subjected to a lot of bullying. As I was of normal or slightly more than normal height, and I didn't wear specs or stand out in any very obvious way, I can only think that the only reason for it was the fact that I was known to have an Indian family and background. I certainly had an Indian name, and by the time I went to my second school, St Paul's, I decided to drop my Indian first name, Ram, and have myself called Roy.

MH: And kept it up until very recently. Did you dress differently?

RB: There was no Indian dress or anything like that, at least not for the boys. My father always wore a suit, my mother wore saris, but only when she went out to a dinner party or was entertaining. What I was trying to do by the time I went to St Paul's was to pass as English, to not allow myself to be identified as non-English or specifically Indian. There were many incidents in which my Indianness became an issue. For example, I can remember being subjected to the most horrific bullying at the time of the Suez invasion, starting with the headmaster, who was extremely irate about India's opposition to it, referring to 'naked fakirs'.

MH: The headmaster?

RB: Yes, and it wasn't a big school. 'Fakir' is a kind of pun. This stems from a remark made by Winston Churchill about Gandhi.[6] Stanley Baldwin was Prime Minister at the time. A fakir is just a holy man, but, rather like the Churchillian 'V' sign, it was interpreted and meant to be understood in a completely different way.

MH: So the head took it out on you?

RB: Yes, and of course that was a licence for the other students, some of whom were otherwise quite friendly to me, to take it out on me. It was mainly physical bullying, kicking at my shins and things like that. It did make my life pretty miserable at that school. I was rather relieved to go to St Paul's and be able to assume a relatively low profile and not be picked on for anything. I did get a reputation with some of the teachers for being somewhat naughty though. I couldn't resist trying to subvert pomposity and pretentiousness. For example, if the chemistry teacher, instead of teaching us about chemistry, was droning on about some textbook So-and-So had written, I might ask him insolently if he had found the book a good read, prompting his fury.

MH: What consequences did the bullying have for your identity? Did you identify as English or Indian, or both?

RB: I identified as neither. I didn't feel good about being called an Anglo-Indian because that referred to a caste of Englishmen –

MH: Was that by your headmaster, your school?

RB: No, I was thinking about myself. I didn't really feel good about calling myself an Indian, and I didn't really feel good about calling myself English, so the obvious thing might have been to call myself an Anglo-Indian.

MH: That's the Raj.

RB: That's right; one use of the term was to refer to English people who stayed on in India after the end of the Raj. Most of the time in England I was treated as an Indian, an Indian in England, and I quickly realised that I wasn't happy sustaining this identity, not only because of what it excluded me from in England but also because, when I went to India, I couldn't really identify as an Indian either. Indeed, the first thing that struck me as a young child was that everyone there was either too fat or too thin, too rich or too poor. I was horrified at the exclusiveness of the caste system and Indian society generally. It did not take me long to realise that this exclusiveness was also characteristic of British society, because it was very, very racist. If you were Indian you were basically excluded. And then my parents wanted to enforce a kind of class exclusion on me as well, that I shouldn't be friends with people who weren't suitable for me. I couldn't go along with this. From the standpoint of the inner questioning I was constantly engaging in, I just could not see any ground for the difference. It was obvious to me that lower-class people did not behave worse; but nor was I an inverted snob, I did not think they behaved better than middle-class people. Rather, my tendency was to identify with the underdog, so I would be inclined to feel very Indian in England. For instance, when the Indian cricket team came to England in 1952 they did terribly poorly, and I supported them. Similarly, when I was in India, I would stick up for the good points about England.

I eventually cottoned on to the fact that no society was perfect, although it did take me a while to come round to that view. Thus I became suspicious about why everyone was demonising the USSR (Stalinist Russia), and so when neither Indian nor English would fit as a description I made myself an honorary Soviet citizen. But I did not really have to wait for Khrushchev's speech in 1956 when I was twelve to realise that all was not right there. Indeed, by 1956 I was so impressed by the American opposition to the Suez adventure that I formed an attachment to the USA. What I was trying to do in a way was explore the good qualities, the things we were neglecting to mention or had forgotten when we were demonising the Soviet Union or being very disapproving of the United States, the things that were left out. This again was prompted by the nascent principle of universalisability. A little later on I was very taken by the idea that a society such as Brazil, where there did not seem to be the same overt racial conflict, might be able to transcend the difference between black and white. Then when I went to Oxford and joined many societies, I quickly became president or secretary of the Latin American Society. However, I soon came to feel very embarrassed about this. I realised that Brazil and much of Latin America was actually founded on a double oppression, first the oppression of the Indigenous or native American Indian people and then the oppression of imported people, that is, black slave labour and indentured Asian labour. In short, they were still very stratified and racist societies.

MH: Both classist and racist.

RB: Yes. Siding with the underdog and going against what seemed to be the conventional wisdom were perhaps my two most characteristic dispositions. And what in a way underlay them both was the fact that I was, and experienced myself as, very marginalised.

MH: You yourself were an underdog, subject to many constraints. Returning now to the number one constraint, your being put on the path of being a doctor: what strategies did you develop to overcome it?

RB: For a while I had a compromise solution: I would become a psychoanalyst, which meant that I would qualify as a doctor but then do the sort of thing that I knew myself to be interested in, studying people. By the time I started doing science, and more particularly biology, I realised that not only was I not good at drawing, but I abhorred dissection; I was very bad at the practical side of biology. I was also very aware that my father led, despite his interest in religious philosophy and the many societies he belonged to, what would be for me a very boring life.

MH: Aspiring to conform, to be conventional –

RB: Yes, and going on his rounds and seeing one person after another with the common cold. I didn't think I would have the patience for that. On the other hand, I was really excited by ideas, I was very good at English and writing essays and I was interested in history and geography and subjects such as that.

Science was very boringly taught; I wasn't completely uninterested in it but I had a penchant for subjects like English and history. After doing O-levels we went to India for the summer holidays, and when my brother and I flew back for the beginning of term I seized the opportunity of my father's absence to go to the school authorities at St Paul's and suggest that they switch me from the science stream to a geography stream, as I felt my main subjects should be geography (which included some economics and a bit of politics), history and English and perhaps a bit of Latin or French. Their response was, 'Oh yes. That is a much better idea, because you are so good at English and history.' So they went along with it. Then my father arrived home four or five days later, found out what had happened and rang up and went to see the headmaster and the other relevant authorities and told them to put me back in the biology stream.

MH: An Indian doctor prevailed over the English public school headmaster. Did you have mixed feelings about that?

RB: I was more interested in my own freedom than my father's victory. My father was very good at bullying such people. Indeed, there were few people he could not bully. He lorded it over my mother too. I admired his forcefulness, but not the bullying. Because of my schools' compliance, I could never really identify much with them and really wasn't much influenced by them.

MH: In any way?

RB: No.

MH: I'll come back to that in a moment. Might not a way forward in your conflict with your father have been to devote yourself to a career in theoretical science? After all, there are scientific aspects to medicine and science has very considerable kudos in Theosophy.

RB: No, my father was insistent upon my being a doctor. Basically what he wanted was for me to first join and then succeed him. He was not interested in me being a pure scientist; he wasn't motivated by a fondness for science but rather by the desire that I should be doing the work in his practice. This was somewhat ironical because my brother, Krishan, who had been ear-marked as an accountant, actually wanted to do it I think. So he fulfilled my father's desire for him, going on to become an accountant.

MH: Might not pure science have satisfied you, however, even though it did not satisfy him?

RB: No, given the way science was taught at school, I wasn't much interested in science; I was interested in people, societies, politics, economics, history. And I was very interested in philosophy. I read a great deal of philosophy.

MH: You end up becoming a philosopher – and in the first instance a philosopher of science at that – to provide a basis for your interest in society.

RB: Absolutely.

MH: How did you get on with your brother?

RB: We were emotionally close and fond of each other, but the concentration of family power meant that there were also, perhaps inevitably, tensions. We also had differing interests and gradually drifted apart. Affection, however, remained.

MH: Do you have any regrets about your time as a public school boy?

RB: If you take it on a personal level, I think it did lead to a neglect of my formal schooling at St Paul's. I didn't actually spend very much time in school. It was possible just to go in, check in for the first lesson of the day, and then move out.

MH: For the whole day?

RB: Yes, I would often go and sit in a coffee bar in Hammersmith to read or talk with my friends; and of course it was a liberal regime that allowed that to happen. I would perhaps have felt differently if the school had supported my desire, my determination, to change streams. So what happened here was a kind of split between me and institutions. I became used to being an outsider, and even though I wasn't bullied as an Indian at St Paul's, I had become an outsider within the school. Moreover, I wasn't particularly interested in the subjects I was taking. I used to perk up when there was a general studies lesson, because I loved doing what we normally had to do, which was to write an essay. So good were my essays that I won the Lord Chancellor's English essay prize, which I suppose is some achievement in a school such as St Paul's. I was interested in the more theoretical side of science, and I realised that, whatever I eventually managed to be able to do, I would have done well at A-levels, so I mugged up on selected theoretical topics in all the science papers I was taking. I was very interested in the theory of evolution and in organic chemistry, which had just witnessed the discovery of DNA. I was excited by all that, and did very well – which was just as well, because my marks for the biology practical were one out of twenty. I have to say that they were so bad in biology because of my aversion to dissection.

MH: Was this perhaps related to your aversion to split, your yearning for wholeness?

RB: Yes, but also I was, at least in these kinds of things, manually indexterous, clumsy. Moreover, the particular dead animal we had to dissect in my A-level exam was a dogfish. I remember it vividly. Indeed, I have memories from a very early age of going past the fishmonger, who had a shop about ten doors from where we lived. And I used to hate the smell, and actually the sight of fish; it is something I found repulsive. The upshot of all this was that because dissection played such a large part in the career of a medical student, it seemed to me that I would never be able to make it, even if I had wanted to.

MH: Dead fish are rather repulsive, but if one likes eating them I guess one overcomes that. Were you a vegetarian at this stage? Were your parents vegetarians?

RB: They became vegetarians when war-time rationing was ended. I remember clearly the day. My father came into the room and announced it. My mother was making chicken soup, which was a favourite of mine, and I was very disappointed! However, since I no longer had to eat fish, or parts of the bodies of dead animals, I soon came happily to accept it.

Having decided that no society had got it right and that every human being deserves a chance, I became very interested in questions of exclusion and difference. It was not just that I tended to side with the underdog, I also looked for those who did not even rate as underdogs; those for instance who were not even in the caste system in India. For me everyone had a right to pursue their dharma. So I came to see my own struggle to be in my dharma as part of a wider struggle for everyone to be in their dharma. I supported and identified with the civil rights movement in America, nations such as Egypt which were being bullied by the West, and so on. And of course I was against all class and caste differences and all the intolerances that these differences are associated with.

MH: When did you become aware of the idea of being in your dharma?

RB: I don't remember.

MH: You would presumably have absorbed it as you were growing up.

RB: By my bed, in the room I shared with my brother, was a little bookcase with a sample of the 109 or so books my great-great grandfather was reputed to have written.

MH: He was a Brahmin priest?

RB: He was a Brahmin. I don't know whether he actually officiated as a priest or not; he would certainly have been a sage. These books were the background to my own father's interest in these things. As I've mentioned, he came from a Brahmin family, and traditionally the Brahmins were the priestly caste.

MH: To return to the issue of your not identifying with St Paul's. On your account, your coming into your dharma was in spite of the school more than because of it. Yet you have what strikes people as a public school persona. You ooze an establishment sort of confidence and charm.

RB: The confidence probably came from two or three other external sources as well – the facts that my father was a Brahmin and that he seemed to get his way in whatever he did, that he had become a self-made man in England, and that my mother was extremely able and universally loved.

MH: And then there are more specific things, such as being familiar with classical Greek. This is one of the things that rubs off on you in public schools.

RB: I didn't actually do Greek at St Paul's. I was always very interested in concepts and often they did not have a good name in English. I basically learnt most of what I know about Greek from my father's books in the first instance, especially medical texts and reference books.

I don't want to deny the possibility of public school influence, but in fact it is probably just as true to say that it was I who had a bit of an impact on St Paul's, though not in the customary way. Every Monday the expected thing was that you should do something called CCF (Combined Cadet Force), which entailed dressing up in military uniform – either army, air force or navy – and then performing various drills, including shooting and things like that. Now I was very sympathetic to pacifism and certainly did not like the idea of war. I was a supporter of CND (Campaign for Nuclear Disarmament). There was an alternative to CCF which was the Boy Scouts, which I joined. But as a Boy Scout you had to go to school on a Monday dressed in short trousers, and I felt a bit stupid doing that in Hammersmith, going on the tube in short trousers. I was well over six feet by then, and you were also supposed to wear a beret, and I certainly wasn't happy doing that. The only alternative was to do PT (Physical Training), which involved a very tortuous form of retribution for those who were unwilling to bite the bullet and do CCF. So a few friends and myself thought up another alternative and tried to get the school to accept it – which it did. This alternative was social work, going around the houses of Hammersmith and neighbouring areas and knocking on doors and just check-ing whether people needed anything or whether they knew their rights, whether they had the television reception they were entitled to, whether they were drawing their unemployment benefit if unemployed, and so on. This was a great success, not least with the school authorities, and it is now part of the school curriculum. Here was the answer for me as an outsider. I was able to take advantage of being on the margin to advance not only my own interests, thus making life easier for myself, but also something that was much more useful generally.

Another example of this was my reaction to the prescribed sports: rugby, boxing and cricket. Now, because of my hay fever, cricket was out for me, I didn't like rugby, and on pacifist grounds, as well as having had enough of bullying at my first school, I didn't like boxing. Again I thought up with a few friends ways of getting the school to accept an alternative. This was golf. My father used to play golf at a local golf club (Fulwell) and one of my fellow students at St Paul's at the time was a Portuguese junior international; this lent some credibility to our suggestion, which once again was accepted. What this meant in practice was that, after a hole or two of golf, I could have the rest of Wednesday afternoons off in my own home listening to music, and at the same time the range of options available to my fellow students had been expanded.

I think what had a permanent impact on me, and one that I regret somewhat, was the split between myself and the institution, between myself and formal schooling. There are two sorts of outsiders, and I was lucky enough to be the first. This is the kind of outsider who is in some way also inside – an insider outsider. Being on the margins can be very useful for such an outsider because, if you think of the margins as on a page, being on the margins allows you to be aware of other pages in the book and other possibilities; you are forced to see many openings that are not otherwise immediately apparent. But I was also inside – I could see how it might be possible to turn the pages of the book – I was actually inside the school, I hadn't been thrown out, and I was in an Indian family, and both school and family provided enduring constraints that gave me something specific and concrete to try to transcend. So I always had a specific target, there was always something I was fighting against. Whereas if you are the second kind of outsider – an outsider outsider, just outside, without any institutions – then you can get completely lost or so demoralised that you cannot engage in successful struggle. I was able to engage in successful struggles.

MH: Did your desire for oneness manifest itself in relation to nature?

RB: If I was asked to choose between the house and the garden, I would always opt for the garden. I spent a great deal of time there. Much of it was actually throwing a ball against the wall and catching or hitting it, but some of it was just enjoying – for instance, the flowers. I remember feeling how nice it would be to be one with the grass, the lawn. My parents had a little bungalow by the sea in Brighton which they bought when I was about seven or eight, and the small garden opened up onto the beach. That was great for me, I could play beach cricket – there was often a game of cricket going on the beach – or alternatively I could just walk along the beach and experience the sublimity of nature. I loved looking up at the sky or looking out to the sea, or just listening to it. I felt there was a depth to nature that you would miss out on if you related to it as an outsider. If you could identify with it, be with it, be one with it, then it would reveal its depth and beauty to you and afford consolation and inspiration. I had access to the sublime in books and in my fantasy land but also, particularly to the sea and the sky, there was the sublime in nature. So I treated it as a most precious resource.

MH: On the face of it you had all the makings of a happy childhood – a holiday cottage, a well-to-do family, a culturally rich environment – and yet I get the feeling that you would actually define your childhood as unhappy, basically because you weren't given your head on the crucial issue of finding the right way for you. If so, it seems to have been paradoxically a very productive unhappiness in the end.

RB: Yes, I remember a slogan that was often trotted out: 'enjoy your schooldays, because they are the happiest days of your life'. Well, mine weren't, mainly because of the subjects I was forced to study. There were of course experiences that my parents shared with me or gave me that I was very happy about; travelling for instance. But the big question of my identity outweighed everything else. I imagine that this is the case for girls of sub-continental families who know that they are going to be forced to marry someone they have not chosen and even against their will. They might have many of the features of a happy childhood, but that will outweigh everything else.

MH: The lack of freedom.

RB: Yes. Because the child thinks of adult life as the period of fulfilment, it accepts that there are many things it cannot do now; but it has the hope that when it is grown-up it will be free to fulfil itself. Girls often have projected the state of marriage, boys are typically asked what they want to do. Actually I also asked myself this question because, while I knew I did not want to be a doctor, it was not clear to me that I knew what I positively wanted to be (other than perhaps that it would be something to do with people). Around the age of fifteen or sixteen, since I was really good at writing and loved doing it, I felt I might become a novelist and actually started writing a novel. I also felt that I was good at arguing and entertaining. What everyone, including my parents, liked me for was a capacity to make them laugh. My dad would often find it useful to have me in the room when he was talking and arguing with associates because I could come in and say something witty or light. Actually this was the great era of British comedy, with shows like *Beyond the Fringe*, and I thought about being a playwright. From what I knew about Jean-Paul Sartre – I admired him greatly – I thought you could just do this thing, write novels or plays, and I recorded sketches with friends. But as my D-Day approached I realised I would have to have another strategy, because you could not just become a novelist or comedian or philosopher or whatever, you had to pass A-levels and then you had to have admission to an appropriate institution. So having got A-levels, I realised that I could sit an entrance exam to Oxford or Cambridge which did not involve science. And so I took the modern studies entrance exam to Oxford and I won an exhibition – a form of scholarship – to Balliol College to read PPE (philosophy, politics and economics).

MH: What did you father think?

RB: He didn't know. One has to remember that I was fighting a Gramscian war of position and I was following the Taoist motto that the way to win a struggle is by preparation, stealth and speed. That was the stealth: you do not tell the enemy what you are going to do, otherwise he would have prevented me. He had even filled in my signature to medical school (unbeknown to me) and King's College Medical School had actually (I think) admitted me. So getting this scholarship enabled me to go to him and say, well look, I am going to Oxford to read PPE, I am not going to cost you anything, you don't have a leg to stand on. So he gave way.

MH: Did he come to terms with it?

RB: Formally he accepted it, but he had his reservations. The simplest form this took was getting one of his friends to persuade me to have dinners at one of the law schools (I think the Inner Temple) so that I could at the same time train to become a barrister, while I was having my little bit of fun doing PPE at Oxford.

MH: Sounds as though he was fighting a war of position too.

RB: Indeed. I remember being interviewed at the Inner Temple and the head of the school or college asked me whether my parents were in law or had any relatives in law. When I said no, he asked, 'What does your father do then?', in a rather exasperated tone. So I told him he was a doctor, and he said, 'Well, why don't you go into medicine?' Little did he know! After my first couple of books came out I took the reviews to my father and said, 'Do you think I might have taken the right decision after all?', and he said, 'Well, I don't know about that. If you had gone into medicine you would have had a Jag by now.'

   Of course, some people kindly say to me, 'You *are* in effect a doctor now because you are a healer, trying to heal people, society, and such like.'

MH: It is hardly what your father had in mind though. He seems to have been more interested in material wealth and status. Did he himself have a Jag?

RB: Well, he had a Rolls Royce for family occasions, a Jag for business, and a sports car for visiting patients. The garage at the house in Weybridge (which was called 'Nirvana') was huge. My parents helped me to buy a Mini when I was seventeen, and later a sports car.

MH: Were you at all embarrassed by such conspicuous consumption?

RB: There are always special circumstances. This is how he wanted to spend his money. Remember, these were pre-ecological times, and we were living on an estate in Weybridge where you had to drive. That was his little bit of luxury. He didn't particularly like going out to posh restaurants or staying in expensive hotels, in fact my parents used to go camping.

MH: You later characterised the phase of the philosophical discourse of modernity you lived through as a child and adolescent as the theory and practice of modernisation, a leading characteristic of which was judgementalism on the basis of a conviction that the developed countries of the West are in the vanguard of a unilinear evolutionary process. Were you aware of this kind of big picture at all before you went up to Oxford?

RB: Yes, the idea was that western societies are the most advanced and map out the path for less advanced societies, that there is a direct progression from the bullock-cart to the car. This was basically a version of history with which my parents identified, however inconsistent it was with the multilinearity of their Theosophy and their own experience of exclusion. For reasons we have gone into, although I enjoyed cars, TV and pop music, I was sensitised to both the costs and the limited nature of the progress actually made. As Gandhi said when asked what he thought of western civilisation, 'I think it would be a good idea'.

MH: What has really struck me listening to you today is the extent of the continuity between your developing identity and your mature one; some of the leading themes from your mature philosophy are present at an early age. You don't pose any philosophical problem of trans-life standards, of commensurability and identity, there is such strong continuity!

RB: Well, I think it is an unfinished struggle. In a way, you see, coming into your dharma is an ongoing process. To be fully in your dharma you would need to live in a society that accepted the principle of everyone being in their dharma everywhere. If you had such a society it would be a eudaimonistic society, a society in which the free development of each is a condition of the free development of all. And to achieve that the first thing you need is survival, which for many people is a continuous struggle, including to some extent for me. But once you have survived then you need to flourish, and that is wholly possible, I do believe, in a spirit of concrete utopianism. We have to overcome the material constraints that prevent humanity having the fine future that it could still have. Ecological sustainability is a high priority for that, and of course having a mode of production, consumption, settlement and care and a way of organising our economic life that does not involve the exploitation of human beings in the ways that our current capitalism does is another.

MH: It is an ongoing quest, but were you confident that you were in your dharma nonetheless at some stage in your childhood?

RB: Well no, I identified my dharma with being free to do what came best to me or easily. So my feeling about my dharma might have been wrong, technically one must allow that. But my feeling then would have been a superficial one – and I think it probably was in relation, for example, to being a cricketer, but probably not in relation to being a philosopher. As a philosopher, though, I have never felt totally happy; it might be that I am in the right profession, but there have always been constraints and struggles. I would say my dharma was perhaps more complete when I was able to be a philosophy graduate and then teach philosophy, than it was when I was an undergraduate, in the sense that I was more in it. I wonder about that, though, because I am not sure what my complete dharma or what my dharma conceived as itself evolving really is. For all intents and purposes you could say, well, he is a philosopher, he has written so many books and there are people who are discussing his ideas. But that does not necessarily make me feel whole, it depends what people are doing with the ideas. I think critical realism is still to some extent marginalised notwithstanding the valiant struggles being waged by people such as yourself to demarginalise it. I think everywhere, unfortunately, we have a long way to go.

MH: I was thinking of your knowing what your dharma is as distinct from realising it. You knew basically what trajectory you wanted to have?

RB: I think that is so, but had I been free to study what I wanted when I went to university I might have opted for psychology or sociology, rather than PPE. Of course, since Oxford and Cambridge were the best universities it was natural for me to think of going there, and I had gone for Oxford despite, or perhaps because of, the fact that my family traditionally supported Cambridge – middle-class families always supported one or the other. At Oxford I could have done psychology, but it involved dissecting rats, and playing around with them. I didn't feel like doing that, and you had to do sociology via PPE. I was really concerned about the problems in the world, I didn't want to do just pure philosophy at this stage, I wanted philosophy that was going to be relevant to something. And in this regard when I went to Oxford I was in for a rude shock. However, at a personal level I felt pretty whole most of the time I was there.

2 Oxford days

Carrying through the Copernican revolution in the philosophy of science (1963–1973)

MH: Tell us, to start with, something about the trajectory of your formal studies at Oxford: what you started off reading, what you ended up reading, and why and how.

RB: In October 1963 I went up to Oxford on the exhibition I had won to read PPE at Balliol College. That exhibition was very soon converted to an open scholarship. I graduated from Balliol in 1966 with a first class BA Honours. Then I enrolled for a DPhil in the economics faculty to do a thesis called *The Relevance of Economic Theory for Underdeveloped Countries*. I was appointed a lecturer in economics at Pembroke College. I spent a further year at Balliol, then won a place in Nuffield College and I was there from October 1967 to the end of the summer 1969. I kept my lectureship at Pembroke. I became a research fellow at the Oxford University Institute of Statistics and Economics in about September 1970 and I held that post for one year. Then I was awarded a junior research fellowship at Linacre College, a fellowship in philosophy – by now I had switched to the philosophy faculty – and towards the end of 1971 I submitted a DPhil thesis in the philosophy faculty under the title *Some Problems about Explanation in the Social Sciences*, but it was too long for the examiners. I submitted a second thesis when I was at the University of Edinburgh, where I had become a lecturer from October 1973. It also was not accepted, I think this was in April 1974, but it might have been May.

MH: I'll return to the fate of your theses. To go back to the beginning: when you arrived in Oxford you were finally free of your father's ambitions for you to become a doctor. It must have been a very liberating experience?

RB: Yes, it was. I found it socially liberating in many respects, but what I found most liberating was being able to talk about what I wanted to, being able to express myself in a field in which I wanted to express myself, where the concept of expression made some sort of sense to me. I remember the very first night after my dad and my mum had driven me up to Oxford and delivered me there in the afternoon. We all assembled in the dining hall, and before that I think we were given a glass of sherry in the common room, since it was our first day there. A couple of my fellow debutantes, freshers I suppose, started to converse with me and we began having a really stimulating conversation over the sherry. At dinner, I found myself sitting next to another couple of people whose conversation I enjoyed, and I think we also had a glass of port there. Then we went back to the common room for coffee, and then all five of us went to one of our rooms and sat there conversing till four or five in the morning. It was not a trivial thing, we were having very exciting free-ranging conversations, and I remember going to bed, feeling, 'Well, I am now doing what I ought to be doing. This is the life I ought to be living.'

MH: Some of the skills you were deploying would have been honed in your struggles at home and at school.

RB: Absolutely. When I had my first couple of tutorials in PPE I found them immensely rewarding. The fact that I was doing something I was intellectually interested in and was able to express myself intellectually was very important. I was no longer stuck with diagrams of the digestive system of a rat, or dissecting dogfish, or formally repeating theories in physics that were put forward in such a way that they had no explanatory content in relation to anything in the world. This was very exciting. Of the three subjects, I think I was most interested in philosophy. I used to thoroughly enjoy the weekly essay. It was often a struggle, but the kind of struggle I loved. It might be something on probability. I would read the recommended books, then I would have to ask a question and work my way through to a sufficiently clear understanding of that field to read a coherent essay. I found it a very stimulating experience.

MH: There was presumably one-on-one tutoring?

RB: It was either one-on-one or one-on-two. Despite my passion for philosophy, at the end of my finals I eventually opted for economics. This was really because I thought that economics was the most important, or rather the most serious, of the PPE disciplines. While I was very good at solving the puzzles that were posed in philosophy and found the experience very rewarding, they were often in themselves totally trivial, such as is there another mind in the world, does this table exist, or do you have two hands? And there I sat reading an essay to my tutor about it! The topics in politics and economics by contrast were intrinsically about something, the answer wasn't obvious, with the only challenge being how you arrive at the answer. I actually thought at the time that I was best at politics, but whereas I got alpha marks in philosophy and economics, in politics in my finals I got gamma marks. At the time I thought this was because I was too creative and free, and probably too radical, whereas in philosophy and economics there were bodies of theory that you had to show competence in and I was at least very competent in those theories. So I rejected politics as a career option to some extent and that led me into economics. The biggest problems in the world were I thought economic ones, and that is the reason why I went into doing a DPhil in economics. While I jettisoned philosophy because of its lack of seriousness and politics because of its lack of theory, it was intuitively obvious to me that the economic theory I had been expounding in my essays and exams was woefully inadequate. In fact the beauty of the tutorial system was that one was encouraged to be critical even about the latest received theories. By the time I took finals in economics, my essays and the discussions I would have with my tutors fully exhausted the tutorial hour and they were having to find spaces in their schedules to carry on the discussion.

MH: Tumoori coming into his own – and Why-Because.

RB: That's right. I took my finals at the end of May 1966 and I think in January we had a mock finals exam and I won a prize, called the Jenkins prize. I felt completely on top of my form from the point of view of writing an exam, because I thoroughly knew the theories involved.

MH: In orthodox economics?

RB: Yes. But this was also true of philosophy, where I was able to be critical in a very small way, because most of my criticisms were of the kind that had already occurred to my tutors or that they were prepared to accept. So I was for them an ideal – a star – undergraduate.

MH: You were very conscientious?

RB: Well, I always went to my tutorials. I had very good tutors. If I could just develop the contrasts a little. By the time I did my finals I was so critical of the received problematics that, as one of the examiners told me later, though he had been informed that there were two outstanding candidates from Balliol, of whom I was one, he had been unable to find any really outstanding papers (he learnt our names only later). By now I had become too critical of the system and I myself did not enjoy the experience of doing finals, because I was already onto the terrain of my postgraduate research. Looking at Oxford as a whole you could say that there are two big contrasts, the contrast between the undergraduate population and the graduate population and then between the students and the teachers. Oxford is very much a place for undergraduates, Oxford and Cambridge are the best places in the world to be as an undergraduate; you lead a wonderful existence if you are lucky enough to be in a college and have tutors who are good and have a good circle of friends. Most original or creative postgraduates, on the other hand, have a very difficult time because when you are postgraduate you come up very clearly against the limits of the discipline. PPE was designed to turn you into a top-class civil servant, able to turn your hand to any brief or service the empire in a variety of roles. But when you are a postgraduate, what you are actually having to do is to become professionalised into a particular discipline. There are very different skills required. When you are an undergraduate it doesn't really matter what you say, as long as you say it well, and argue it cogently. But when you are being indoctrinated into a profession such as law or analytical philosophy or ortho- dox economic theory, your argumentative prowess and whatever skills or orig- inal insights you have are totally secondary to working within the existing problem-field. In the field of development economics this was cost-benefit analysis under the sign of the theory of modernisation, and when I went into the faculty of economics as a postgraduate my supervisors and the other econ- omists I knew were very concerned to enrol me in some research project of their own, which might be cost-benefit analysis in East Africa. A very nice guy who was the other tutor in economics at Pembroke, Arthur Hazelwood, tried to get me into this; he wasn't coercive at all, but that is basically the kind of thing my superiors wanted me to be doing.

MH: Do work for them?

RB: I very much resisted this. After doing finals, two other finalists of that year and I launched a PPE reform group that developed a critique of PPE. The precise nature of the critique is something we needn't go into in detail here, but from my retrospective point of view, trying to capture what I felt at the time, the gist of it was that PPE may have been a great experience but much of it was not serious in the Hegelian sense.

MH: So in terms of your struggle to come into your dharma, the big picture is that Oxford provided a wonderfully exhilarating and liberating context for you as an undergraduate, but then as a postgraduate you encountered the orthodoxy of the discipline, the tyranny of normal science, the mandarin outlook of aca- demia.

RB: Absolutely, and I think you can say that I was already running up against the limits of the tutorial system while I was an undergraduate. In January 1966 I was completely in my element, but by June I was thoroughly browned off with everything. I remember the last day of my finals. Most people were sitting around drinking champagne, but I drove straight back to London. I wanted to see my girlfriend at the time, but also just to get out of Oxford. In fact I was fed up, what I had been doing did really feel like a constriction. I remember I had a friend who had a nervous condition who didn't take her finals. She might have spent some time in a mental establishment, as they were called, in Oxford. I remember thinking, when I went to see her, that her condition was a result of the pressure, in the form of an essay a week and then the finals, on a very creative person. If I had not taken my finals when I did, I would not have been able to do them. I think I had probably reached the point of being too critical for my own good, first in politics and then more generally.

MH: How did you manage to be too critical? Were you drawing on influences from outside the orthodoxies?

RB: At this point in time I would say inside. I was arguably writing better answers than my tutors could have written within the context of the established framework, but of course the established framework is never as consistent, as coherent, as seems to be the case. At the moment before revolutionary science becomes necessary, just taking the system to its limits is important.

MH: Immanent critique?

RB: Yes.

MH: At a talk you gave in India in 2002 you are introduced as having written your first book when you were twenty.[1] Did you indeed write a book at this time, and if so what was it on?

RB: This would probably refer to the first draft of *Some Problems about Explanation in the Social Sciences*, written in the summer of 1967, when I was 23. (Of course I had, as already discussed, started writing a novel earlier, when I was about 17, called *Regurgitating Psyche*, which was pretty soon discarded.)

MH: Your tutors, you say, were excellent. Who were they?

RB: I do think I was exceptionally lucky in the tutors I had. In philosophy my main tutors were Alan Montefiore and Anthony Kenny. Montefiore had extremely wide-ranging interests and was very tolerant. He tutored at Balliol for thirty years and is still an Emeritus Fellow there.

MH: You thank him for reading a draft of A *Realist Theory of Science*.[2]

RB: Yes. Kenny had an extremely good analytical mind. He became Master of Balliol in 1978, and is currently President of the Royal Institute of Philosophy. In different ways they were both ideal tutors. They were very serious in the sense that they actually believed and to some extent acted on what they were teaching. So they had a kind of theory and practice consistency going, and for me their seriousness was above all evident in their asking, and being amenable to discourse about, big questions in politics. A very nice guy called Bill Weinstein, currently Emeritus Fellow at Balliol, and a consultant on corporate strategy, was my tutor in politics. My main tutor in economic theory was Richard Portes, and in economic organisation Wilfred Beckerman, who is now a prominent critic of sustainable development. All these four or five tutors had one thing in common: they were excellent teachers. I had friends in other colleges who were not nearly so lucky. When I became a member of the senior common room at Pembroke, I could see that, with a few exceptions, including my friend Arthur Hazelwood, students there were very unlucky. Of course at Balliol we achieved exceptionally good results. In my year there were three Firsts, but in the following year I think there were about thirteen out of a group of fifteen. I remember one guy getting a First who had borrowed my undergraduate essays on the eve of his finals. My essays were very much in demand, both as a resource and to revise from. This was in the days before the internet.

MH: What was it like living in college?

RB: In Balliol at first I had a nice room, sharing a bathroom and a kitchen with two others. Then I had a suite of rooms. All these rooms came together with a late-middle-aged bloke who was basically a glorified servant. He used to come in and wake you up in the morning. He was called your scout. It was not so long before that time that undergraduates used to bring their own servants with them! People were sent down, that means thrown out of the college, for being found with a member of the opposite sex in their room after ten o'clock. Ten o'clock is ridiculously early. My room in the first year was directly opposite the chapel, and the Dean, who was also the person who took services, was responsible for ensuring we were not up to any hanky panky. He would stand there from a quarter to ten on the look out – I could just see him looking at my room – and I had one or two very close shaves. I quickly realised there was no problem if you were prepared to tip the porters, as long as your friend left, not exactly at ten but perhaps eleven-thirty, when the Dean had gone to bed; then for half a crown the porter would let her out, or let you out if you were visiting. In my second year there was a coal-hole that I and a friend made usable so that we could come in after ten o'clock. It went into the cellars and up our stairs; the entrance was in St Giles Street. It was as if the system was inviting you to find a way round it, but if you were caught it could be serious. There was one occasion when the mother of a girlfriend of mine went to visit her daughter, and I was in her room at seven in the morning and she went and reported this to the Dean. I was gated for three or four days. The mother was a bit of a pain. When she saw me, she turned to her daughter and said, 'Geraldine! How could you? What about your Queen, your country?' And she carried on in this way for two or three hours, and later launched into a tirade with the Dean, who must have thought, 'I have to take some action'. The sort of action that might normally have been taken if you were caught infringing a rule was rustication, which meant being sent down for the rest of the term, so I was lucky (perhaps the tirade made him soft on me). There were people who were sent down even from Nuffield, which is a postgraduate college.

MH: What a privileged lot you were, though. Tell us some more about your PPE reform group.

RB: As a postgraduate one was aware of a movement to change the antiquated rules governing Oxford collegial life. And this did happen very quickly in the late 1960s. By the mid-1970s almost all the colleges had become both-sex ones, and the gating laws were all abolished. This was in part an achievement of the Oxford revolutionary socialist movement, which made internal demands on the system. Together with two friends, one of whom, Trevor Pateman, went on to become a critical realist (I subsequently examined his PhD in the philosophy of language and education at Sussex), I was very interested in the reform of PPE. We wrote a critique of it and within a year or two the structure of PPE had been transformed. You could now do sociology, you could do Hegel, you could do Marx, continental philosophy, and these were permanent effects at the Oxford undergraduate level.

MH: Did you get a reputation as a rebel or troublemaker?

RB: I think at Balliol I was certainly known as being very clever, but I was also known as enjoying life to the full, which I did. I didn't work exceptionally hard except in my last undergraduate year. I probably did work as hard as, or harder than, most but otherwise what I would do was spend one day writing an essay, and another day writing another essay, leaving the rest of the time free for a mix of preparation, intellectual discussion, socialising, going to parties and that sort of thing. I was politically radical, but I wasn't notorious or anything like that. When I got to Nuffield, then I did become somewhat notorious as a rebel and a radical.

MH: Before we go into that, can you tell us more about the undergraduate work you were doing?

RB: I suppose the basis of PPE was very much laid in the work of John Stuart Mill, who was an adept at all three. The ideal was to become, more or less, a modern equivalent to Mill. There was very little discussion of Hegel and Marx, who certainly weren't recognised as major thinkers. Most people who did well in philosophy wouldn't even have done any Kant. It was sufficient to do Descartes, Locke, Berkeley and Hume, that was it. Philosophy was very philistine in that way. For economics you had to do basic neo-classical and Keynesian economic theory and problems in the British economy since the war. To go back to philosophy, you had a moral and political philosophy paper, on which there was a kind of consensus at the time that was represented by a text by S. I. Benn and R. S. Peters called *Social Principles and the Democratic State*; and a paper on modern philosophy, which was basically Descartes and the British empiricists. You had to do two compulsory papers in philosophy, in economics, and in politics and then you had two other options. I took philosophical logic. This was a very exciting and interesting subject at the time. You did a little bit of formal logic, but it was really based on the Oxford philosophy of John Austin and the later philosophy of Ludwig Wittgenstein. One was reading texts by Peter Strawson such as *The Bounds of Sense* and *Introduction to Logical Theory*, which I still think is a very radical and challenging book.

   The other option I took was economic development, and there I had as one of my tutors Paul Streeton, who was a Fellow of Balliol. He was quite a bigwig in the whole field of development studies. He himself was a disciple of Tommy Balogh who had also been a Fellow of Balliol and now had some sort of visiting or emeritus status there. Tommy Balogh was Harold Wilson's economic guru, and very soon after the Labour party came to power in October 1964 I remember seeing him in a very inebriated but ecstatic frame of mind. He was a bigger than life character. He was a Hungarian economist, like Nicholas Kaldor, but he had been a real critic of the civil service and had written many articles that were very critical of orthodoxy in the field of development economics. You were very aware that he was the guru of Harold Wilson because, while I can't remember ever seeing them together, you also saw Wilson at Oxford. What actually happened on that first night in October was that Balogh and Wilson decided unilaterally, without consultation with anyone else in the Cabinet, that there would be no devaluation of sterling, that they would defend the currency to the hilt. In that decision the fate of the first Wilson Labour government was sealed, because it meant that there could not be an ('indicative') economic plan of the kind that George Brown had been working on and people such as Beckerman had supervised in France. There was no growth potential for the British economy any more, because everything was sacrificed to defending the currency. Of course eventually the pound was devalued. However, to speak about it, to consider its pros and cons was taboo. Nicholas Kaldor, the Treasury's chief economist, went along with the Balogh–Wilson decision, and might even have approved of it. But that of course merely set the context for the capitulations of the Labour government in 1976 to the IMF, and the onset of monetarism – what could be called high-monetarism under Denis Healey and then of course under Thatcherism. And that was the beginning of the end of the welfare state in Britain, compared to what you still have in Sweden and the other Scandinavian countries. That fate was sealed on the very first night of the Labour government. Wilson was known to be one of the best and brightest undergraduates that Oxford had ever produced; he got one of the best Firsts ever, in PPE. He was an extremely clever person and yet what a sell-out to the principles behind PPE. First, it was completely the wrong decision, because all the other goals for the Labour government would have to be sacrificed for it. But then to enforce a complete embargo on discussion so that there was no possibility within government or Labour circles of raising this question again, that was a betrayal of the very idea of rational, even more so that of open and democratic, government. Of course, what they were worried about, because Britain had a balance of payments crisis, was that if you devalued speculators would think that whenever a Labour government came to power there would be a devaluation and therefore a run on the pound, which would make the situation worse for any Labour government in the future. That was the rationale for it. But exports would have been cheaper with the devaluation, and imports would have been more costly; this is how the American economy has been keeping afloat, at least until very recently, effectively by continual devaluations determined by the market and central policy.

Harking back to the point about privilege, I have to say that my first economics tutorial was not actually with the people I mentioned as my main economics tutors but with Derek Robinson, who was not quite such a prestigious Fellow at Balliol. He worked in the Institute of Statistics, where I myself was subsequently to work. When I went into his room for the first time, as soon as I entered the phone rang and he picked it up and said, 'Oh hello Frank' – and that was Frank Cousins, the Minister of Technology. And it was like that, you were very aware that it did not matter which side or aspect of the class divide you were on, or which particular institution you belonged to, the hierarchies of power all converged in Oxford. I liked Derek Robinson, who became a friend of mine. People like Tommy Balogh and Paul Streeton didn't. In terms of economics Paul Streeton, who I think had been a student at Balliol, had attempted to formalise some of the characteristic errors of development economics and there was quite bit of that kind of stuff by Tommy Balogh. Then there was the debate about Milton Friedman and his critics, who included Paul Samuelson. I remember I gave some papers at a postgraduate seminar that Tommy Balogh had come back to run at Balliol, and he didn't really like them, even though I was arguing his sort of pitch. I think he was disapproving of me because I was trying to be, in his mind, cleverer than him, or trying to upstage him. Whatever little critical liberties you were allowed at a postgraduate level, this was always subordinate to the authority of your supervisors and institutional superiors.

MH: That's very common in academia. Because of their structural position academics are prone to be ontologically insecure, and their whole identity is bound up with building a reputation for being at the forefront of their field, so they often find the notion that anyone might be brighter or more talented than themselves difficult to come to terms with.

RB: Exactly. Having entered the Faculty of Economics as a postgraduate student, I was excited because I had been appointed two exceptional supervisors: Paul Streeton, who had done the closest thing there was in that sort of context to a philosophically sophisticated critique of economic theory or what there was of it from the point of view of development economics; and Ian Little, who had a fantastically high reputation in Oxford and indeed generally because he was the author of the standard text on welfare economics called *A Critique of Welfare Economics*. So I thought, well, this is great, here are two very good philosophical minds who are going to help me, and they will read my texts and point me in the right direction. But they were completely unsympathetic and totally uninterested in what I was doing. Ian Little, who was at Nuffield, didn't read anything, and Paul Streeton sat on a draft of my thesis for over a year. When I finally had a conversation with him, he said, 'It's not really economics you know'. It was clear that economics for him was cost-benefit analysis, particularly in the field of development economics, and all these wonderful projects you could be involved in; and he was of course totally uncritical about the tools he was using for the cost-benefit analysis. 'No, it's not really economics, is it?', he said. 'Wouldn't you be happier if you switched to the philosophy faculty, or another faculty?' Mercifully I had also given this text to Alan Montefiore, after waiting for about a year to get some sort of feedback from Streeton and Little. He read it quite quickly – I must admit it was a huge text – but within months anyway, and he said, 'Well this is great, but I'm not really competent to comment very much' (although he did make one or two comments). 'You should switch to philosophy. You should have as your supervisor' (because I was saying a lot about philosophy of science in this text) 'Rom Harré.' And now we are talking about the academic year 1969–70.

I was glad to switch to philosophy, but I was nervous about switching to Rom Harré because I had read a few of his books of the 1960s and they seemed to me very orthodox, and also he seemed to be a very strong individualist. I have to say that I very rarely went to lectures; you can get by in Oxford as an undergraduate without going to any lectures, everything is geared to your tutorials. But I had been told by a friend that Harré was the nearest thing to me that there was, that he was a very dynamic guy, a good lecturer, and with very wide-ranging interests. So I knew a little bit about him at a remove. Anyway, to my great relief, when I went to meet him in 1970 and handed him my text – I can't quite remember exactly which version it was, it was probably a development of the one Montefiore had had, I know it consisted of six huge folders – he read it. I was also aware of a book that for Harré was a major breakthrough, his *The Principles of Scientific Thinking*, which had just come out;[3] there was a quantum leap between that book and the books he had written before it in the 1960s. It was intellectual love at first sight. It was a tremendous relief for me; here was freedom from another huge constraint, the constraint of professionalisation into normal science or an academic discipline as taught normally. I was aware that anyone writing that book with those ideas was not going to be a problem, and of course he gradually read the text and really I can say that he accepted it. But he did not actually give me any supervision. I was already working on the next stage of the synthesis, which was basically a bringing together of his critiques of the sufficiency of the Humean theory of causal laws with my own critique of the lack of necessity of it, a critique that was already developed in my text. I first put the two together in the manuscript, *Empiricism and the Metatheory of the Social Sciences*, and then later more simply and straightforwardly in *A Realist Theory of Science*. I do sometimes find references implying that Rom Harré gave me instruction or something like that. It was never the case. It was a meeting of equals. We had a great mutual respect for each other and became very good friends.

The basic problem I faced in working on a postgraduate thesis on the relevance of economic theory for underdeveloped countries was that it was a topic that was actually impossible to state given the economics profession at the time, because the postgraduate was inculcated with the notion that it was wrong to ask questions about the relevance or the realism of any body of theory. The interesting thing was to express that theory in as succinct a way as possible, to represent it in a few equations on the blackboard, and to work out their logical consequences. That kind of algorithmic was what economic post-graduates did; that was the creed of the economics profession – 'don't ask about the realism, otherwise you could blow everything apart' – that was the naive justification of it. 'We all know that we are not living in a world of per-fect competition, we are not living in a world of a single commodity or two commodities, it is much more complicated than that. So don't ask about it, just see what our tools can do. Don't ask questions about how good the tools are in any way.' The aim was either to be a consummate mathematician and show how you could manipulate these symbolisms, play with these algebraic and computational representations of the fundamental axioms of free market economics, neo-classical economic theory; or to be an ardent practitioner, applying them in practical contexts. Already traditions such as Keynesianism, which had only recently been dominant, were on the wane, regarded as hav-ing nothing more to say. That was up to the politicians. It was just a technique, possibly a rather dubious technique, to use, so you weren't encouraged to work any more in Keynesian economics. I was an office-holder of an undergraduate society in Balliol, to which we invited people like Joan Robinson to come and speak. Joan Robinson was a Maoist, which was lovely and refreshing, but it wasn't regarded as economics. That was a little bit of fun on the side. Obviously I was very questioning of that kind of approach to economics. There was the work of sociologists of knowledge such as Thomas Kuhn. I was already incorporating the critique of the anti-monists in the philosophy of sci-ence, people like Kuhn and Paul Feyerabend, into my thesis, as well as my own anti-deductive critique, and supplementing and synthesising the critique of other anti-deductivists such as Harré.

However the fundamental problem with the methodological discussions of economies was that there was no concept of ontology there. I was aware that this was something that would have to be broached.

MH: There was a taboo on it.

RB: Yes, a taboo on ontology. Looking back, I can reconstruct this more rationally now. I went from economics to philosophy of science, but when you look at the textbooks in the philosophy of science, your Poppers and Hempels, you cannot see anything about the real world there either – not when they are talking about explanation and conformation or falsification and the like. So I went back to philosophy and critiqued the epistemic fallacy, in other words the denial of ontology, at its roots. When I was trying to write an economics thesis most of my criticisms turned on a figure that was absent, the implicit ontology, what these texts were saying or presupposing about the world. It was a struggle. I very much enjoyed writing, I enjoyed the texts I was reading, and I was in a very stimulating social and political environment. But precisely because I was very much part of the environment I was critiquing at the level of metatheory, I was very much identified as a revolutionary. So I knew what I was up against, and I knew that I should not expect any favours from the orthodox doyens of development economics.

By the time I gave my six-volume manuscript to Rom Harré I was already aware that what I was writing was actually the basis of three books. I was writing philosophy of science, philosophy of social science and ideology-critique. The whole thing was about empiricism as a metatheory of the social sciences (and that is what I actually called a development of it a little later). I gave it the title of *Problems about Explanation in the Social Sciences* and submitted it as a DPhil in 1971. Most of the problems I had between that 1971 text and the publication of *A Realist Theory of Science* late in 1974 concerned getting this first critique into a manageable form. The overall project was an attempt to cover the entire ground subsequently traversed by *A Realist Theory of Science*, *The Possibility of Naturalism* and the third chapter of *Scientific Realism and Human Emancipation*. Of those three parts, the part I was most impressed with in the early 1970s was actually the critique of ideology: things like the isolation of empiricism as involving the reification of facts and the fetishism of conjunctions, and showing the resonances between the system of thought and the social order and the utility of using Marxian-type ideology-critique. I would really need to look at the text of *Problems about Explanation*, but my memory is that the role of the necessity for ontology and the role of transcendental argument is downplayed; they are not really there in their explicit form, and I think I can best explain how these later things arose in the context of an account of the influences on my intellectual development.

MH: Yes, how would you characterise the main intellectual influences that went into the gestation of your DPhil thesis or theses and eventually *A Realist Theory of Science*?

RB: To be a little bit formal about this, I would say there were ten main influences:

1 the anti-monistic tradition in the philosophy of science;
2 the anti-deductivist tradition;
3 what can be called the theorists of the concrete;
4 sociology of knowledge and the critique of ideologies;
5 Marx and particularly his conception of praxis, which formed the basis of the transformational model of social activity (TMSA);
6 structure and the whole idea of the contrast between structure and events, as you could begin to find in the work of Claude Lévi-Strauss and the structuralists, but especially of Noam Chomsky (who gave one of the few lectures I went to as an undergraduate in Oxford), and Louis Althusser, who was then at the height of his influence;
7 language;
8 the natural philosophers;

9   the metacritical context – I went back from Marx to Hegel to Kant and also had a fresh look at Descartes;

10   perspective: Nietzschean perspectivism, Frantz Fanon's theory of revolutionary violence, the theory of crisis generally, Antonio Gramsci and, as a kind of corrective or supplement to Fanon, Gandhi perhaps.

Of course any such list will depend to some extent on one's starting point. This is how it looks when I take myself back to writing texts in Nuffield as a sort of consciously revolutionary student. There is a certain amount of irony in talking in these terms, but nevertheless I was a critic of capitalism and a critic of structural constraints of the sort that I was up against in my academic work.

MH: Right from the outset?

RB: From 1966, 1967 – it was a gradual thing. In 1966, when I wrote my finals papers, I was thoroughly imbued with Wittgenstein and Austin, I knew a little bit about Kant, Hegel and Marx, but I might not have even been familiar with the name Thomas Kuhn. His *Structure of Scientific Revolutions* came out in 1962, and while I was a postgraduate student at Nuffield, Paul Feyerabend and Imre Lakatos were having their famous debates in the London School of Economics. I was quite close to those contexts; from the moment I finished PPE I was reading everything I could about science, as part of looking into the scientificity of economics. The extraordinary impact of Kuhn and Feyerabend involved the recognition that it is not just the case, as Popper argues, that falsification plays a momentous role in science, but that meaning change and inconsistency are of its essence. So I could begin to view scientific knowledge as I described it in *A Realist Theory of Science*: as a transitive dimension, as a social process, and one that is set in the context of wider social processes, which are of course in the world. That was the great insight that I took from the anti-monists I read. My reading of Kuhn and Feyerabend came after my reading of the very interesting work being done in the more analytical philosophy of science, professional work by writers such as Wilfred Sellars, Hilary Putnam and so on, and including, I might say, some ordinary language critique – the work of Michael Scriven struck me as being particularly insightful. We should perhaps discuss that under theories of the concrete.

   Now this anti-monist strand on its own could not have done the trick, as there was nothing to stop the collapse into extreme relativism, which is what happened with Kuhn and Feyerabend; and the reason it happened was that they lacked any notion of an intransitive dimension, of the real world, of ontology. And so in reflecting on what was wrong with the anti-monists I was noting correspondences with what was wrong with economics. I did a lot of close textual analyses of some philosophers of science and social science and you could actually see an implicit ontology that was completely false; an ontology that had only to be expressed to be seen to be false. The extraordinary thing about the dominance of these implicit ontologies was that they were informed by the Humean theory of causality. If you actually stated its implications or that of the Popper–Hempel theory of explanation based on it in the context of, say, economic theory or some other specific body of social scientific theory that was at all problematic, it soon became evident that something was very wrong, that something did not fit. But the way these problematics keep going is by divide and rule – 'this is one subject, that is another: that is next week's topic' – and so you never really got down to a focus on the core theories that underpinned them all, and to a focus on the core theories precisely as underpinning them all. These core theories were the Humean theories of causality and of experience of the objects of what it was that was constantly conjoined.

Of course, I did not attempt to rubbish the anti-monists, or anything like that. I was very grateful for their contribution and the stimulus I had from reading them. The contrast between what Kuhn and Feyerabend were talking about and what was talked about in Oxford philosophy was enormous. You weren't just talking about knowledge in the abstract, you were talking about concrete knowledge, scientific knowledge, some real form of knowledge in a real social process. The whole thing had flesh, it moved, whereas the discourse of standard Oxford philosophy did not.

So the first line of influence had to be taken in conjunction with the second line of influence, and this was the anti-deductivist line. And it was already clear to me that you could not make sense of a notion of laws or principles in a domain such as economics unless you construed them tendentially, as something that only tended to happen in actuality. Then the question was what was it that tended to happen? It was obvious that the kind of ontology one needed was a depth-ontology that involved structures, mechanisms and fields, something other than events. This issued in the distinction between the domains of the real, the actual and the empirical, and it was in that context implicitly and to some extent explicitly that I started looking more closely at the writings of the anti-deductivists and particularly Harré's *The Principles of Scientific Thinking*. As I've already said, I quickly conceived that the first thing I had to do was supplement Harré's critique with my own.

MH: What was wrong with Harré's critique?

RB: The anti-deductivists were all trying to say that there was something more to a causal connection or a law than a constant conjunction of events. What was this something more? They were basically saying that it was a model. This was a very Kantian theory. They were saying that knowledge according to the positivists had no structure, but that you could not talk about a scientific law unless you had structure, that Kantian element. The problem for me about this line of thinking was that unless you had a notion of the real world there was no way you could ultimately arbitrate or choose between different models or conceptions of structure. You want one model and I want another, so they are equally good, and once again you collapse back into a form of relativism. The anti-deductivists did not make the obvious move of going from the model to the referent of the model because it was totally taboo to talk about the real world. I realised that, to do justice to their critique and to the anti-monistic one, you had to have ontology there, and of course that is the way I had been moving already in thinking about laws. To say that a constant conjunction of events was not necessary for a law meant that a law had to be something else that in itself had nothing essentially to do with a constant conjunction of events. That was an ontological distinction. Quickly the epistemic fallacy fell into place. And the lack of necessity (as well as sufficiency) of Humean criteria for law, and the necessity for ontology, were two of my three main differences with Harré at the level of philosophy of science. The third concerned the question of how you actually argue. There did not seem to be a principal method of arguing, because after all that is what Harré's account of science implied: it was all about the imaginative deployment of models, and another person might emphasise social context or frameworks or paradigms. How did you know in any case that science operated in this way? Well, there were people such as Mario Bunge, who just looked and described what scientists did, and that is another influence I will come to. But this certainly was not good enough for an Oxford DPhil, you had to prove it, and for that purpose I had adopted a transcendental mode of argumentation. For a couple of years after the publication of *A Realist Theory of Science*, Harré actually accepted transcendental realism,[4] and then, for reasons that we can come to later, in my view fell back to a pre-transcendental realist model.[5] I had further differences with Harré when it comes to the philosophy of social science, which we may also come to later.

Perhaps I should briefly clarify my three main differences with Harré at the level of philosophy of science. First, the Humean theory of causal laws as constant conjunctions of atomistic events or empirical regularities is not only not sufficient, it is not a necessary condition for a causal law (and a fortiori for all the theories of orthodox philosophy of science based on the Humean account). That is to say, the causal connection is neither contingent nor actual. There is an ontological difference between causal laws and patterns of events, which is brought out when I talk of the difference between the domains of the real and the actual.

So the second difference between Harré and myself at the level of philosophy of science concerns his lack of the notion of ontology. He is a transcendental idealist, rather than a transcendental realist; whereas for me, the presence of structure in the world, as well as in our knowledge of the world, must be recognised and accommodated. And, as a condition of this distinction, we need also the critique of the epistemic fallacy or the conflation of ontology and epistemology.

The third difference concerns the nature of philosophical argument, how we get at our conclusions in philosophy. There is no conscious employment of transcendental argumentation or commitment to the principle of immanent critique in Harré's work. On the contrary, he deploys relatively ad hoc and metatheoretically ungrounded methods of argumentation.

The three differences at the level of philosophy of science concern the lack of necessity as well as sufficiency of orthodox accounts of science; the absence of ontology and concomitant commitment to transcendental idealism; and the lack of a principled method of argumentation.

MH: It is sometimes said that Harré is the co-founder of critical realism with you. What is your response to that?

RB: I suppose the suggestion must concern itself only with first-level or basic critical realism, which may be regarded as compounded of theses or positions in the philosophy of science and the philosophy of social science.[6]

In respect of the philosophy of science, as I have already argued, Harré's position is Kantian, rather than transcendental realist. There is no critique of orthodoxy at the level of ontology, the critique is restricted to epistemology. And even here the method of argumentation is, as we have seen, suspect. Moreover, neither Harré nor his fellow thinkers, such as Charles Varela, appreciate the way in which the lack of necessity of Humean criteria for orthodox accounts of science provides an extraordinarily strong and powerful case for a species of realism that can altogether break from the problem-field of Humean empiricism, in which Harré, like Kant, continues to be mired.

Our positions have always diverged in the philosophy of social science. When I first met him, he was committed to a methodological individualism. His approach to structure has usually been voluntaristic. And his ontology of language has characteristically been idealist. In typical neo-Kantian style, a dualistic schism and Manichean contrast between the socially constructed world of society and the empirically given world of nature has pervaded his thought. In short, whereas in the case of philosophy of science there are continuities as well as breaks, there is a huge gulf in our accounts at the level of the philosophy of social science, as he would himself confirm.

Moreover, to imply that he was a co-founder of critical realism would suggest a level of collaboration that we have never enjoyed.[7] Finally, the absurdity of this idea may be seen from the fact that he has never claimed to be a critical realist and has always asserted, when not opposed to it, at least a degree of difference from it (for example at the International Association for Critical Realism [IACR] conference in 2008, to the extent of calling himself 'a neo-critical realist').[8]

The doyens of most of the anti-deductivists were Austin and Wittgenstein, who were also the chief mentors of what I call the theorists of the concrete. These included people who had been Oxford philosophers or interested in Oxford philosophy, such as Peter Geach and Elizabeth Anscombe, and I would mention in particular, as a theorist of the ideographic, or the unique and particular, Michael Scriven. But the work of Michael Polanyi, *The Tacit Dimension*, and other books by him also falls into this category.

The fourth big influence was the sociology of knowledge and critiques of ideology. By now I had a conception of the transitive and intransitive dimensions and was beginning to see that, not only did scientific knowledge and knowledge generally have to be situated in the social world – and the influences here would include Kuhn and the Edinburgh school of sociology of knowledge, especially Barry Barnes and David Bloor – but they had to be situated in the world itself, that is ontologically, as being, and materially, as (an emergent) part of nature. Moreover, the social world presupposed critique – and remember I was always at the same time working on or thinking about the philosophy of social science. Indeed, initially the most important thing for me, and the first of all the strands of influence to be developed by me, was the critique of ideology, as I have already said. Eventually I realised that I would have to give up trying to put that in a very simple form because I did not have the time and energy. I had to press on with the positive aspects of my personal dialectic, so its residue is to be found in a chapter in *Reclaiming Reality* and the third chapter in *Scientific Realism and Human Emancipation*.

Then the fifth influence was Marx.

MH: When did you start reading him?

RB: I was very intellectually interested in Marx in my undergraduate days. Indeed, I had already taken an interest in Marx in socio-political terms as a teenager. But for me as a postgraduate student Marx had become of practical relevance, because when I entered Nuffield the social world was very polarised. And Nuffield – Oxford generally, but Nuffield more than any other college – had very direct links between the academic community and the key decision makers outside. George Brown and Jim Callaghan were visiting Fellows, and they used to come, and we were supposed to socialise with them. The first people I became friends with in Nuffield – I was already of the left – were students from the Third World: Trevor Munroe, who a few years later founded the Workers' Liberation Party in Jamaica, later called the Workers' Party of Jamaica (a pro-Moscow communist party); Athar Hussain, who was one of the collaborators of Ben Brewster and other Althusserians; and another Indian called Prabhat Patnaik, who went on to a career in India as an academic economist strongly critical of neo-liberalism and became prominent in the Communist Party of India (Marxist). Of course before arriving in Oxford these people were already to some extent organic intellectuals in their own context. What was most important to them were things such as the black power salute that Tommie Smith and John Carlos gave at the 1968 Olympics. We studied the news of the Vietnam war every day, and what was happening with the Cuban and other revolutions and insurgencies all around the world. This was what immediately concerned us. We were part of a broader Oxford revolutionary student movement, and I was recognised to be the intellectual, as it were, who was writing the critiques and the texts; and I used to help them with their pamphlets. The Nuffield left had a special position here. From the point of view of thinking about science one obviously needed to look at Marxism; it was obviously going to be a tremendously relevant resource. When I started reading Marx seriously, I found the youthful writings and texts such as the Introduction to the *Grundrisse*, which had only just been published, immensely stimulating. It was obviously in Marx that you had a conception of praxis. I began to see my own life, like that of the group, as politicised; so I could no longer be friends in the same way with colleagues on the other side of the political divide.

The sixth sort of influence was structuralism. It was tremendously exciting to read the works of people such as Lévi-Strauss, Althusser and Chomsky. It was clear that the objects of scientific knowledge they were concerned with were something other than atomistic events. All three of these structuralisms were more or less consciously critical of empiricism. It quickly became obvious to me that the 'other thing' that was the bearer of tendencies and powers would have to be structures. Then you wanted to know in science about the way structures worked, so you were concerned with the modus operandi, the generative mechanism, at work as a property of the structure and how it produced events. I was never an Althusserian, though like everyone else at the time I was enormously impressed by his work.

The seventh sort of influence was language. You could not help but be influenced by language if you thought there was any truth in what the later Wittgenstein and Oxford philosophy was saying, because for them the solution to all problems lay in the analysis of language. But this interest in language, which took me into hermeneutics and semiotics and overlapped with my interest in structuralism, also raised the question of the limits of language. It seemed to me patently obvious that society is constituted by more than just language; that society is about real oppression, real acute poverty, real deaths, real wars, real battles, and that there is a huge distinction between the word 'battle' or any number of sentences about a battle and a real battle. It is important to remember in this context that in the formal part of my studies I was working on three fronts: philosophy of science, philosophy of social science and the critique of ideology. In the philosophy of social science the limits of language was obviously going to be a very important topic.

And then the eighth influence was natural philosophers. These were philosophers such as Samuel Alexander and R. G. Collingwood. There was a traditional, pre-Oxford-linguistic discourse about what science did, which, when it fused historical narrative and metaphysical speculations, as exemplified, for example, in Collingwood's *The Idea of Nature*, could be very invigorating and wonderful up to a point. You were actually talking about nature. But you could also find this kind of thing as well within more orthodox philosophies of science; for example, the work of Bunge, who was saying very sensible things about what scientists did. The great problem was that it was just their account, they had no way of demonstrating that it was more than that. When, for example, analytical philosophers wanted to say, 'Well, we are not interested in that, we are pursuing the implications of the analysis of knowledge or what counts as knowledge, or we are doing something properly philosophical', then you had to have a way of immanently critiquing them, of engaging with them, of making them serious. (I don't know if I would have used the term 'serious' at this stage.) This was also true of the reflections of writers such as Michael Polanyi, who was one of the very few who talked about emergence. I remember that, even as late as 1985, when I was negotiating with Verso for the publication of *Scientific Realism and Human Emancipation*, Peter Dews was deputed by *New left Review* (whose publishing house Verso was), and presumably by Perry Anderson, to say to me, 'Well, emergence is not a scientifically acceptable concept.' Yet that was a major part of the realist *critique* of science. Polanyi was one of the few people who talked about emergence, and yet it was divorced from any philosophically rigorous way of proving or establishing it.

And so I became interested – all these influences are going on simultaneously – in the ninth line of influence, which was the metacritical one. This involved going back from Marx and reading Hegel and then Kant, and discovering that transcendental arguments were the key with which I could unlock empiricism while immanently engaging it.

MH: So you went to both Hegel and Kant via Marx?

RB: No, I would have read them to some extent before getting into Marx.

MH: Including Hegel? You came to him independently?

RB: It is difficult to say, but undoubtedly by the time I was really interested and seriously reading Marx, including *Capital* and trying to make sense of what Marx was trying to do, I was also interested, as you could not help but be if you were really interested in Marx, to go into the Marx–Hegel relationship. I became really interested in Kant as well, and of course the first step in the melt-down of Oxford linguistic philosophy was Strawson's *The Bounds of Sense* (1966) which defended a non-empiricist method against the methods of John Austin and other analytical philosophers, which were empiricist: they said in effect, 'Just look at the way we use language, take a few examples and you have your resolution there'. *The Bounds of Sense* was a systematic attempt to understand Kant in Kantian terms. Strawson was regarded as the doyen of the Oxford philosophers at the time. He had established the respectability of using something like a transcendental argument. Very few philosophers were consciously doing that, but I seized on it at a relatively early stage.

Then, of course, before Kant there was Descartes, who everyone agreed was the founder of modern philosophy. Something like the cogito, 'I think therefore I am', did indeed seem to me to express what much modern philosophy was about. Now Wittgenstein had succeeded in critiquing the dominance of egocentricity in so far as his private language argument basically showed that society is ontologically prior to the individual. What I wanted to argue was that, while society is indeed prior to the individual, the natural world is also ontologically prior to society and thus to any human being, at least any human being as we know it. And I wanted to ask what are the presuppositions of this thought of Descartes, 'I think therefore I am', and that led and fed into my critique of the dominant philosophies of science as ideologies.

Then the tenth influence can best be introduced in the following sort of way. Even if you had transcendental argumentation, interesting questions remained as to why Kant discovered it or why and how you were using it. It was very obvious to me that in a politically, socially and economically polarised world perspective is a very important determinant of what one actually believes. So Nietzschean perspectivism was among my influences. A question obviously arose: what was the correct or best perspective? My friends from the Third World at Nuffield and I decided it would be important to read texts relevant to revolutionary struggle in the Third World, of the sort that was going on in Vietnam. Fanon was the great theorist of revolutionary violence, of the cathartic effect that violence could have on the individual. And to some extent this was also very popular among the non-Third-World peer group that quickly formed around us, including people such as Ben Cousin and Caroline New.

MH: It is interesting that you identified as Third World when in important respects you weren't really Third World, you were First World middle class.

RB: In any event we had Third World allegiances, and we were at the core of the movement. One of our group was an Indian and another a Pakistani, and I found it congenial to identify with my Indian background. When we had black power leaders coming, they tended not to say, well, you don't look very brown or black to me. I was always assumed to be on the right side, so this was a little bit of elitism. I was very critical of elitism, but psychologically, if the door is open to you and you want to go into that room, then you go through it. But don't forget I had suffered racial oppression myself as a child.

Now undoubtedly revolutionary violence can play a vital role, but some of my friends thought that was basically it. So they were always up for a confrontation whenever they could get it. Remember this is the era of Mao's Cultural Revolution. Those who took a contrary view were cold-shouldered. This happened to me once or twice to my disgust. These were fraternal arguments, but I could see the effect it was having; there had to be a broader strategy. Intellectual struggle was part of it, so I began to think in terms of all struggles being basically struggles in wars of position and manoeuvre (I was reading Gramsci) in which you were trying to outflank your opponent, preferably without violence. You could do this. I believe that all the great revolutionary moments that we know, when they actually happen, do not involve very much violence at all. It might come subsequently, because the revolutionary cause is incomplete or because it is not carried through, or for some other reason. Later I became interested in how you could adopt an altogether different approach. But even then I was aware of, if you like, the transcendental features of consciousness, that when you are engaging in violence you can always reflect on it, and when you are reflecting on it you are not (in that moment of reflection) being violent and, in the state of non-violence so achieved, are less likely to be violent at all. That is a clue into a Gandhian non-violent strategy.

MH: You were into this already in about 1970?

RB: Yes. Properly conceived this is a strategy that is a way of waging war, but a non-violent or non-warlike, peaceful way of waging war – or, we might say, of waging peace, peace in the interests of social justice. Then the question could be, at the minimum, which way is the more effective? Gandhi called his theory *satyagraha*, which means the way of the truth, holding onto truth, truth-force. So we have the idea that the self-conscious monitoring of what was happening at the surface level could, as it were, embody a more profound truth and give you a greater purchase in your war of position and manoeuvre. This could be conceived, as I think Gandhi did, and I was later to do (in my theory of co-presence), as a matter of principle; or it could be viewed, as I was inclined to view it at the time, as a contingently tactically superior position. Then you could, if need be, choose a violent response, but it was not a matter of dogma, it was a matter of tactics and strategy. However you can only articulate that position, which does not eschew violence, from a stand-point of something that is itself non-violent. Here, of course, you already have the idea of stratification again; here we are talking about a stratification in consciousness and a stratification in levels of political strategy. Looking back on it, as I have noted elsewhere,[9] I think the great mistake of the revolution-ary movements I was associated with in the 1960s and 1970s was to think you could overthrow capitalism merely by mobilising social hatred. That might produce a revolution, but would it produce the good society? If you are going to build a society based on love and co-operation, the end must be prefigured in the means. Or, as Gandhi put it, 'You must be the change you want in the world'.

MH: I'd like you to come back now to the issues surrounding the rejection of your DPhil theses. What precisely happened, and how would you explain it?

RB: In autumn term of 1971 I submitted a thesis called *Some Problems about Explanation in the Social Sciences*. The name I subsequently gave it after it had been rejected as a DPhil thesis, *Empiricism and the Metatheory of Social Science*, is a better description of it. It was about 130,000 words long. My supervisor, Rom Harré, was in America and I think he might have forgotten to apply for an extension of the word-limit, which was 100,000 words. The thesis was basi-cally a draft of what *Scientific Realism and Human Emancipation* (*SRHE*) would later be. It had three chapters, each longer than the one before. The first was to become 'Scientific Realism' (*SRHE*, Chapter 1) and *A Realist Theory of Science*; the second became 'Critical Naturalism' (*SRHE*, Chapter 2 and *The Possibility of Naturalism*), and the third on the critique of ideology became 'The

Positivist Illusion' (*SRHE*, Chapter 3). But the first chapter did not start with a transcendental argument from experimental activity in science, it started with a transcendental argument from language. So it is quite interesting I think even now. Anyway, I was a little apprehensive, I suppose, but basically I was feeling confident that I had made a significant contribution to knowledge. The day that my oral examination was due to be held, in early March 1972, I think, Rom Harré rang me at about eight in the morning. I thought he might be ringing me up to wish me good luck or something, but what he said was a bombshell: the examiners had refused to examine it because it was too long. Since they had had it for several months, I was pretty disgusted at this. If they had only just looked at it the night before, that would have been even worse, but what I suspected was that they had had a look at it and were fixing on an excuse not to examine it, possibly because they did not find it easy to assess the arguments within it or at any rate did not want to debate them with me. The first line of defence, if you are faced with something very radical, is not to argue with it, to ignore it and hope it will go away. And I think that is what they tried to do.

MH: Who were they?

RB: They were David Pears, quite a respected philosopher who was an expert on Wittgenstein, and Peter Hacker who became very famous for producing one of the orthodox interpretations of the later Wittgenstein. I was very upset to say the least when Rom Harré told me this. I talked to a few friends, and I think almost that day, or perhaps the next, I drove down to London with Gareth Stedman-Jones, a friend at Nuffield who was a couple of years older than me but had always been very close to the revolutionary kernel in Nuffield. I went with him because he had a literary agent. So I met this literary agent who took a look at it and sent it to Routledge. The editor of the Routledge series was Ted Honderich, who became relatively well known as a philosopher. He wrote to me after about a year saying this is a really formidable work, we would very much like to publish it, is there any way you could make it a bit simpler in places? So I wrote back saying I was actually producing a text that I hoped would be much simpler – by then I was writing *A Realist Theory of Science*. I had decided that it was too much to cover the whole territory I was working on in one book, and that I should concentrate on the positive account of science.

MH: How did the examiners get appointed?

RB: The faculty are supposed to appoint them but your supervisor should really play a role. From what they had written, neither of the examiners were competent to judge my work. Indeed, most Oxford philosophers did not know anything about Kuhn and Feyerabend or about science, and they weren't really that much interested in social science.

MH: Two Wittgensteinians are hardly the sort of philosophers one would choose as examiners of your work if one wanted to ensure it was given a constructive reading. Did Harré fight back?

RB: He was personally (though not institutionally) very supportive after the event. He might have recommended someone else, but he probably did not.

MH: What did he think of your work? Did he read it?

RB: Yes, Rom read every bit of it and he would sometimes make a little marginal comment on it, but basically he was extremely supportive to my face in everything he said. He was now writing with Paul Secord *The Explanation of Social Behaviour* and giving lectures on it. He more or less twisted my arm to go along, so I did go to many of them. Sometimes when I was there he would take up some point from my work and advertise it to the class. He would say, 'As Roy Bhaskar says, we have to distinguish the real and the actual'. He would say this in a rather offhand way, though I think he did also actually understand and believe it. He also probably thought he was doing me a very good turn, but of course the result was laughter. People thought, what could be more absurd than distinguishing between the real and the actual! I was mortified and had a word with him, saying please wait until it comes out. I had realised from discussing my ideas with people that, as Feyerabend later put it, it takes time to develop a good theory – if you let it out too soon, then you lose it. I could have spent a lifetime in the economics faculty arguing about laws and tendencies and have got absolutely nowhere. When you are engaging in a strategy of immanent critique, you have to be very careful about what your target is, and then you have to carry it through, it has to be a total critique. You isolate what you are trying to attack, you concentrate your forces on it and then you carry it out. It has to be total, everything has to be worked out.

MH: You have a wonderful gift for this.

RB: Anyway, I told Rom Harré to shut up, but I don't think he really did; I was not going to his lectures any more. By now I was living in Herefordshire, close to the Welsh border, and I was working on my own. After I went up to Edinburgh in October 1973 I quickly completed *A Realist Theory of Science*, and took it down to Oxford.

MH: So you had basically decided to work up the manuscript that became *A Realist Theory of Science* as another DPhil thesis. Is that what Harré advised?

RB: No. I was very excited about ontology, I was very excited about transcendental arguments and I knew what I was doing now. The moves that I was making seemed so obvious I could not believe no one else had made them –

resuscitating the ancient science of ontology or a new form of it, using a transcendental method; it was waiting to happen. And people were talking of a Copernican revolution being in the air; Rom Harré used these terms. This was obviously a real Copernican revolution, because I was turning Kant around using his own method. I knew nobody else had done this, and so was very excited about what I was doing. I wrote the text in quite a short time; I think I wrote chapters one and two in a couple of weeks in the autumn, the last term of 1973, and then in a couple of weeks in the first term of 1974 I wrote chapters three and four. Then I took it down to Rom Harré and gave it to him, and he kept it overnight. There were tears in his eyes when he handed it back, saying, 'Well, if they don't give you a DPhil for that, then no one can ever get a DPhil in Oxford', something like that. I had the thesis bound, and then submitted it to the faculty. Then the examiners were appointed, and you have to say there was no other philosopher of science in Oxford other than Rom Harré at that time. Supervisors weren't allowed to examine.

MH: It had to be an internal examiner?

RB: No, it did not, but it was the Oxford tradition only to have internal examiners. The examiners were appointed, I went back to Edinburgh and then in April went down to Oxford for my viva. I went and met the examiners, I knew who they were of course –

MH: Who were they?

RB: Geoffrey Warnock, who later became the vice-chancellor of the university and was Austin's favourite pupil, and Bede Rundle, who was a logician at Trinity College. I was completely armed for every possible line of criticism. But actually there was no criticism. Instead, it was: 'Do come in, Mr. Bhaskar. We would like to congratulate you on this piece of work. We cannot find anything wrong with it, in fact we agree with it all.' I was really taken aback. 'There is only one problem about awarding you the title of DPhil. We are not quite sure how you satisfy this statute', and they took out this big book of statutes. 'The work has to be an original contribution to knowledge, but we already know all this stuff. We cannot find anything new in it.' I was completely thrown. On almost every page I say exactly, very precisely, what the advance is that I am making. I was dumbstruck. They said, 'If you could take it back, and just make clear exactly how you are adding to our knowledge, what we do not already know, then I am sure there will be no problem.' They probably knew that I would not do that, and they hoped it would just go away and be forgotten. But actually this was the other line of defence against a novel system of thought: one line is to ignore it, the other is to say you accept it and that it is in fact already there.

MH: What did you *say*?

RB: I was completely dumbfounded. I had gone in with my mind all cluttered up with ideas about how to respond to every conceivable criticism. I did not see the full importance of being empty-minded until much later.

MH: Was Harré there?

RB: No, but I told him. I had given, or very shortly afterwards I gave, this text to a few people to read, including Perry Anderson, who was the editor of *New left Review*, at Verso. One of the other people I gave it to was trying to set up a book company in Leeds, the boyfriend of Theresa Hayter, Bob Gregory. Bob Gregory didn't read it, but he said he would publish it. So it was quickly snapped up.

MH: What happened to the interest from Ted Honderich and Routledge?

RB: He wrote to me, after it was already under contract, roughly to the effect that if anything he preferred the earlier work, regarding *A Realist Theory of Science* as tending to idealism in places. I think this was probably because of its reference to natural necessity, which he perhaps did not sufficiently differentiate from logical necessity. Generally, however, the response to *A Realist Theory of Science* ranged from cautious approval to outright enthusiasm. Perry Anderson wrote to me, saying this is a work of the moment, your prose has extraordinary eloquence. Rom Harré was very upset that it had been rejected. The book came out in November 1974, but we decided to put 1975 as the date of publication, because that allowed a whole year for it to be a new book. It was immediately given a very good review in the *Times Literary Supplement* by Stefan Körner. My colleagues at Edinburgh were very supportive; many of them did not even ask me what had transpired, they knew from my expression that something terrible had happened. Generally, the reception was very favourable. It included the two foremost Kant scholars in England: William Henry ('Richard') Walsh, the head of my department at Edinburgh, and Stefan Körner, who wrote the *TLS* review. They both liked it.

MH: You once told me that Perry Anderson felt that it was so radical that you got what you should have expected – rejection of the thesis I mean.

RB: Many people said it was too good, and I was aware of that myself. But I was personally crushed, extremely upset. There were various strategies open to me, though. One strategy was to confront the examiners. But I was already out of Oxford and it seemed there was no way I could win there, so I tried to outflank them by getting it published immediately, which is what happened, and then it was published to excellent reviews. What I thought at the time was, well, the examiners will be mortified to realise that they have done this, but of course I did not encounter them again in the flesh and I think they probably quite soon forgot about it. Of course, I realised that not having a DPhil wasn't the end of the world. As I said to Walsh, the most celebrated of philosophers, Strawson, did not even have a First. That was common knowledge in Oxford. Very few Oxford dons had a DPhil at all. I didn't think it would be an insuperable obstacle at the time, but I was very upset.

MH: How do you account for its rejection?

RB: One reason is that, as most of my friends thought, what I was writing was too radical to be accepted within the conventional framework, and the immanent critique touched points that it just wasn't acceptable to question within that system. I think that is part of the truth; but another part is that I did not belong to the old boys' network in Oxford. When I went to the senior common room in Pembroke and to high table at Nuffield I did not feel part of the club. Many of the Fellows were getting extraordinarily drunk in the middle of the day and they weren't doing any work. Oxford philosophy was tremendously complacent. I could perhaps have joined the club by just concentrating on linguistic philosophy, as I was good at that sort of argumentation, but that wasn't something I could really justify doing with my life and whatever talents I might have. So I did not go to high table much, I did not sit in the seminars that might have been politic to sit in, and I did not offer to do papers in front of Strawson, just as I had not wanted to do cost-benefit analysis.

MH: You didn't play the game.

RB: I didn't get professionalised into normal science.

MH: It reminds me of a saying of Albert Einstein to the effect that really creative work always meets with violent opposition from mediocrities.[10]

RB: Also of course, and this is something I have not thought about until recently, another reason could have been racism. And then there was politics – because I was well known to be a Marxist and to identify with the revolutionary left. At the height of the student revolutionary movement the proctors – the organ of discipline in Oxford – were always summoning me on one excuse or another. It was a war. Another thing I think should be mentioned is that I probably did not sufficiently prepare the ground for the new approach. Of course, a number of people who knew me and broadly what I was working on, for example John Mepham, were eagerly awaiting my work, feeling that I would say something significant. But the actual themes had not been floated, and you could argue that had I floated some of them in an article or two it might have made a difference. A few straight articles in orthodox philosophy of science might have helped.

   A further factor has to be that I did not get the support that I really needed from Rom Harré. He should have increased the word limit initially and made sure that the examiners were going to read it seriously. He could have said to them, you have to read this thesis and you have to understand what he is saying. I think he could have done more for a better result. The system in Oxford was that there was a faculty committee that nominated the examiners, but probably subject to the right of the supervisor to veto them. So the question might arise as to why Harré was so confident, if indeed he was, that they would give me a fair crack of the whip. This raises an interesting question about his thought at a personal level. What I myself would have done as a supervisor is try to ensure that the examiners are the right people, or at least competent to examine the thesis; and, if there was any doubt, go and ask them, test their knowledge of the area, find out. But he did neither. I think this goes to the basis of an objective weakness in Harré's thought, his voluntarism about ideas. This was shackled on to an elitism about Oxford, but it also reflects an unfortunate personality trait, which was that, coming from New Zealand and being put in the hot-house atmosphere of Oxford philosophy, he and his wife Hettie went out of their way to conform. They would vote Tory, and Harré was always the absolute model of an Oxford don. He would dine in college wherever possible, always go into college for lunch, and take responsibility for choosing the wines and organising senior common room or high table dinners. He adopted the whole lifestyle of an Oxford don to an extraordinary degree, almost to the point of caricature. He craved the social recognition of his peers and the community in Oxford, which he never really got. He felt he was always looked down upon as something of an oddball and, as a result, was permanently insecure.

MH: Perhaps he was to some extent a victim of what is known in New Zealand and Australia as 'the cultural cringe'. The cringer is commonly thought to be a person who thinks most things antipodean are second-rate, but underlying that posture is an inability to accept in a mature way that there are always going to be some things in a new-world country that are indeed less than world-class.[11] So when abroad your cringer feels very insecure and tries to compensate, to be more Oxbridge than the Oxbridgeans. But, paradoxically, the more he does that, the more attention he draws to his problem.

RB: Yes, your cringer is a country bumpkin from one of the colonies. Harré subscribed to what he called the open souls doctrine – he did at this time anyway – which is the idea that you can find out by talking to people what they think and believe and you can always argue with it; this can get you a long way, he thought, because there is nothing more to society and social forms, including linguistic and ideational forms, than people and their accounts. But actually there is: once you start looking at the content of their accounts, there is a lot more to society that heavily constrains who and what are included in the conversation, who and what are recognised persons and topics, what subjects and lines of argument are acceptable. Harré was oblivious to all these questions, and this was a defect in his thought. In the debates I have had with him, he would start off by saying I was his star pupil – after I had just given what I thought was a devastating critique of his position. We always had very good debates and I enjoyed his company intellectually because he was lively and willing to argue. But I think he had a deep insecurity. People are prone to ask me, 'Why didn't you go to Oxford and get your chair?'. One reason is that deep down – subconsciously – Harré did not want me there. He would have viewed me as a rival, rather than as someone who was going to support him, which I always did. He had to be the centre of the show and he did not want anyone around who might upstage him. It is a great pity at many different levels. I did not at that time, and also subsequently, have good backers within the analytical establishment.

MH: What was the relationship between the text of the DPhil thesis and that of the book we all know? Did you make many changes?

RB: The thesis was published virtually unchanged, and it hasn't been changed since.

MH: What a sorry episode in the history of Oxford University. A wider question that comes up about the rejection of your thesis in so far as it was ahead of its time is why it had taken so long for the Copernican revolution to manifest in the philosophy of science. That is some lag!

RB: There are two aspects to this Copernican lag. There is the lag after Copernicus. This may be explained partly by the fact that self-consciousness in a practice is only necessary when practice is problematic, as in late twentieth-century or contemporary social science. Then there is the lag after the publication of *A Realist Theory of Science*. This is explained partly by the practice of, in Kuhnian terms, normal philosophy of science, in which a piecemeal approach is adopted to essentially fragmented questions, with causality disconnected from explanation, and explanation from confirmation, etc. However, there are signs in current discussion of dispositional realism and the evidential basis of laws that the two main ontological distinctions of *A Realist Theory of Science*, between the domains of the real and the actual, and open and closed systems, are being taken seriously; and that ontology – and with it the cardinal distinction between ontology and epistemology – is coming back into vogue (though not always with sufficient transcendental grounding).

MH: Can you now say something about your orientation to religion? Were you religious in a broad sense when you went up to Oxford? How did your views change?

RB: What I would say is that, although I was always interested in the transcendent and transcendental, by the time I went up to Oxford I had a very secular cast of mind. Earlier, although by the time I was twelve or thirteen I had ceased any kind of worship, I had an openness to what we couldn't or didn't understand, which we could say was religious. At Oxford I was intellectually satisfied because there was enough to get my teeth into, whereas in my very early days religion was the most expansive framework I had within which to think things about the world, and that was gradually supplemented by political and social frameworks. And then I noticed that institutionalised religion was often or mainly on the wrong side in all those other frameworks, so I left it behind. I was very dedicated politically – as I have indicated.

MH: Yes. One further thing on the political front, what was your response to the burgeoning feminism of the times?

RB: I had myself suffered direct racial oppression as a child, and I was very aware of women's oppression from the case of my mother, from the time she was a young child right the way through. So when feminism began to come up as a political movement, naturally I sided with it one hundred percent intellectually; but I had a rude shock, having always been on side existentially, to realise that it was not just self-evident to feminists that I was going to be on their side. I had to pay my dues. Much of the time it did not matter, because these things were not too strictly observed. Sometimes I went to feminist meetings and took part in them, playing a very modest role; but I also had the experience of being thrown out of one meeting because I was a bloke. And then I realised that sometimes even when you walk through doors you have to be careful about who you are leaving behind, to whom the doors are not open. This really struck home to me in 1970 when I went to America, where the feminist movement was much more advanced than in England. I had always been able to talk in a completely free way with my feminist women friends in Oxford, but it was not possible to have the same sort of dialogue with their American counterparts. Actually, I think what I later critiqued as left elitism and substitutionism was partly responsible for this state of affairs. Of course, all this was in part a necessary defensive reaction to the exclusions of women in a sexist society.

3 Beyond empiricism and transcendental idealism

Transcendental realism and the critique of classical modernism (1973–1975)

MH: You dedicated *A Realist Theory of Science*, your first book, to your mother. You mentioned last time that she was dying of cancer as you were writing the book, which must have been traumatic for you. Can you tell us more about this episode in your life?

RB: My mother had had cancer for about seven years. The last time I actually talked to her, the last time she was conscious, was when I was driving to Edinburgh via London to have my interview for the job I subsequently got there. It was just before Easter Sunday, I think it was a Wednesday in April 1973. I saw her in hospital and I was so happy because she seemed fantastically alive and vital and was talking in an enthusiastic and excitable way. Then I realised that was because she was on morphine, which was the last throw and basically it means there was no hope. I drove back to where I was living in Herefordshire and then on Easter Sunday she lost consciousness and I drove to the hospital in Teddington. It was a little cottage hospital. My father was one of the senior doctors there – in those days the National Health Service (NHS) practitioners who were involved in the cottage hospitals used to do operations; they doubled as surgeons. She was unconscious. I stayed until Monday morning, then I realised I had to get back to the cottage in Herefordshire; among other things I wanted to see what the outcome of my interview had been. On Monday night she died. On Tuesday morning I received a letter telling me that I had been appointed to the job. I had felt that I probably would be, because at the interview the three professors, Walsh, Acton and Ronnie Hepburn, who was head of department and was interested in Wittgensteinian sorts of issues, had seemed suitably impressed, and at the end Ronnie had come up to me and asked me what my stipend was. In that kind of context I did not even remember what a stipend was, so I said, 'About the normal.' So actually I was appointed on a very good salary. In my mind my mother's death and going to Edinburgh were closely associated. The events were synchronous in the strict sense, and I interpreted it as a synchronicity. Edinburgh was like a gift from my mother. It was a great release for me. I was free of the Oxford old boys' network and all its snobberies and affectations, free from the necessity of doing my thesis, and free from economic dependency on grants and things like that. Of course, after three or four years I found Edinburgh itself limiting. Also it was a long way away from where most of my friends were, and I found myself doing many long weekend drives to London. So that was the way I interpreted my mother's death. My mother's illness was itself strange, because my father, though an NHS doctor, would not admit to either of his grown-up children that their mother had cancer, and nor did she. It was an extraordinary thing –

MH: She didn't tell you?

RB: She didn't say. We knew, but it was a sort of taboo topic at the time.

MH: You never talked about it at all with your family?

RB: No, we did not. For instance, there was an Indian cousin of mine who came over, and she desperately wanted my father to give my mother some other non-orthodox western form of treatment. My father also knew homeopathy and she pleaded with him to at least try that, but he was absolutely resistant. It was a peculiar turn of events, and of course my mother died very young, she was in her fifties, and she had been ill for an awfully long time. I remember as she became very ill she was desperately wanting me to tell her something; she kept pointing to her throat and I knew she was saying, 'Tell me'. What she wanted to know of course was that I had got my DPhil, because she knew I'd submitted the first thesis. Of course, I couldn't tell her, so I always skirted round the subject in some way. And then of course when the turn of my second thesis came, it too was unsuccessful, so I wouldn't have been able to tell her that either. But I interpreted her also to be saying, 'Speak out generally. Do not take oppression lightly or silently. Use your voice. Speak to the world.'

MH: Did you feel energised by her death?

RB: No. That was the meaning of it – that's how I interpreted it subsequently – but actually I became very depressed for about three or four months. I became more or less anorexic and I was given various pills for this, none of which worked. But by the time I arrived in Edinburgh I was OK.

MH: How did your father cope with your mother's death?

RB: My father had been very devoted to my mother, going every day during her illness to be with her for as long as he could. But he told me afterwards that he could not live, as he put it, without a woman. So a very short search ensued and he lighted upon the ex-girlfriend of a friend of his and married her. She was called Brenda. My father insisted on my being his best man, and I performed all those duties. My brother quickly fell out with Brenda but I tried to maintain a sort of peace, understanding why my father had needed to do this. That in a way also made the whole episode of my mother's death more traumatic, because everyone said to my father: how could you do this? They viewed my father's second marriage as a kind of betrayal of such a wonderful woman.

MH: When did your father die?

RB: 1991.

MH: I will come to that in a later interview then. Can you say more about how you found Edinburgh after Oxford?

RB: It was a wonderful contrast. The air was fresh and my colleagues were very supportive and appreciative. I was now in a position of responsibility and enjoying it. I enjoyed, for example, giving stuffy characters like W. H. Walsh, a distinguished Kant scholar, and H. B. (Harry) Acton, a run for their intellectual money. Acton, a noted Hegel and Marx scholar, but also something of a Cold War warrior, was one of the three professors, and it may be that I was only accepted in the department because the other two kept my political allegiances completely quiet from him, or so I was led to believe. As a junior lecturer I was supposed to call Walsh 'Professor Walsh'. He invited me round to his house. I was a friend of his daughter but had to keep that quiet. When he found out that she was going out with my Jamaican friend he was horrified. Of course, you can't be friends with someone you call Professor Walsh. He actually liked to be called Richard, and after some minor social loosening up, everyone was on first-name terms. Before long there was quite a clamour for me to succeed Walsh, who was nearing retiring age. But his wife nobbled him. She thought that having a young revolutionary of Indian descent as his successor would ruin his chances of a knighthood. She wanted him to be like Strawson and Popper and Ayer, all of whom were awarded knighthoods. Even if the whole department wanted me, the door was closed. My dharma was being freely expressed now in my writings, and my first book had been well received. I was being invited to conferences and elite colloquia around the world, one in Houston, Texas with Charles Taylor, David Hamlyn, and Paul Secord, for example, and another in Barcelona with John Searle. But how long that would last I did not know, and of course now I was also a little uneasy about being a member of any elite. But I was free to read and write in Edinburgh and to have my own life. I was being paid enough to live well.

MH: You were married by this stage?

RB: Hilary[1] was a member of the revolutionary left in Oxford and I started going out with her at the end of 1968, beginning of 1969, and then from 1969 to

1970 we lived in a little rented house in a place not far from Oxford called Chiselhampton, because I had now moved out of Nuffield. It always seemed to happen that when my parents phoned up Hilary answered, and when her parents phoned up I answered. We were both first children, and while subsequent children in our generation were by and large allowed to do what they liked, there was still an assumption in the case of us first children that you should be married if you wanted to live together. Also my mother was dying of cancer, and Hilary was the first girlfriend of mine that my parents liked. I was similarly liked by Hilary's parents. Mainly to make things easier we decided to get married. We did so in September 1971, and while I was working at the Institute of Statistics we lived in a flat in St Anthony's College, which had far better food than most, including and especially a nice bistro. And then the year after that we bought for a thousand pounds a cottage in Herefordshire on the Welsh border, and this takes us through 1972–73. When I went to Edinburgh she went to Newcastle, and although there were periods when we were very close after that, she basically went her way and I went my own way. At Edinburgh I had girlfriends, in Newcastle she had boyfriends. She used to come up and see me now and then. We took a decision that both should be free to have an independent career. On feminist grounds I couldn't really argue against it. We remained very good friends and I would help her with her various political projects.

There was a time when I actually wanted to have children, and when I was in Edinburgh I used to volunteer to go baby-sitting for my friends. I got on tremendously well with some of the young families about my age who had children. One of them became a girlfriend of mine. It was a very weird thing, I did not like the situation, but the children were lovely. There was a French lecturer in Edinburgh who came to seminars I was holding on structuralism – this was in keeping with the times – and his wife came too. She was extraordinarily beautiful, a Hungarian-French Jewess. Anyway they both started coming to my talks, they were great enthusiasts. They invited me round to dinner. Then the husband let it be known that he was going away for a couple of weeks. Then she invited me round, and I was delighted because I was looking forward to good conversation with someone I liked. However, it soon became very obvious what I was supposed to do. And then she insisted that I come and live with her and her children as a surrogate husband and father. She had three children aged between about two and six. They were lovely, and remember, although it wasn't pressing on my consciousness, I was aware that I probably had a subconscious desire to have children. The eldest boy became extremely attached to me and everyone thought I was his father because I was a bit dark and all the children had a dark complexion. They acted to me as if I was their father for those three or four weeks. I think they would have liked to go on holiday with me, but I drew the line at that.

MH: As you explained last time, you turned to philosophy ultimately because human emancipation presupposes genuine knowledge of the real forces that chain us, and the possibility of such knowledge of the world was widely denied. In *A Realist Theory of Science* you wrote that

> we are not imprisoned in caves, either of our own or of nature's making. We are not doomed to ignorance. But neither are we spontaneously free. This is the arduous task of science: the production of the knowledge of those enduring and continually active mechanisms of nature that produce the phenomena of our world.[2]

Am I right in thinking that this is the fundamental message of the book?

RB: Absolutely right, this is the way to freedom from ignorance. But, of course, knowledge is not the only condition of freedom, and later on in my work I had to go into some of the other conditions. Obviously I knew I would have to do this, but the theme of the critique of ideologies that masquerade as and stand in the way of knowledge was already very important. I think the transcendental revindication of ontology and the understanding that the scientific process involves a transformation of our beliefs, and gives us access to a world that is not immediately apparent, is vitally important for general emancipation, and that is the enduring message of the book. One has to bear in mind that *A Realist Theory of Science* was only the first third of a more global project, as we've discussed. I knew it would have to be followed up by a book on the philosophy of social science and also, so I thought, by a book that would carry through the critique to the level of ideology-critique. I saw it as part of this broader project; it would explain empiricism and idealism, the false theories we held about knowledge and even more importantly about being. It was a first step in a process of ideology-critique, a process that was to be carried through to my meta-Reality books when I went into the philosophical discourse of modernity globally, the first phase or moment of which – classical modernism – is critiqued in *A Realist Theory of Science*.

MH: What else would you say is original to *A Realist Theory of Science*? That is, what would you say are its really radical claims? What distinguishes it from mainstream scientific realism?

RB: I think the best way I could answer this is by saying that I think it was like a revolution waiting to happen. And I can perhaps best illustrate this by going back to the question of my influences that you asked me last time and the contours of that answer. The anti-monistic and anti-deductivist strands provided powerful insights into what I was to call the transitive dimension of scientific activity and ontological stratification, respectively. Of course, they followed the Kantian path of involution, making scientific structure a function of mind or of the scientific community rather than seeing it as a real feature of the world. But nevertheless the concepts of scientific process and scientific structure were already there. At the same time you had philosophers such as

Strawson coming up with transcendental arguments. So the basic way I could appropriate Kant's method was already there waiting for me. Perhaps the main thing that was not waiting for me was ontology, and that is I think the really crucial missing ingredient. I will come on to this by talking a little more about some of the other things that were already there.

The idea of structure also loomed large in social theory. It was not satisfactorily theorised philosophically, but through people such as Chomsky and Lévi-Strauss, structuralism had become fashionable and the idea that science needed to deal with structures was in the air again. There was not a clear disambiguation between scientific structure, ontological structure and structure in the mind. The last was very much Lévi-Strauss's and Chomsky's way of looking at it, Chomsky with some excuse because the structures he was talking about were linguistic structures. But nevertheless you had the concept of structure there. What is distinctive about transcendental realism in this area is that, within a conception of an intransitive world, it distinguishes three different senses of structure, or three successive forms of it. The first conception is that in which there is a simple oppositional contrast between a structure and an event. Structure is that which generates and explains the event. The second conception is structure in the sense of the multi-tiered stratification of reality. Here the distinction between structure and event is applied iteratively and so extended in principle indefinitely. The third conception is the sense in which, in the context of that multi-tiered stratification, we can talk about a structure as emergent, as having come into being. Later, in *Dialectic*, I came to see structures in the first sense as themselves moving and changing.

Then you had the idea of complexity, particularly in relation to events. There was the old debate about the problem of historical knowledge, and this also can be applied to knowledge in everyday life. It seemed to me impossible to fit any ordinary or historical event into the sweep of the deductive-nomological model; events are complex. And then of course there was experience always rattling around. But what was this about experimentation? If you look at the writings of the classical British empiricists, such as Locke or Hume, or at Kant, you can quickly see that, at least when they were concerned with questions pertaining to the justification (as distinct say from the explanation) of knowledge, by experience they meant experimental activity. But the whole idea that experimental activity was the same as ordinary sense experience was nonsense, because of course the sorts of things that go on in a scientific experiment in a typical laboratory are very recondite to the ordinary lay person and to untutored common sense. So, besides ontology, another major ingredient that needed to be added was a serious analysis of experimental activity. Even this had been partially prepared for in the work of Elizabeth Anscombe and Georg Henrik von Wright, who had talked about experimentation as an intervention in the world. Now clearly the only point of intervening in the world is if you are going to produce something that would not otherwise happen, and once you take that seriously it becomes absolutely disastrous for empiricism, pivoting on the Humean theory of causal laws as, or as involving, a constant conjunction of events.

Another thing that I brought to the scene or that you could not find immediately there – it had to be repackaged – was the idea of emergence. If you took
a human being seriously and if you wanted to defend the possibility of social
science, as I certainly did, it was clear that you would have to argue that
human beings and social science are somehow emergent from nature. So you
needed a conception of emergence.

Then the way that I understood transcendental arguments was always in the
particular discursive context of theories of science that palpably held sway. At
the same time I had to do a DPhil thesis that was acceptable to the establishment. The only way to achieve these two objectives was through immanent
critique. As we've seen, the particular vantage point from which I was
approaching the issues initially was economics, and this also played a big part
because there was already an ongoing debate about the relationship between
economic theory and the world, with the standard answer being that there is
none; that, in other words, economic theory has to be pursued in some sense
for its own sake. This raised the problem of its status, and I came to think of it
as kind of praxiology, as a theory of efficient action. But of course that itself
presupposes something about the world. I tried very seriously to apply the textbook deductive-nomological models and so on of philosophy of science to
economic phenomena, and came to the conclusion that this was completely
hopeless; there was no way they fitted. So what was very obvious to me – the
constant for me as a DPhil student in economics through to the writing of *A
Realist Theory of Science* – was that the Humean theory of causal laws could not
be correct. I would like to stress to anyone trying to do original work that it is
really important to ensure that you have the sort of critical focus that this
gave me. It is important to be clear about what it is that you are actually attacking. To situate the epistemic fallacy as a fallacy, to show how the Humean
theory of causal laws just could not apply, even to the extent that the anti-
deductivists thought it could or that Kant and that whole tradition allowed,
that was very important.

Then of course there was the conception of human beings that underlay the
whole project I was critiquing. This was a very minimalist one that saw human
beings as essentially passive spectators of given phenomena. And so the epistemic fallacy, the underlying model of (tacitly gendered) man and the closure
presupposed by the Humean theory of causal laws were always at the forefront
of my mind. I was not particularly thinking that transcendental arguments are
a fine thing in a general sort of way. Rather, I was thinking about how I could
use this mode of argumentation for the practical ends that I wanted to achieve:
the critique of empiricism and idealism, including the transcendental idealist
superstructure on empirical realism. (It should of course go without saying
that none of this was designed to impugn the continuing value and relevance
of reading Hume and Kant.)

MH: You talk about a revolution waiting to happen. Would it be more accurate to say
there was a revolution underway in the philosophy of science and you carried

this through, synthesising all the elements that were around and adding vital new ingredients such as the revindication of ontology?

RB: Yes, that is what I am saying. It is important to remember that science is not simple, it is an arduous process. Scientists have to work at it practically and of course mentally, theoretically. But what they are trying to do is uncover something that people never knew about before. So science is surprising, science is wonderful, science has the capacity to transform the world as we know it. Yet it was never an infatuation with science itself that drove me, it was rather a feeling that it is part of life, and a part that all my peers think is extremely important: they themselves think it is of paramount importance, so let us understand what is happening in science.

Of course the whole point of experimental activity, even when it can only be done in thought, is precisely to give us access to the structures of the world. But how exactly does it do this? Everything that happens, happens in accordance with Newton's laws of physics, but these laws are not the only things that go to explain events. Moreover, you cannot test Newton's laws – the principles of Newtonian mechanism, for example – except under very special closed conditions that we have to produce experimentally and then control, and that means that there is an ontological gap between those laws and the patterns of events. This was the basis for the distinction between the domains of the real and the actual.

MH: So you wouldn't agree that the focus of transcendental reflection in *A Realist Theory of Science* on scientific practice as a paradigmatic practice informing us about reality makes transcendental realism 'scientistic'? Or that it is satisfactory to read off one's ontology from science, as for example Mario Bunge[3] does and Alexander Callinicos[4] recommends?

RB: The important thing I think is that, first, transcendental realism does not underwrite any particular science or any particular practice of science; it is quite consistent with a critique of scientific practices in a particular domain. Rather, what it does is ask what must the world be like for the scientific practice – experimental activity – that our tradition takes as paradigmatic to be possible, intelligible, successful and ongoing. Now of course there are also other practices, and scientific knowledge is not our only value; this is something that I explicitly signalled in *The Possibility of Naturalism*. But the arguments in *A Realist Theory of Science* consist in critiques of empiricist and idealist accounts of science and of scientific knowledge, and if you do not think science is important you need not be bound by them. But if you claimed to think that knowledge is not important I would not understand you. I could, for example, ask you whether you are telling me that knowledge is not important. If your answer was yes, I would ask whether what I said was true. You would then have to make a claim about knowledge at some level. However, I can understand what is meant by people who critique the value placed on knowledge, because of course there are many other things in life besides knowledge – many other things necessary for happiness, for example. It also has to be said that you do not necessarily have to have a very high valuation of science to accept *A Realist Theory of Science* because what it says is that, so long as science in general occurs, then the world has to have a certain shape or categorial form. So you just have to be interested in the nature of reality; the argument goes from science to ontology. In no sense is transcendental realism scientistic. First, it does not underwrite any particular scientific practice; it is not saying, for example, that some piece of experimental physics is correct. Second, it does not argue for the supremacy of science over other human values. Furthermore, I think most of the uses of transcendental realism lie in the critique of scientific, or allegedly scientific, practices and are oriented towards better scientific practice, that is immanent critique will constitute or be a part of the various sciences. Now the second part of your question was –

MH: Is it satisfactory to read off one's ontology from science?

RB: Any speech action, like any discursive philosophical project, is in a certain context and my context was one in which analytical philosophy and linguistic philosophy with a tacit empiricist ontology and therefore tacit empiricism or transcendental idealism was dominant. My objective was to critique it. To do that I had to engage with the people who were practising it, my critique had to be immanent and that is why I picked on the transcendental argument-form, because through it I was able to seize on a premise that my opponents accepted. This allowed me to show them that experimental activity was inconsistent with the Humean theory of causal laws, for instance; so something – either experimentation or the Humean theory – had to go. That is the sort of thing that a Bunge does not do. He looks at science and he might say that obviously the Humean theory of causality is wrong, or it needs reformulating or it needs to be put in a wider context, but unless you already accept that the science he is describing is epistemically valid then the argument is only going to go so far. Someone could always say that what he is describing is not science. Or that his analysis is insufficiently deep. For it will always be possible to reconstruct any piece of genuine science, if you hone it finely enough and redescribe it in an appropriate way, as consistent with almost any philosophical thesis. If you only describe what happens inside the laboratory after an experimental situation has been set up, then it looks as if science is Humean. And of course, if you foreswear transcendental argument, as Callinicos recommends, you are then in no position to critique science itself.

MH: I turn now to the objects of scientific thought, which you construe as causal powers. *A Realist Theory of Science* seems to imply that right at the outset you denied what you later came to call the 'brute' or 'exhaustive' physicality of being:[5]

> The philosophy of science has noted, quite correctly, that the objects of scientific thought are 'ideal' or 'abstract' with respect to [ordinary] things and events. But the transcendental realist sees such objects as real. For him the world is composed of real things and generated by real mechanisms. It is the world itself, not our thought of it, that is abstract and ideal.[6]

The last paragraph of the book says that, although we could not know it if there were no material things, 'electrons could exist without material things'.[7] And of course we have the position that a social structure, like a magnetic field, is 'irreducible to but present only in its effects'.[8] Such views are not well received by some critical realists who think of themselves as materialists. What can you say to allay their misgivings?

RB: You cannot of course posit the existence of electrons unless they have an effect on material things and that is the way we know them. But at the same time I think one has to be very wary of restricting one's ontology to the domain of middle-sized material things like us. In any case material things like us have reasons, we have misgivings. What is a reason or a misgiving? It is certainly not material itself. You might say that I can only identify your reasoning through certain sounds that you articulate or generate, but you just cannot identify the reason with those sounds. It is the reason or the misgiving, not the sound, that counts in the explanation of what happens in the social world. The idea that this is dualist is wrong. The dualism is rather on the other foot. What it does involve is the notion of emergence, that we have an ontology, an account of being in which some explanatory structures are emergent from others. If you subscribe to an exclusively materialist ontology, an ontology of material things, in the physical sense only, then you cannot make sense of the emergent powers that are most characteristic of human beings, or of social structures, or very generally of all those social and material states that depend upon, or are in part the outcome of, patterns of human interaction involving such things as reasons. What happens is that the materialist, who says that all that exists in the world exists at basically one ontological level, is forced into a de facto dualism because they actually have to argue at another level, deploying an emergent language, a language of reasons. Such materialism cannot sustain its ontology. So it is a self-refuting and dualist position.

MH: It could be that some misunderstanding arises from the notion of 'material causes'. Ideas and meanings are material causes in the Aristotelian sense in which you deploy that concept in the transformational model of social activity, for example. It seems to me that that kind of 'materialism' is sometimes mixed up by critical realists with metaphysical materialism. When, for example, Doug Porpora argues that social relations are 'material',[9] this is often interpreted metaphysically but perhaps he means in the Aristotelian sense.

RB: Well, on Aristotle's theory of causes, according to which you have material, efficient, final and formal causes, every event is supposed to display all four. The material causes are the antecedent social structures, including social relations at different levels, together with the pre-existing structures of physical objects, including artefacts.

MH: Are social structures just 'material causes' of action? Or are they also formal causes, as Ruth Groff has suggested?[10]

RB: Social structure is among the social material causes of praxis, in Aristotle's sense. But these material causes are stratified, and social structures are deep and enduring social material causes, which are aefficacious on and in any praxis or round of social activity. So they are not just conditions of, but conditions in, praxis and thus in Aristotle's sense, formal causes also. In any given social context they define and limit what is to count as an appropriate action. They are pre-existing conditions which are aefficacious in and on and during praxis, and in and on it from within, as well as without, they inhere in us. It is vital to see that social structures not only pre-exist, but are ongoing, and ongoing precisely in virtue of our activity. They are thus social material causes which are also formal, and none the less ontologically real for the fact that they are not material things (but what produces changes in them).

MH: I turn now to the nature of the transitive and intransitive dimensions and the distinction between them. People find this difficult to grasp. One of the problems perhaps is that the distinction as originally formulated is in relation to science, but you are already thinking in terms of its more general application, with the transitive dimension embracing everything currently being affected by human praxis. Thus the intransitive objects of science are absolutely intransitive ('not produced by men at all'[11]) whereas those of social science are only relatively so (there is causal interdependence to varying degree) except in so far as things are existentially intransitive (fully determined). Because of this kind of complication – the transitive objects of science themselves have an existentially intransitive dimension – some are inclined to think that the distinction is a pragmatic one that is useful in orienting our thinking about the scientific process rather than a fundamental ontological one. You are on record as saying that you drew too sharp a distinction in *A Realist Theory of Science*.[12] What are your thoughts on this whole issue now?

RB: One has to see the distinction between transitive and intransitive dimensions as drawn from an epistemological point of view, and that is the way I was looking at it then. That is to say, the important point was that there is a domain of objects that exist and act quite independently of any knowledge. So the emphasis was on existential intransitivity and irreducibility against both the epistemic and the ontic fallacies. When I say that it was drawn from an epistemological point of view, I mean that I purposefully abstracted from everything that pertained to the sense in which beliefs themselves are real and from the social world as itself an object of study, including the beliefs within it. Later on I would obviously have to include beliefs within being. The reason I used the terms transitive and intransitive was because they were relatively free of the connotations that existed around beliefs (or at least knowledge) and being, and in particular the connotations around epistemology and ontology. They were most favourable to the establishment of ontology, because what I wanted to say was that science is a process in motion – that is its transitive dimension – but that what it studied was something that existed and acted quite independently of it. I knew that I would have to qualify that when it came to the social sciences. However, it still remains the case that epistemologically, at any moment of time, beliefs and knowledges have an other, an object, a referent that exists independently of them at that moment of time. That is to say, there is always a distinction between beliefs and what they are about.

MH: That is existential intransitivity?

RB: Yes, and it establishes a permanent wedge between epistemology and ontology. But this wedge, which is the transitive/intransitive divide drawn from the point of view of epistemology – the transitive side of the divide – does not mean that that belief itself is not real and cannot be explained once you are thinking ontologically. Another way to put this is to say that the notion of epistemology is proleptically, and necessarily, dualistic – it always implies an ontology, from which, as epistemology, it remains distinct. But the notion of ontology is not dualistic, it does not itself have any necessary reference to epistemology. However, although the transitive/intransitive distinction registers a permanent wedge between beliefs and what they are about, this is I think much less far-reaching than the idea of ontology per se which incorporates the idea of a distinction between ontology and ontogeny and a notion of ontology that will encompass the social world and beliefs from the start. However, of course once you have the idea of an object-domain that exists intransitively, then you can talk about how we access it. Thus it is only when we have drawn this distinction that we can begin to do justice to the empirical.

MH: The question of access pertains to the transitive dimension which, unlike existential intransitivity, is not a permanent feature of existence conferred by the irreversibility of time. You see it rather as geo-historically relative, as constituted by the emergence of human beings and the first act of referential detachment?[13]

RB: Absolutely. But one might wonder whether we could use this distinction in studies of other animals, for example animals that learn. Learning could be a more general feature of the environment. And then you could think about constructing arguments, even transcendental arguments, from particular types of learning.

MH: There could be embryonic transitive dimensions for many forms of life.

RB: Yes, learning could be a very general feature of the universe. That is a speculation.

MH: I now want to ask you about transcendental arguments, the main argument-form you use to elaborate a realist ontology. As David Tyfield has suggested, Kantian transcendental arguments can be construed, like yours, as embracing immanent critique, that is, of *Humean* experience.[14] In which case would it be correct to say that the crucial move you made was to deepen the focus from experience to social practices as conceptualised in experience, thereby giving transcendental arguments purchase on a mind-independent world in so far as people are themselves causal agents in the world?

RB: For me transcendental arguments are a species of retroductive-analogical argument distinguished by a number of considerations, the first being that they have a philosophical subject-matter. I can bring this out by indicating how they relate to retroductive-analogical arguments. A retroductive-analogical argument will say there is a domain of phenomena here, this is what makes that domain of phenomena intelligible. A transcendental argument as I use it will say there is a human activity here which is conceptualised in our experience, the nature of the world as structured and differentiated makes this activity intelligible. So it has that form. This means that it is fallible, epistemically relative; it arrives in a particular social context. A retroductive-analogical argument does not have to refer to anything to do with human experience, whereas a transcendental argument does. The minor premise of the transcendental argument is the basic feature of experience as conceptualised in a certain way. One concerns oneself with a minor premise in so far as one wants to criticise or develop or perhaps defend some account of that experience. David Tyfield is absolutely right that significant transcendental arguments always have a critical context; more generally, if you want to produce an original transcendental argument in philosophy, it is always going to be in an immanently critical context. The minor premise here has to be some form of human experience that your opponents accept; for example, experimental activity, understood in a certain way. The approach is immanently critical in so far as you are critiquing established or dominant accounts of that activity. What you will then be doing is bringing out the implicit presuppositions of a form of life that has already been ongoing. So you can say that even if scientists who are engaging in experiments think their activity under Humean descriptions, actually what their activity in practice presupposes is non-Humean; and so you have the beginnings of what I later called a Tina formation.

MH: Does that mean that every argument that is retroductive from any activity conceptualised in any way is going to be transcendental?

RB: No, it is not quite as simple as that. You do have to have the immanent critique of some notion about human activity as conceptualised in a particular way. But characteristically we would only call an argument of that form transcendental if it operated at a level that was sufficiently abstract. So we would not normally call an argument about housing or furniture a transcendental argument. But you could very plausibly construe many of the arguments in Marx's *Capital* as transcendental because they deal with more general or pervasive features, the sorts of feature that are, or are close to being, categories. This brings out another characteristic of these arguments: that they operate at a syncategorematic level, that is to say, they talk about things in general, not a particular thing. Then of course the class of transcendental arguments also includes, as a sub-class, dialectical arguments. So actually transcendental argument denotes a distinct class of arguments that are fundamental in social science as well as in philosophy.

As part of a discursive strategy of immanent critique not everything critical philosophers say is going to take the form of transcendental argument. Indeed, in general, besides providing a transcendental argument that shows that the selected activity presupposes something that is inconsistent with, that is excludes the given account of, it they will normally also be concerned to make various reductios or point to internal aporiai and inconsistencies in the position they are attacking. Transcendental arguments have not been well studied in the period after Kant, just as dialectical arguments have not been particularly well studied after Hegel; they were studied in classical Greek and medieval times when dialectic was not operating in a context of transcendental arguments.

MH: Do transcendental arguments work in relation to other social practices such as music or religion, or do they have to take their departure from science?

RB: In relation to religion Émile Durkheim, for example, gave an interesting answer to that in his book *The Elementary Forms of Religious Life*. A transcendental argument about music would give you knowledge of the world, and it would be part of science, the science of music or musicology. A transcendental argument in the context of music will look at it from the point of view of the intelligibility of music. It won't help someone trying to compose like Beethoven, but it will help someone trying to understand Beethoven better.

MH: Do you want to comment further on the issue of the purchase of transcendental arguments on a mind-independent world?

RB: In terms of the mind-independence of the ontology of transcendental realism, I think I cannot over-emphasise the role of the practical. In experimental activity it is our role as causal agents that is vital, not our role as thinkers, and that immediately gets us out of the purely mental sphere. Of course, my conception of the transitive dimension was very much inspired by Marx and his notion of work and labour, but interestingly enough also by Wittgenstein and his private language argument. Basically Wittgenstein said you cannot be an atomistic individual – an individual monad – and make sense of language and meaning; you have to do it by being in the context of the social. And what was very important to him was not just an abstract social but the social and practical: social practice, social activity. *Philosophical Investigations* begins with an account of builders building, or laying blocks and slabs. That is absolutely vital; this is where the truth of materialism that we are physical beings – causal agents – fits in. Most philosophy had completely abstracted from this. Of course, Wittgenstein did not pursue the implications in full, but that is the real importance of his private language argument. You could say that there are two aspects to this argument. First, as I mentioned last time, there is a world out there independent of my mind. This is not explicitly differentiated into what exists independently of my mind (the pre-existing social) and what exists independently of any mind (the purely natural). We have the thesis that society is ontologically prior to the individual; but this aspect also immediately connotes existential intransitivity and realism. The second aspect involves characterising, further specifying, the nature of the world out there. There are other people in the social world out there and this pre-existing social world depends in part on their causally aefficacious activities, that is to say, this world is dependent on the material activity of causal agents. This specifies the form of the sociality of the first part of the argument. Of course, once you understand the physicality of the interactions that human beings enjoy, then you can also go into social interaction as speech-action and other forms of action between causal agents who can think, and then we get a more complete picture.

MH: Kenneth R. Westphal has recently argued independently (that is, without, it would seem, reading your work) that Kant's own precepts, methods and arguments, when consistently carried through, refute transcendental idealism and point in the direction of a transcendental realism similar to your own.[15] Does this accord with your own view, both then and now?

RB: Yes it does. There are two things that I would like to say here about Kant's work. The first involves the endemic aporiai of transcendental idealism: that actually unless Kant accepts the reality of the categories and the understanding then we cannot even have knowledge of the phenomenal world. It seems to me that Westphal is developing the kind of point I made about the categories and the understanding in relation to the flux of experience, which is great. Unless you have a distinction between the objective manifold and the subjective sequence of experiences, you are not going to have anything that is going to look like the terms of an empirical invariance – you are not going to have the manifold. If we include stray events, stray experiences, we are not going to have an empirical invariance. You can argue that the main contribution that Kant made was the idea of stratification within mind. However I want to point out that, in the second place, his immanent critique of Humean experience still involves the idea of Humean causal laws. It still involves the idea of an empirical invariance of events as being necessary for a law, and that has the disastrous consequence that our freedom as human beings is placed outside the world as studied by science. So there is no scientific route to emancipation, the possibility of a science of human beings is undercut, and we have a split world. In *Dialectic* I do actually explicitly argue that Kant's own precepts, methods and arguments, consistently carried through, entail dialectical critical realism, hence also transcendental realism.[16] What Kant particularly wanted to do, of course, is to show how freedom and morality are consistent with the science of Newton. He never questioned the universality of that science, which he interpreted actualistically, and that was a truly disastrous mistake. The empirical realism is the more important thing in Kant, the transcendental idealism is relatively secondary. Of course, transcendental idealism in general, from Kant on, has had this wonderful intuition that scientific knowledge and thought are structured, but the involution of structure means that there is no way we can ever regard that structure as anything other than arbitrary: this is my story, one possible story against others. Of course, we now know in some areas of science that the Newtonian categories are inappropriate; we do not accept them any longer even in physics at the level of Einstein's theory of relativity or at the level of quantum physics, let alone the human sciences.

Categorial realism is so important, not just in the context of Kant but in the context of philosophers of science such as Popper, who assume that the categories are within the human mind or, to put this in a more sociological form, within society: they are things that we impose either individually or as a community on the world. If you believe that then you go back on transcendental arguments, and ultimately you won't have a ground for saying that a particular process or law operates in the world. Modal realism too is so important. As the wonderful saying by Paul Eluard you drew my attention to has it: 'There is another world, but it is in this one.'[17] It is not this one, but it is in it, it is a possibility. As a possibility it is enfolded within the things and structures that we have in this world, and so this world could be different. Modal realism is indispensable for concrete utopianism and for human freedom, and even for the aefficacy of critique, because you have to be able to say I need not believe this, there are other possibilities. The specific form of modal realism is dispositional realism, to which transcendental realism is also committed. This asserts the reality of causal powers, liabilities and tendencies.

MH: In a paper that attempts to situate your early work in relation to current debates within Anglo-analytic metaphysics and the philosophy of science, Ruth Groff has recently suggested that *A Realist Theory of Science* (*RTS*) comes close to espousing

> what Alexander Bird has called the mixed view regarding the existence of dispositional and categorical[18] properties. The mixed view, in contrast to

either dispositional monism . . . or categorical monism, is the view that there are some properties that are purely dispositional, others that are categorical. . . . A fourth position . . . is that all properties are both. Bhaskar explicitly allowed in *RTS* for the possibility of properties that are purely dispositional, but I see no textual evidence to suggest that he held that *all* properties are purely, or even fundamentally, dispositional rather than categorical. Thus I conclude that the dispositional realism of *RTS* would fall into the category of 'mixed'.[19]

Is this a view with which you concur?

RB: Yes. What is distinctive about transcendental realism is that it involves a three-tier analysis of causal powers. Not only may causal powers be possessed independently of their actualisation, we must distinguish their exercise from their actualisation, so as to allow that they may be exercised without being actualised (that is, manifest in an empirical invariance), just as they may be actualised without being experienced or perceived by human beings. This is of course an index of the distinction between the domains of the real, the actual and the empirical. The result is a dynamic depth dispositional realism in which the real acts, even if it is not manifest in a Humean-type sequence, that is, irrespective of the closure or otherwise of the system in which it acts – what I call 'transfactually'.

MH: In relation to modal realism, Eluard's saying should perhaps be amended to say that there are other worlds, not just another world; that is, the possibility in this one is infinite.

RB: Absolutely. You see, modal realism as understood in critical realism is concrete rather than abstract. It is not just that the world could have been different, or that there could be different worlds, as David Lewis, for example, and the counterfactual theorists have it – which is true but not very interesting – but that in our world, the world that we have and know, there are alternatives. But the very idea of an alternative is something inconsistent with actualism, and this is why the big negatives – the negative point, the negative critique – of transcendental realism are so important: to clear away, to get rid of, empirical realism, anthropomorphic accounts of science and being, the epistemic fallacy, and perhaps above all actualism.

MH: You wrote: 'On the conception of philosophy at work in this book both the ultimate premises and the immediate conclusions of philosophical considerations are contingent facts, the former (but not the latter) being necessarily social and so historical'.[20] This has been taken to mean that you are committed to epistemic relativism within science but not philosophy. How would you respond to this?

RB: That is not correct. The premise – for example, experimental activity – is necessarily social, but the conclusion is not, it might be about the world as such and in general. Moreover, you can detach the conclusion from the premise in the same way as you can detach the conclusion of a retroductive-analogical argument if it is acceptable. There is no way I can prove transcendental realism; as I say in *A Realist Theory of Science*, it is not even the only possible account, but it is the only one consistent with the phenomena that I analysed.[21] We detach those conclusions because we cannot get by in social life without using detachment, without accepting our conclusions when they are as well justified as we can possibly make them, such that we feel that they are good enough to act on.

MH: This is transcendental detachment?

RB: Yes. I don't talk about it in *A Realist Theory of Science*. It is very close to referential detachment, except you are not detaching the referent, you are detaching the conclusion of your argument. You are detaching it, not because it is necessarily infallibly true, but as the best account that you know of in that domain. Without some such procedure, argumentation would have no point at all and we would be stuck in an endless regress because, whenever we wanted to establish anything in philosophy and we could not detach it, we would just have to go on, as Hegel did. You would have to say that you cannot have any knowledge at all except of the totality, and if you accept with critical realism that the totality is open and unfinished, then you can never have any knowledge. That is absurd. If someone said I really believe that you can never have any knowledge, I would say that is absolutely fine, you stay with that, but I am talking to those people who believe empiricism and act on it. And in a subsidiary argument I would want to see what you act on. Because undoubtedly you would be acting on something like empiricism; you would not be acting honestly.

MH: It is important, hermeneutically, to try to understand any work both in its own terms and context and as a moment in the broader development of a thinker's thought. You have said and implied in a range of contexts that *A Realist Theory of Science* was already implicitly dialectical. Can you indicate some of the ways in which this is so? Would it be true to say that the dialectics came from life before they came from books (we discussed earlier how you were practising an embryonic dialectical method from very early on)? Of course, some of the key concepts of transcendental realism – the transitive and intransitive dimensions; the domains of the real and the actual; transfactuality and tendency; the relational conception of social forms; the 'holy trinity' – are implicit in Marx (whom you were reassessing as a scientific realist), a fact that must be presumed to lend support to the implicit dialecticality thesis. When you wrote *A Realist Theory of Science* were you aware of absences in transcendental realism that could themselves be absented by immanent critique – that is, that transcendental realism itself could be developed dialectically – and to what extent did you already think this important or even necessary?

RB: I think I would want to answer the part of the question about dialectics coming from life before books in a double way. Yes, this is what I was doing, in life as well as in books. When I wanted to outwit my father's control of me in relation to choice of vocation, I was picking on grounds that he would concede but finding cases he didn't include when he was thinking about it, so I was looking for the absence there. Similarly, in *A Realist Theory of Science* I was looking for what was really missing. As a child this was of course at an intuitive level; I hadn't really formulated what I was doing, or at least not to any great extent. In the second case, although it might have been more conscious, it was still something that was not discursively formulable in the context of received ideas about dialectic and dialectical method; there was no way I could have actually said what I was doing and it took a long time before I felt that I could. It was only when I had finished *Dialectic* that I felt at all happy about being able to situate this approach, and to situate it dialectically.

In relation to whether I was aware of absences that would or should be absented, here one has to say yes. As I pointed out last time, *A Realist Theory of Science* was only one third of my total project, the other parts being philosophy of social science and ideology-critique or sociology of knowledge. I knew I was going to have to get round to those two. I was very conscious of the fact that I was abstracting from the way in which in the social sciences beliefs themselves are affected causally and causally affect in turn the objects of knowledge. More generally, that we would have to look at beliefs as part of the intransitive dimension and thus of ontology in its own right. So I was abstracting from crucial aspects of the social. I was also aware that I was abstracting from change and from questions of internal relationality – what later became 2E and 3L. And of course even in the triptych of the overall project, I was abstracting very consciously from the whole context of debates about Hegel's and Marx's dialectical method. As early as 1978 I was writing, for *New left Review* it so happens, an article on dialectic, materialism and science. It was going to be a critique of Galvano Della Volpe, Lucio Colletti and Sebastiano Timpanaro, but I never finished it. Even the articles I published, for example the dictionary entries I wrote on dialectical themes, abstracted from serious engagement with absence, contradiction, and dialectical method. But I was working on it, and it took thirteen years of hard labour for me to lick the problem of absence and see that I had to situate it as an ontological category and then reconstruct the understanding of being informing my whole project. It had to be deepened to take into account all the phenomena of processual reality – the first level of structure I identified in *A Realist Theory of Science* had to be seen as itself changing, the traditional principles of substance and causality had to be dynamised – and that meant that critique also had to be deepened.

MH: In terms of dynamisation, the key implicitly dialectical concept in your first book is tendency?

RB: Yes, it is the key concept in the dispositional realism I put forward. You have powers, but a power in motion is a tendency. This gives the concept of power a three-dimensionality that other accounts, even those of Chomsky and Harré, lack. Dynamisation was also to allow me to concretise my understanding of scientific method a little, to put the logic of scientific discovery I articulated in transcendental realism in a more explicitly social and less, so to speak, idealised context. This does not mean that there was anything wrong with the account in *A Realist Theory of Science*, just that it abstracted by and large from a lot of messy sociological considerations that the later account took on board. The logic of scientific discovery – the description of a non-random pattern in nature, the imagining of a plausible model of a generative mechanism, the elimination of alternative accounts, the identification of the generative mechanism at work, and then of a new level of structure – that model is to be understood as occurring within the epistemological dialectic I articulated in *Dialectic*. Or another way to look at *A Realist Theory of Science* is to see it as being primarily concerned with ontology and the stratification of being, and the epistemological dialectic as complementing this with an account of what the scientist understands and experiences subjectively. In *A Realist Theory of Science* I explicitly referred to the logic of scientific discovery as a dialectic, a dialectic which of course incorporates also a dialectic of explanatory and taxonomic knowledge.

MH: The earlier account seems to deny a key feature of the later one and also of the account in the philosophy of meta-Reality: creativity ex nihilo. It places heavy emphasis on material causes: 'man never *creates*, but only *changes*, his knowledge, with the cognitive tools at his disposal'.[22]

RB: The earlier account does indeed seem to exclude ex nihilo creativity. But its thematisation of emergence – of the reality of the 'secondary qualities' and irreducible novelty – prepares the way ontologically for such a notion; and it must be borne in mind that, although it gives an account of science as a social process in motion, it does not seek to give an account of the source of change, except by invoking a general notion of human creativity. What is not there in *A Realist Theory of Science* is a full statement of the transitive dimension. That depends upon the development of a philosophy of social science, which was the brief of *The Possibility of Naturalism*, and a full account of how you would critique a system of thought as an ideology. *A Realist Theory of Science* was not a full critique of empiricism. It satisfied only one third of the criteria that I give for ideology-critique in *The Possibility of Naturalism*. Although there was a great deal of talk about motion, it did not analyse how motion actually occurred; it was silent on the categories of negativity and process that were to come in *Dialectic*. What you can say in general is that, in the logic of scientific

discovery in Chapter 3 and throughout the book, there is much that antici-
pates *The Possibility of Naturalism* and much that depends upon but does not
actually anticipate the work in *Dialectic*. I had an intuition that absence was
going to be important, but that is all. It was a long time before I could formulate what is philosophically necessary for any full understanding of change.

MH: Are there any senses in which transcendental realism is implicitly a philosophy of meta-Reality as well as dialectical?

RB: Yes. Take the critique of atomism in Chapter 2. It is very important for everything that happens in critical realism subsequently, but especially in the meta-
Reality books. While *A Realist Theory of Science*, as I point out in the
Postscript,[23] does not explain the abstract model of human being that underlies empiricism and idealism, the beginnings of an answer are sketched in its
discussion of the two poles of the basic problematic of classical modernism: an
abstract, actualist, account of universality and an atomistic, punctualist, egocentric view of the world, such that we have atomistic human beings or isolated egos set in opposition to a uniform and unchanging world. That is of
course absurd. But it is an absurdity that was prevalent at the beginning of
modernity in the works of Hobbes and Hume and in the models that underlie
the accounts of science and knowledge that modernity generated, and that are
still prevalent in the textbooks as accounts of explanation, prediction, falsification, and so on (see *A Realist Theory of Science*, Appendix to Chapter 2), and
in the aporiai they generate, such as the problem of induction (see ibid.:
Chapter 3.6). Even Kant assumed that there is a level at which the empirical
is simply given to us, in which we are completely passive, and then, superim-
posed on this level, a mind that can synthesise and make sense of it, that is
active and can do things. In contrast, *A Realist Theory of Science* argues that we
are active agents engaged in various processes of transformation in a complex,
differentiated and changing world constituted by different levels, all of which
in principle can be scientifically understood, as can our own action. I wanted
to situate the possibility of freedom as a power of human beings capable of acting out of their bio-psycho-social nature and from their complex constitution
and back on the materials out of which they are formed.

This is consonant with recent work in anthropology, broadly conceived.
Thus Brenda Farnell[24] argues that it is not sufficient merely to relocate the
body at the core of theories of social action, but that the body must be conceived dynamically, as *engaged in movement*. Embodied human agency, conceived as a generative causal power grounded in our corporeal materiality,
thus provides the conditions of possibility of our cultural being, while our cultural life determines the form or mode of expression of our own materiality. In
short, persons are irreducibly bio-psycho-social beings, always manifesting
their intentionality in the physical world out of which they emerged.

Central to my approach in *A Realist Theory of Science* is a critique of our
received notions of a thing and events, and correspondingly critiques of our

conceptions of identity and of universality and therefore unity. Both point the way forward to meta-Reality as a philosophy of a rich differentiated and developing identity that constellationally embraces non-identity and difference.

Another pointer in the direction of meta-Reality was the concept of depth-stratification. Just as we have to think of beings at different levels, so we have to think of our ordinary life as constituted by different levels of structure and different levels of agency. Relatedly, the idea of a false understanding of science coexisting with a good or sound practice of it leads on to the concept of co-presence and the conceptualisation of the Tina formation in *Dialectic* and of demi-reality in transcendental dialectical critical realism, and so to an understanding of emancipation as the shedding of heteronomous orders of determination to release the good or true enfolded within them. The concept of the transcendentally real self is not yet there in transcendental realism, but it was already very clear to me that you had to analyse the self in a different way. This connects with the theme of non-duality in meta-Reality. This functions as a kind of reductio of the crude subject–object model that sees subjects over here and objects over there. The reformulation within transcendental realism and subsequently within dialectical critical realism already makes it clear that subjects arise from a world of objects that are causally acting and reacting back on them. So the new model is differentiated, it is complex, it is dialectical and it is stratified. But what happens in states of non-duality is that the focus on the object as distinct from the subject, and vice versa, collapses. It does not mean that the beings collapse but just that in that state there is no separation between them. When you are reading the newspaper, actually reading it, in that moment of reading it, it is not an object distinct from the reading, there is just the reading; existential intransitivity is lost. But then you cannot do what we call science. To do science means that you have to reconstitute a discursive world; but non-duality is nevertheless a part of being, and without it you cannot begin to do science. Science is a discursive superstructure on a non-dual basis. The discursive superstructure is very important, and that is what *A Realist Theory of Science* addressed. In meta-Reality one is talking about states that transcend discursivity, and so this potentially completes the account of science and scientific practice, indeed completes, as it underpins, the whole set of issues that are built on or around the subject–object distinction. Indeed, this may all be viewed as proleptically contained within the transitive/intransitive distinction that is constructed in a clear but minimal way at the beginning of critical realism. Together with notions of depth-stratification, emergence, the irreducibility of novelty and unity-in-diversity,[25] it gives you – *A Realist Theory of Science* gives you – in rudimentary form many of the tools you need for critical depth-emancipatory discourse.

MH: I was going to ask if it ever seemed an attractive option for you to become a professional philosopher of science, but from what you have just said about the developmental logic of *A Realist Theory of Science* it would seem the answer is definitely no. This is a book that had to go on, and as we know it did. It was already going on well before it was published.

RB: This is true, but at a more immediate and subjective level I was aware after *A Realist Theory of Science* came out that I did not want to be like Popper or Hume, who did their really original work at a young age and then basically spent the rest of their lives reformulating it. I did not want to be like that. But of course, as I have said, *A Realist Theory of Science* was only a third of a total project to demolish the ideologies standing in the way of human freedom and what I was later to call the eudaimonistic society. I would have felt divided if I had ever accepted the option of being a narrowly professional philosopher of science. I would have been an Unhappy Consciousness. So I did not do it.

4 The critical realist embrace
Critical naturalism (1975–1979)

MH: Tell us something about your personal life and career during the years covered by this interview, the second half of the 1970s.

RB: I started off this period at Edinburgh. I've already recounted something of my life there, how it was a liberation after the graduate world at Oxford but became limiting after a time and how there was a move in the department for me to succeed Walsh, but the way was blocked. My career was actually going very well at this stage and I wasn't particularly anxious to get a chair, or to settle down in any way. I wanted rather to go on. I'd had an exceptionally good reception in the University of Sussex when I went there in 1977 to give a paper on the possibility of social scientific knowledge and the limits of naturalism, which was published the following year in the *Journal for the Theory of Social Behaviour*. The University of Sussex was a revolutionary campus. Feyerabend had been there as a visiting Fellow; his tenure might have overlapped with my visit, but I didn't meet him on that occasion. The reception was so very good that I went back two or three times that year and eventually they offered me a one-year fellowship, which I accepted, and I took sabbatical leave from Edinburgh for that year. In 1979 I went down to Sussex, and I lived most of that year in Brighton. Some time in 1980 I got a flat in Battersea in London and, whenever I went to Brighton, I would drive there and back.

MH: When you turned to the philosophy of science a key motivation was to discover what light an adequate philosophical account of the natural sciences could shed on the search for truth and freedom in the social sphere – 'the project of human self-emancipation'[1] that had been manifesting itself to you since childhood; whether it would permit a resolution of the crisis in the human sciences, their emancipation from the ideologies stymieing them for the work of emancipation. I take it that *The Possibility of Naturalism*, with its central question, 'to what extent can society be studied in the same way as nature?' was thus, in terms of your drive to come into your dharma, a book that had to be written. Indeed, as you mentioned last time, you were already planning it and a sociology of knowledge or ideology-critique sequel on *Philosophical Ideologies* when you were writing *A Realist Theory of Science*.

RB: Yes, absolutely.

MH: I take it that the fundamental message of the book is accordingly similar to that of *A Realist Theory of Science*, with the emphasis now on the sociosphere: social science as a way to freedom from ignorance as one of the conditions of human free flourishing. Contra the gathering relativism of the age, scientific knowledge of society is possible and social science, which unlike natural science is internal to its subject-matter, necessarily takes the form of explanatory critique and so directly impinges on the project of human emancipation from reproduced structures of domination that constrain our essential freedom.

RB: Yes, absolutely.

MH: As I see it, the possibility of naturalism is derived from (1) transcendental argument from human transformative praxis (intentional agency) and (2) immanent critique of the antinomies of social theory: naturalism/anti-naturalism; reification/voluntarism; holism/individualism; body/mind; causes/reasons; facts/values. And it is lent support by consistency with transcendental realism, which critical naturalism constellationally embraces (hence its long title: transcendental realist critical naturalism[2]). Am I right in thinking that the main new move in all this was the widening of the minor premise to embrace human practical activity as such, not just scientific practical activity? As you explain in the 1989 Postscript, it is part of your strategy of immanent critique, since intentional agency 'is a good anti-naturalist premise'.[3]

RB: Yes, I agree with all of that. Your formulation is correct in terms of the discursive strategy of the finished product. One could add that my initial approach to the possibility of naturalism was via my first book. In *A Realist Theory of Science* I had produced a radically new account of knowledge and science, including its social preconditions. The question now was what could one do with it, a question that must also be seen in the context of my pre-existing triple project embracing the philosophy of social science and ideology-critique of the philosophies that were so dominant.

What *could* one do with a book like *A Realist Theory of Science*? The first and most obvious thing is to look into its transapplication to different contexts, to see whether and how far it is also applicable to, for example, the social sciences, but perhaps also the biological sciences (as I was to do in *Scientific Realism and Human Emancipation*) – or perhaps even to something more specific, such as cybernetics; or possibly to a domain of human practice, such as for instance law or architecture. A second approach would have been to delve further into the concrete, because undoubtedly my focus in *A Realist Theory of Science*, as it was in the work I did subsequently, was theoretical as distinct from applied science. Indeed, although I had gone into the stratification of nature and emergence in some detail, I did not really do much more work on applied science or the concrete, at least until *Dialectic*, and then again it was rather theoretical work on the concrete. So another form of application or better, development, of transcendental realism, would have been to go into the concrete, to look in depth at applied science. It is this kind of work I have turned to over the last six or seven years, especially when I was working in Scandinavia and the Nordic area. Then again one sub-division of that, intersecting with the first approach, would be to go into various regional sciences in much greater detail, and to some extent I am also doing that now. Of course, since *A Realist Theory of Science*, many other critical realists have been doing that anyway, at least implicitly. People generally come to critical realism from some specific context, a context in which theory may be stuck or there may be problems in research or practice; and in using critical realism as a tool in that context they are led to elaborate (or tacitly presuppose) a regional critical realist theory of that context. This is something that is testified to by the many divisional entries in your *Dictionary of Critical Realism*.

While I did engage in transapplication enterprises and went deeper, at least to some extent, into the concrete, the main emphasis of my subsequent work has been on the theoretical deepening of transcendental realism. This took the form mainly of a deepening of ontology rather than epistemology. I think of this deepening as work that transcendental realism necessitated. Its developmental logic is registered in the MELDARA schema. The project of *The Possibility of Naturalism* was the first stage in this; it took me onto the terrain of 2E, the terrain of negativity, contradiction, processuality and social relationism and transformationalism. And of course I already knew that it would when I started working on the book, that you could not just take critical realism as developed from physics and chemistry and apply it mechanically to social science, because that would be begging the question as to whether the subject-matter of the social sciences is indeed comparable to that of the experimental natural sciences (paradigmatically, classical physics and chemistry). Undoubtedly you would find some kind of fit there, but so would a social constructionist or some other form of poststructuralist; Hempel and Popper and the deductive-nomological philosophers had also thought they had found a fit. So what was required was actually a transcendental realism for the social sciences that was somewhat independent of existing critical realism, and again what I did was try to pick on a premise that would be acceptable to people almost everywhere. That was intentional agency. I have to say 'almost everywhere' because there were positivists who denied it, and that is why I needed the double approach of transcendental argument from intentional agency and an immanent critique of the antinomies in which social theory and science were stuck.

This double strategy, on the basis of the transcendental realism already posted as it were, is reflected in the double specificity of the results. Every science is going to be specific, on the one hand, to its subject-matter – you cannot just have an epistemology or theory of method in isolation from a specific subject-matter, some specific domain of the real; and, on the other, to where the science or scientist is in its research process, in its epistemological or transitive cycle of discovery and explanation. I think it is very important to remember that work in the human and social sciences in particular is doubly specific in this way. It is always going to be guided by the particular subject-matter you are studying; if you are studying education, or health or military history you are going to have to have slightly different ontologies and therefore slightly different methodologies. The methodologies are going to be a vector partly of your specific ontology but then partly of something else that is also very specific, which is where you are in your own concrete research process. There is not a single simple methodology; the methodology that critical realism entails is always going to have this double specificity.

This specificity can be seen in terms of a kind of double inclusiveness. First, the critical realist orientation gives you a maximally inclusive ontology, because for critical realism there is nothing that is not real. Now this does not mean, if you believe in animism, that the world is populated by witches and devils. However it does mean that it is populated inter alia by your belief in witches and devils. Ontology then is maximally inclusive. Critical realism does not say in advance that something is not real, or even that it might be real but is not worth studying. That is up to the researcher to ascertain. So too, in the second place, it is up to the specific researcher to determine exactly what tools, what part of the total metatheoretical, categorial and conceptual toolkit offered by critical naturalism needs to be deployed, and what exactly needs to be tinkered with and developed according to the specificities of the research of particular subject-matters. Moreover, the researcher's interest will depend on where the researcher is in the epistemological dialectic of the particular science or concrete research enquiry, or even (embedded within these) the researcher's career. Thus, there is nothing that critical naturalism says in advance against number-crunching. If you do not have any data then the first thing is to get some data. Similarly there is nothing against theory-construction. The house of an epistemology that is going to be adequate to physics and chemistry, on the one hand, and the social sciences in general, on the other, is going to have many different rooms.

Now with this double (ontological and epistemological) inclusiveness in mind, we can then look at what alternative or rival philosophies of social science do, and we will see that normally they fasten onto only one particular bit or phase of the research process and, in so far as they are doing ontology, theorise only the sort of thing they are expecting to find at that particular level. So the Humeans – the empiricists – look for constant conjunctions. The neo-Kantians are thinking about the importance of structure in mind and the social community, so they are looking for that. The hermeneuticists come along and say, well, the nature of social reality is very different from natural reality and the structures that you neo-Kantians are thinking about are constituted by language. Their basic argument is that that is how society is, so you have empiricists and neo-Kantians focusing on the transitive dimension and the hermeneuticists focusing on an intransitive dimension of the social as constituted by linguistic or conceptual matters. Then the social constructionists come along and couple a neo-Kantian epistemology with a hermeneutic ontology and you have the doctrine that the only thing that can be known is what we constitute in our linguistic experience. Then you realise that what all these different philosophical vantage-points are talking about is correct in so far as it goes, in so far as one focuses on one specific area of investigation or one moment of the total enquiry. However, what critical realism tries to do is give a picture of the whole. This means that critical realists can embrace the insights of other positions and need not fear anything from them. Critical realists are welcome to join in, but so too are social constructionists, empiricists, neo-Kantians and any other variety of philosopher, social theorist and researcher. This could be called the critical realist embrace.

MH: I like that!

RB: We do not demolish our opponents at this level, we embrace them. When you are talking with them, you do not say, 'What a terrible liberty, just focusing on language and ignoring the other aspects of social life!' or anything like that. You share their enthusiasm for the particular linguistic feature they have fastened on and invite them to be part of a critical realist research team and then they will soon start saying, for example, 'Oh critical realism – I can do critical realism doing what I do as a social constructionist (or whatever), now let me do it.' And then, when their guard is down, a critical realist colleague might say, 'Why don't you try economic structure as well as linguistic structure, and look at these interesting statistics, or look at these interesting interviews I've done.' In this way I think critical realism can provide an ontological, epistemological, and methodological framework for everyone working on a research project in the social sciences. All we ask of those people is that they don't stop other people doing what they want to do.

MH: All the tendencies within philosophy and social theory you have alluded to are replicated within critical realism to some extent. Are you saying in effect that it is entirely appropriate that people should work within them for, as we know, pushed to their limit, their developmental logic will take them along the authentic critical realist way, straight down the middle and over the top? So all you need is to really want to know.

RB: Absolutely. Someone might ask, 'If we can just do what we were doing anyway what is the point of becoming a critical realist?' To answer this we have to take a slight detour – which is not really a detour – into the forms of critique of alternative or rival philosophical accounts of the subject-matter of the social and human sciences. One that I have always stressed is immanent critique, and of course what might be nice for a researcher who is just seeing the light about critical realism is to do an immanent critique of philosophical positions at work in their subject area. There might be so many possible immanent critiques that they could get a little lost, but there is a form of immanent critique that is very powerful, which I would recommend. It is what I have called the Achilles' Heel critique. In this form of critique you seize on the most important premise for a particular position and show how that premise and all the beautiful insights that are hoped to be sustained by it cannot in fact be sustained on the basis of that specified ontology, epistemology and methodology. It is a real blow to the empiricist, who believes that all knowledge about the world comes via constant conjunctions of experience, to realise that this cannot do justice to experimentally produced experience, which is the only sort of experience that the natural scientist is normally interested in. Likewise, it would be a blow to a Marxist, for example, if you could show on the basis of their epistemology that they cannot sustain the concept of class consciousness. It would be a blow to the hermeneuticists and social constructionists if you could show that they cannot sustain the intelligibility of language on their assumptions. So that is the Achilles' Heel critique, and it is the most powerful instrument for arriving at a more inclusive conceptual formation.

MH: The moral of all this is that if we are going to build the eudaimonistic society we really have to use our heads.

RB: We have to use our heads anyway, because when you want to correct a belief you have, or rid yourself of an illusion, or critique someone else's false belief, you are doing this. You are oriented against the false belief in favour of one that you hope will succeed as the result of an intentional rational project. That is the only way we can do it; we cannot suppose it is going to happen beneath or behind the back of intentionality. Of course, we know that our intentional projects won't cover all the conditions that apply, but it is the hope of human emancipation that we can do this thing, we can survive and flourish in a eudaimonistic society as a result of our rational self-conscious endeavours. To those who are very swayed by the pull of local sociologies oriented against reason I would point out that the legitimate complaint that Third World people, women and ethnic minorities might have is not against reason per se but against one particular form of reason. Reason is for me dialectical and concrete, that is to say, it is always contextual and locally specific as well. That is absolutely essential, and what they object to is a dominant ideology – instrumental rationality – which is an ideology we are against.

MH: Margaret Archer's 'analytical dualism', which endorses the transformational model of social activity, holds structure and agency to be essentially related yet ontologically and analytically distinct. This sounds like your concept of 'duality' rather than any kind of 'dualism'.[4] By unpacking its temporal dimension, she has suggested significant refinements of the transformational model of social activity. Am I right in thinking that your subsequent double 'negative generalisation' of it in *Dialectic*, which preserves the activity-dependence of structures even where the activity is that of the dead, takes her elaborations fully on board? So here we have a case where *The Possibility of Naturalism* definitely needed dialecticisation.

RB: Yes, in *Dialectic*, at the pages you have in mind, I refer to and praise Margaret Archer's elaborations.[5] Having said that, the argument in *Dialectic* in relation to negative generalisation was constructed before I had read Maggie's work on morphogenesis, and is already implicit in the elaboration of the TMSA as four-planar social being in *Scientific Realism and Human Emancipation* which, although it was published in 1986, was written in 1983. But when I read her work I saw that it did provide a very powerful argument against what she called central conflation theory. I was very grateful to her for that. I had done the work on the negative generalisation but I think she showed me in very stark terms that there was no way that my position was the same as that of Tony Giddens. I think the negative generalisation of the TMSA in *Dialectic* has to be complemented with another form of generalisation, which I suppose is there between the lines in *Dialectic*, but which only comes to the fore in the philosophy of meta-Reality. This I would call the preservative generalisation, because in any moment of transformative negation there is always going to be something that is preserved; or to put it another way, in any praxis there will be something transformed and something preserved. The whole emphasis of *The Possibility of Naturalism* through to *Plato Etc.* was on the transformative moment, or transformation and production – on human beings as producers of change. It is what I as a critic of Kant actually focused on. However, ecological and other considerations necessitate another orientation, which is caring, sustaining, and nourishing, and a feminist could say that I have neglected that side. But of course in a fully balanced account both should be there as two aspects of the duality of praxis. We need to put sustenance on the same level in our consciousness as transformation.

MH: Maggie has subsequently elaborated a thesis of 'the primacy of practice' in the realisation of human agency. She argues that the properties and powers of human beings are neither pre-given, nor socially bestowed, but realised through (emergent from) our practical transactions and relations with our natural, practical, and social environment. As such they have 'relative autonomy from biology and society alike, and causal powers to modify both'.[6] Do you have any problems with this view?

RB: I have no problem with either the thesis of the primacy of practice or the overall contours of Maggie's account. In fact I use a version of the thesis of the primacy of the practical in the way I argue for the principle of axial rationality (in my recent, not yet fully published, work). I argue that axial rationality stands alongside universal solidarity as a principle or presupposition which can be appealed to in the rational resolution of conflicts, especially those which seem to involve scientific (disciplinary, professional) cultural or moral incommensurability. People everywhere learn how to cook, drive cars, handle guns and use computers – this is a *learning*, which depends on our capacity to identify and correct mistakes. From this we can derive a basic universal principle of critique and self-critique, which, when coupled with the presupposition of universal solidarity, stating that we can in principle identify with any other human being, a principle which can be motivated, and transcendentally established, by the fact that we could have been them, gives us an organon or procedure for carrying out the basic critical realist theorem of judgemental rationality. However, this basis, deriving from the practical order, is learned, and is always in a social context, historically relevant and shifting – it is both transitive and always socially and culturally conditioned, contextualised and mediated; it is not 'foundationalist'. Furthermore, I would argue that, though we are born with certain innate capacities and infinite possibilities into a world of infinite possibilities, we always come into the world with a concretely singularised endowment and into concretely singularised circumstances – capacities and circumstances which at once constrain us and enable us to transcend these constraints. Moreover, we are born as dependent needy beings, dependent upon a context for our physical survival and the acquisition of the practical skills which Maggie rightly stresses, a context which is always at once social and cultural – which is the strength of the Vygotskian position which she tends to underestimate – as well as natural.

MH: Bob Jessop has recently argued that the transformational model of social activity, as developed in *The Possibility of Naturalism* and defended and elaborated by Maggie Archer, 'adopts a flat temporal ontology, neglects space, and treats the poles of structure and agency in terms of a relatively undifferentiated concept of society and people rather than engaging with specific sites of structural constraints and different kinds of social forces'.[7] Is it your view that this identifies real deficiencies in the model, and to what extent has your later work redressed them?

RB: I think he is wrong to say that space and time are ignored or neglected. I was very conscious of both from the word go in *The Possibility of Naturalism*, and I talk about the space–time dependence of social structures. It is true that in the simple model of the transformational model of social activity I do not specifically put space and time in anywhere, but of course transformation and reproduction have to be conceived as processes at a point or place in space and across or over time. In *Scientific Realism and Human Emancipation* I develop under the rubric of the social cube or, as I later called it, four-planar social being,[8] an elaborated ontology of the social world in which space and time are explicitly incorporated, and this is further developed in *Dialectic*. So I do not agree that they are neglected. Obviously they are very important in the philosophy of social science. Second, what seems to be involved in his comments is the idea that you should not talk about praxis or structure or agency or unacknowledged conditions or contradictions without talking about specific instances of them. But I don't think you can talk about specific contradictions, for example, unless you have a concept of a contradiction. Most people who talk about contradictions have a wrong concept of contradiction. This is what the work of underlabouring in *The Possibility of Naturalism* was all about, getting the basic concepts, which would need to be refined subsequently, into good shape. I did the subsequent refining, but then of course they have to be concretely applied and that is what Bob Jessop and people like him are doing.

MH: In elaborating a causal theory of mind in *The Possibility of Naturalism* you allow for three possibilities, which you say we as yet have no means of deciding between: (1) mind just is a complex set of powers historically emergent from and present only in association with (certain complex forms of) matter; (2) there is a material substance that is the bearer of these powers, a position that reduces to a materialist stratified monism; and (3) there is an immaterial substance that is their bearer, a position that reduces to dualistic interactionism.[9] How do you see these 'equal possibilities' today? Could not (1) be characterised as a 'stratified monism' (a concept you used again in *From East to West*[10]) as well as (2)?

In intentional causality, you say, 'mind' affects 'matter', that is, psychological states affect neurophysiological states. This is a transcendentally necessary condition of human praxis, but, because we do not know what the mediating mechanism is, you introduce a concept of 'transcategorial causality'.[11] Some find that this manner of speaking concedes too much to the mind/matter dichotomy you wish to overcome and risks slipping back into idealism. Thus Kathryn Dean in a recent draft paper comments:

> Bhaskar's use of the phrase 'radically new principles of organisation' suggests that his account of 'mind' remains materialist, so long as we have a broad, multi-modal understanding of materiality which does not set it up as the 'other' of ideality. Yet, throughout the chapter [Chapter 2], Bhaskar's dichotomising of 'mind' and 'matter' implies that there is an idealism at work here. Note, for example, the claim that 'causality . . . holds between beliefs and matter' and the conception of agency as 'mind' putting 'matter in motion'. Beliefs and mind are here, apparently, conceptualised in non-material terms; as, somehow, the 'other' of matter rather than as specific organisations of matter.[12]

So far as I can tell, in your later work you do not find it necessary to invoke transcategorial causality. Are the kind of concerns Kathryn expresses the reason why?

RB: The whole point of the synchronic emergent powers materialism model was to show that reasons can be causally aefficacious in the world. So the emphasis was very much on emergence, the emergence of the human and social sphere. But it is important to avoid a misunderstanding here. It is sometimes maintained that I provide philosophical support for an autonomous psychology that has no need to resort to sociological explanations. This is not true. I have no truck with the notion of an autonomous psychology in that sense. I do speak of the 'autonomy' of psychology and the psychological in *The Possibility of Naturalism* but only in the sense that, though constrained by the sociological and the physiological, it is not reducible to them. It was very clear to me when writing that book that human beings are, as the World Health Organisation has put it, a 'biopsychosocial' mix[13] and I explicitly use 'sociopsychology' and related concepts.[14] In *Scientific Realism and Human Emancipation* I distinguish between natural, mixed and social determinations and stress that human agency, 'moored socially in a complex of social relations and physically at determinate locations in space and time' is mixed.[15] The whole point was really that psychology is always going to be influenced by biology, geography, history and sociology. Actually, what is called for in *The Possibility of Naturalism* are regional, geo-historically specific or sensitive psychologies. I would not deny that there might be universal principles operating in a transhistorical way at the psychological level. But in so far as one can find psychological universals of that sort they are always going to be in a specific changing context. So you might as well build a context into them from the start.

In *Plato Etc.* I indicate that I do not talk about transcategorial causality any more and do not need to, because the point of the argument for synchronic emergent powers materialism was that reasons are aefficacious on the natural world. That is normally what we call matter.[16] Nonetheless, critical realists who think of themselves as materialists sometimes regard me as falling short of their position. I think the reason for this lies in the fact that materialism has historically been a way of orienting oneself against religion and against explanations of phenomena that cannot be justified in terms of reason, but have to be accepted on faith. I am one hundred per cent a materialist in that sense, in which materialism is basically acceptance of the scientific world-view, but I would also rather not say that that is materialism; nor do I see it as necessarily atheistic, though it will be critical of religion. We see exactly what a scientific approach to explanation means when we look further into the kind of materialism that people on the left are inclined to accept. There seem to be two principal planks of this. First, they have to be against vulgar reductionist materialism to defend the possibility of a social science at all. So they are against reductionist materialism, as am I. Second, they have to be against individualism and totally opposed to methodological individualism, as am I. However, if you go into the sort of social materialism that I find sometimes addressed to me these days and counterposed to what is imagined to be my position, the claim is that my meta-Reality thesis of the primacy of self-referentiality takes us back close to an individualist position. But this is not true at all because I have always held that it is the task of the emancipatory project to transform or eradicate the oppressive social structures we inherit from the past. The primacy of self-referentiality only comes into it when you ask how we are to do that. At the end of the day you can only do it through human action, and human action is precisely the place where the social sciences touch base with materiality. That is the only place in the social sciences, other than the artefacts produced by human action, where the social sphere actually touches base with materiality. So social materialism is a peculiar orientation to counterpose to my position. The project of an emancipatory social science depends on, has as its premise, intentional human agency. This is the presupposition, not only of Marx, but of the whole range of emancipatory social science. And that presupposes the causal aefficacy of reasons in the world. In the last instance this comes down to the causal aefficacy of a good argument or a good reason on your belief and your own praxis in the world, and thus on the world generally.

MH: A good reason is not necessarily the 'other' of matter.

RB: That is true; one has here a situation in which, obviously, the opposition between mind and body – the dualism of mind and body – has to be re-thematised. The mind-body problem has to be critiqued as part of the emancipatory project of returning to a richer version of the 'whole-body mindedness'[17] all humans enjoyed prior to what I call with Max Weber and Karl Jaspers the axial revolution in the first millennium BCE. Part of this critique will be to see these reasons, which will always be in a social context, as aefficacious on the world through intentional agency. The argument presupposes the irreducibility of reasons, intentional agency and the rest of the sociosphere to the materials in relation to and on which they are causally aefficacious. And if you take emergence as roughly having a threefold meaning or justification, namely, their unilateral existential dependency on lower-order structures and systems, and the taxonomic and causal irreducibility of higher-order states to lower-order states, you can say that the materialists who criticise my position are wanting to emphasise the dependency whereas what I have tended to emphasise is the emergence. Whatever you want to call the emergent product, it is clear that mind and thought in the last instance are the means in virtue of and by which the material (physical) world is transformed. You cannot get away from mind there. In order to have emancipatory science you need a causal notion of mind.

It is vital to defend the irreducibility of intentionality to physics and chemistry or biology if we are to have the possibility of rational argument and therefore of science. The sort of argument I produced in *The Possibility of Naturalism* is the condition of any science, not just social science; but of course, most importantly from the point of view of the materialist project, it is a condition of the possibility of any social science that we defend the emergent causality, and a degree of autonomy, of the intentional realm. If the intentional realm was some kind of automatic superstructure of the non-intentional realm, we could not have a science at all, let alone a social science; there would not be any rational point in having a science, and all the momentous and terrible things we have done to nature and ourselves would be inexplicable and unattributable.

Just invoking materialism without specifying exactly what the sense is does not get you very far. It is often claimed that ideas and ideology have a material existence ultimately rooted in physical matter. But what is physical matter? If you go down one level of the stratification of nature you come to atoms that are weird in terms of our normal conceptions of concrete materiality and in fact turn out to be not a-tomic at all! If you go down another couple of levels you are dealing with distributions in space and successions in time. You are very far removed from 'concrete materiality'. The world of quantum fields and quarks is not the world of concrete objects and solid material things. What the belief in brute physicality as exhaustive of the world depends on is in fact a species of commodification; it is an ideological materialism that commodifies and fetishises the properties of concrete material things. By downplaying or denying the possibility of intentional agency, it is just as much oriented against the possibility of social science as is supernaturalist idealism or the resort to faith in totally transcendent, supernatural causes. In many cases I would rather not use the terms 'materialism' and 'idealism': I would rather just talk about 'science', 'realism' and 'ontology'.

I am a little wary of doing this, however, because, in so far as you have a dispute between idealism and materialism, there are two levels at which you can make out a case for orienting the balance in favour of materialism. The first is that we are material things, and in science we confirm things, at the moment anyway, through their impact on material things. The material world of solid objects in which we live provides the framework in terms of which we adjudicate all the other claims to reality. Second, we do have a successful theory of how human beings emerged from less complex material things, the theory of evolution. In both these senses, the sense in which we are unilaterally dependent on the physical and biological world from which we emerged and the sense in which we use it as our framework in the domain of public assessability of scientific validity claims, materialism is valid. Both must be correct because things must have been implicit in what they emerged from. I think there are dangers in religious idealism. But there are also dangers in materialist secularism. The philosophy of meta-Reality offers a way of transcending both.

The case for orienting the balance in favour of materialism takes us close to the claims of *historical* materialism. It depends upon focusing on the implications of the relationship of dependency in the hierarchy or stratification of levels of reality – from the physical (including cosmological), through the chemical, biological, human (psychological), to the social, cultural, and so on. This hierarchy is such that human cultural systems are (unilaterally) dependent on human social systems, that is economic, political, family and community, and military institutions and forms. Such human social systems are in turn (unilaterally) dependent on human material systems, that is systems of production, consumption, care and settlement, which are in turn (unilaterally) dependent on (human) life-support systems, such as for example, functioning ecosystems, species of living organisms in their environments and climatic systems. These are of course in turn dependent on more basic geological, chemical, and ultimately physical structures and powers. This defines the sense in which certain material necessities have to be satisfied for any form of social or cultural life. However, the manner in which such prerequisites are satisfied is always socially and culturally dependent, and the way they are efficacious, negotiated, mitigated or transcended is always dependent, at least partially, upon a co-determining emergent higher-order level of reality. The 'material' here is a constraint in a complex play of forces and structures, but a constraint that must always be satisfied in the social world, and satisfied before anything else, and for anything else to be possible.

MH: What about the first part of the question, the possibilities concerning what mind is that you originally postulated?

RB: Mind is just a complex set of powers historically emergent and present only as far as we know in association with certain complex forms of matter. That is all we can say. I am not so keen on the possibility that there is a material substance that is the bearer of these powers, a position that reduces to a materialist stratified monism, unless this emergent domain can be very clearly situated scientifically. I was trying to bend the stick in favour of the view that the human and social sphere has to be studied in terms of radically new principles of organisation, deploying concepts, some of which were already familiar, such as the concept of intentional agency, and others of which were not so familiar. Whether we are familiar with the concepts or not, the study of this domain is going to have to be the study of an emergent product and cannot be reduced by psychologism, biologism or anything else to something more simple. This is not to say that biology is unimportant, but that we cannot reduce the social sciences to the play of the gene pool. That is vital to the whole project of the possibility of naturalism. And if you think about it, it is vital to all parties to disputes on these issues, including the science of biology. For the science of biology advances as a result of a reasoning, intentional process in which we presuppose for the rationality of that science that intentionality has causal aefficacy on the world, in particular on our pre-existing beliefs. Even for this it has to be aefficacious in the production of sounds and marks and all the material things that we want to do.

MH: I want to come on to the whole issue of facts and values, explanatory critique and ideology mainly in the next interview, because it receives much fuller elaboration in *Scientific Realism and Human Emancipation*, though it is important to register here that your basic thinking in this complex area was already laid out in *The Possibility of Naturalism*. Bracketing that, then, what would you say are the most original or radical theses of *The Possibility of Naturalism*?

RB: The resolution of the antinomies of structure and agency in the TMSA; individualism and collectivism or holism in a relational conception of the subject-matter of social science; and meaning and law in a qualified critical naturalist conception that does justice to both, and also isolates the limits of both naturalism and the linguistic paradigm, articulating a conception of social life as concept-dependent but not concept-exhausted. Then, relatedly, the synchronic emergent powers materialism that I sketched, the defence of the causality of reasons and the evaluative and value-entailing character of factual discourse, and the orientation to theory–practice consistency and relevance, a role that I summed up as philosophical underlabouring. Further, the exploration of the possibility of social scientific (and psychological) knowledge, which at the same time issues in a critique of alternative philosophies of social science, especially positivism and hermeneutics. Finally, as *A Realist Theory of Science* attempted to isolate the conditions of possibility of positivism, so *The Possibility of Naturalism* attempts to isolate the conditions of possibility of hermeneutics and the most characteristic hermeneutic circles.

MH: There is an extraordinary passage at the end of *The Possibility of Naturalism*, Chapter 3, in which you try to situate your achievement metatheoretically, to put your deduction of the possibility of naturalism, building on the transcendental realist philosophy of science, in context of the major scientific advances of modernity. You situate it within a four-fold decentring of humankind initiated by Copernicus:

- of the earth from the universe (Copernicus, astronomy);
- of earth-bound humanity from the universe (Darwin, biology);
- of human society from the human subject (Marx, sociology, geo-history), social practices from the intentional actions that reproduce them (TMSA);
- of mind from consciousness (Freud, psychoanalysis, psychology); the stratification of mind (psyche) and of purposes (project/a life): a person as a decentred unity.

And you suggest that there are two further aspects of this decentring (from the TMSA): establishment of a philosophical ontology or intransitive dimension; and of a materialist (non-idealist) epistemology or transitive dimension, entraining critiques of the leading philosophies of the social sciences.[18]
 This underlines for me just how seriously you take the achievements of the great modern scientists. Would it be true to say that your main role has been to render explicit, via transcendental argument and critique, what was already implicit in the scientific process? Is there any room for Einstein in the account of decentring? In relation to your own contribution to it, specifically your rejection of the Kantian view of the categories, does transcendental realism leave open the possibility that there may be a priori forms of intuition and categories of understanding?

RB: The passage in *The Possibility of Naturalism* you refer to should be taken in conjunction with what I say in *A Realist Theory of Science* (see p. 198) about the (tacitly gendered) modernist conception of man as one of three mutually reinforcing models underpinning the world-view I am critiquing there, the others being the classical paradigm of action (or more generally the whole cor-puscularian framework of which it was a part) and the celestial closure Newtonian mechanics had effected. Now this world-view already involved a profound break from the pre-modernist conception but it is itself in crucial respects conceptually incoherent, as I show in *A Realist Theory of Science* (see Chapter 2.3). The final decades of the twentieth century witnessed two fur-ther conceptual revolutions in physics (revolutions which have been only imperfectly reconciled). Einstein showed that we no longer live in a world of absolute space and absolute time; quantum physics showed that the atomistic conception of things must give way to something which is altogether more peculiar, but is perhaps best thought of as a field with some irreducibly sto-chastic properties, and that events must be thought in a non-punctiform way as distributions (in space) and succession (in time). One implication of this is that physics cannot be used to bolster atomistic individualism or a monistic conception of space and time any more. However, it is also important to remember the critical realist principle of methodological specificity, that one always has to produce specific arguments for emergent domains as to what their fundamental categories and methods are, so that we should never have tried to transfer conceptual systems and techniques from physics to the social field – and one should not do so now. As to the scope of the a priori, the exam-ple of corpuscularianism shows that we can indeed (within limits) use rela-tively a priori considerations to critique the conceptual framework of a science, but I doubt very much whether there are absolutely a priori forms and categorisations at a scientifically meaningful and significant level – the appro-priate forms and categorisations come as part of an irreducibly empirical process of discovery and conceptual transformation.

MH: Finally, tell us something about your manner of writing. I understand that, starting with *Dialectic*, you have spoken all your books into a dictaphone from notes. How did you produce your manuscripts before that? Did you type them or write them by hand? Are the various manuscripts extant?

RB: Actually there was a procedure I developed when working on *A Realist Theory of Science* and, indeed, the manuscripts that pre-dated it. This was to write everything out by hand. I wrote very quickly. If there was a mistake on the page, if the writing was not flowing, I would feel that there must be something wrong with it. So there are indeed manuscripts, and they are mostly extant in a warehouse in East Anglia, unlike many of my furnishings and clothes, which were sent to the broker's yard to be sold or auctioned. You can see very small, but very neat handwriting. I would give the final version to a typist. At Oxford I had a typist called Mrs. Browne. She typed several of my manuscripts. She started typing for me in 1967 or 1968 (I think), but it gradually became more and more difficult for her to read my handwriting, which was getting smaller, so I began to use a dictaphone in about 1969. I always wrote everything out by hand and then spoke it into a dictaphone. I wrote these manuscripts at a rapid rate, and some of them are quite long, one or two are the size of a big book. Then I dictated the manuscript into a dictaphone. When I was in Edinburgh I decided that I had to write things more legibly, so I wrote bigger, and *The Possibility of Naturalism* was typed by someone else.

MH: I don't fully understand the relationship between the dictaphone and the writing.

RB: I spoke from handwritten manuscripts into a dictaphone, then the typist played the dictaphone. These dictaphones came in two parts, a part you spoke into and a part you played like a tape recorder. So the typists would listen to that and they would have earphones and pedals for stopping and starting the tape. It was a technology quite widely used in those days before computers.

MH: You were speaking from a complete manuscript?

RB: Yes. I didn't just make it up as I went along.

MH: So there was no change in the way you did *Dialectic*? I'm being particular about this because it is widely and in my view very unjustly believed that *Dialectic* is badly written, and I've heard it said that the 'fact' that it was the first book you spoke (from notes) rather than wrote might have contributed to this. Did you write it first?

RB: I re-wrote it several times, re-doing earlier drafts. The only change that happened was in the editing of the typescript. I have written complete manuscripts by hand for all my books with the partial exception of the meta-Reality volumes. In the early days if there was a mistake I could easily mark it on the typescript or I would sit next to the typist and tell her what corrections to enter. But in the case of *Dialectic*, because of the many new and difficult concepts, there were too many corrections to do things this way, so I carefully entered them all by hand. The typist, I remember very well, was a woman called Sue Kelly who was an amazing typist, almost as fast as Jenny Cobner (!!).[19] Sue was a very brilliant woman. She had never been to university and her real love in life was dogs. She had a house on the London side of Croydon, where she lived with her husband or partner who was a minicab driver for Addison Lee. I was doing some teaching in Brighton and Sue's place was on the road between Battersea, where I lived, and Brighton – I was driving most places in those days. Anyway, she lived in a big house with about thirteen dogs of all varieties, and she used to walk them. These were her own dogs, but in her spare time she used to work in Battersea Dogs' Home. She had lots of cats as well.

MH: What was brilliant about her?

RB: She had a brilliant mind. The tragedy was she was born into a working-class background in which women just did not go to university. She was familiar with most of my concepts.

MH: She understood your concepts?

RB: She didn't try to understand them rigorously, but she understood their point and how they functioned in a rough-and-ready way.

MH: So she's typing away, and all of a sudden she hears 'ontological monovalence'!

RB: And that's new.

MH: What does she type?

RB: Well, she might look up 'ontological' and 'monovalence' in a dictionary, or 'syntonic' or whatever it was. As I concede and everyone says, it is a difficult text. So when I was looking at the typed manuscript I started to edit it much more and I did alter sentences.

MH: So the editing of *Dialectic* was if anything more thorough than was the case with your previous books?

RB: Yes.

MH: Did Sue get most of these concepts right first time round?

RB: Yes, but that's not why I said she was brilliant. I think anyone who is intelligent, can type well and is practised at transcribing can pick up most of the concepts aurally and put them in a written form. But she actually understood them in a basic, spot-on sort of way.

5   'Prolegomenon to a natural history of the human species'

Explanatory critique (1979–1986)

MH: The 1980s saw the crystallisation of the postmodern as a global discourse. In your later written assessments of postmodernism, you praise it for its critique of abstract universality and its emphasis on difference and diversity, its critique of modernity and Eurocentrism, but strongly criticise it for its rejection of any kind of universality and its consequent actualism and for its judgemental relativism. Fredric Jameson already in 1984 offered in effect a real definition: 'the cultural logic of late capitalism'.[1] Your own work was very much devoted to moving beyond that logic. While postmodernism's political trajectory was rightwards in the direction of anti-communism/anti-Marxism and an endism that saw liberal democracy and capitalism as unsurpassable, that is, counter-revolutionary,[2] you continued to work metacritically within the conatus to freedom linking Descartes, Kant, Hegel and Marx and remained committed to a form of revolutionary socialism. Thus while postmodernism was rejecting the European Enlightenment holus bolus, you (while by no means uncritical of it) were elaborating versions of several of its 'grand narratives': those of emancipation through the advance of knowledge and, in your work towards *Dialectic*, of the tendential rational directionality of geo-history, issuing in the possibility of a new eudaimonian enlightenment. While postmodernism was prone to view ethical categories as mystificatory traces of power relations, you were bent on elaborating an ethics grounded in truth. You must have felt you were swimming against the tide, if not kicking against the pricks?

RB: No, I didn't really, funnily enough, because I had tremendous confidence in the power of basic critical realism to critique the tendencies you refer to, and this was something confirmed to me again and again in debates – of which my published debates with Rom Harré and Ernesto Laclau are examples. Let me give an example of this kind of context. Rom Harré organised a society called 'The Friends of Good Psychology' to which he regularly invited social constructionists and postmodernists such as John Shotter (with whom I was very friendly) and Ken Gergen, to come and talk. *Journal for the Theory of Social Behaviour* has followed this example, giving equal place to social constructionism (of all varieties), as it does to critical realism. Harré himself co-edited it with Paul Secord until Charlie Smith took over in 1983. Harré's views on philosophy and social science underwent several changes, so that in different books one can identify radically different positions, but they were (at least in respect of social science) basically idealist and mainly individualist, at least until his late Vygotskian turn. I would go along to such events, sooner or later I would feel it necessary to intervene, and there would tend to be no answer, or at least very little in the way of a rational response, to the sort of thing I said (or so I felt). So critical realism appeared to possess a kind of intellectual hegemony. I felt that the critique of actualism and the isolation of the epistemic fallacy, together with the revindication – indeed the establishment of a new science – of ontology were probably the most important things that enabled me to prevail. I could say, well, what you are doing at the level of epistemology and of discourse contains an interesting enough suggestion about the social world, but there is also a part of the social world that might be constituted by structures and so on, a part which might cast light on your problem-area (or the tenability of your suggestion) – let us investigate that too. A little later, by the time I had written *Dialectic*, I had come to see that the critique of ontological monovalence was just as important as the critique of the epistemic and linguistic fallacies. However, it was not so useful from the point of view of critiquing poststructuralism and social constructionism, because many of their adherents accepted change and a non-Platonic analysis of change, or at any rate accepted it as a phenomenon – almost as much as their arch-concept of difference.

However, although I was outwardly buoyant, underneath there was also a slightly dejected feeling. Much of the time, at least while I was writing, or in a seminar, I could be in a little capsule, or set of capsules, in which intellectual arguments held sway. But it was also the case that it was the guys who lost the argument who got the promotions and the material security that I lacked. While I may have won intellectual victories, my antagonists were busy building nest-eggs for themselves. However I did have a firm conviction that there was a certain rational directionality in history (which I went on to try to elaborate in *Dialectic*). Their victory at the level of material gains or even social recognition would not count for so much in the long run, or so I thought.

MH: Where were you physically at this stage?

RB: Physically I was mainly in London living in Battersea. I lived in three different houses in Battersea.

MH: Did you still have a job?

RB: I retired from Edinburgh University in 1982.

MH: In order to do what?

RB: I had been invited to apply for a chair in philosophy at Leeds, Peter Geach's chair. I went for the interview and there were six or seven other candidates; I thought I did quite well, but as the day wore on I had a feeling that I really didn't much care for this, and I am sure that many of the people in the department – although there were allies there – felt they didn't much care for me either. It was at the time of Thatcher's first cuts, and I did not follow it up. Later I was told that they were willing to make me an offer, but for some reason I did not receive it until after the position was otherwise filled.

MH: So the broad picture is that you were freelancing, not holding down a full-time academic job?

RB: I was effectively full-time freelancing, but I was also teaching in Oxford, for which I was getting paid meagre rates. On the other hand I was also going to prestigious conferences and colloquia in places like Hanover and Houston. However, what I really wanted to do was to complete the tripartite project that I had set myself in the late 1960s. By the time *The Possibility of Naturalism* was published I was already working on *Dialectic*. In fact I had a contract from Verso for a book on this topic, I think in 1978 or 1979, and I was also commissioned to write an article for them. The book was going to be called *Dialectics, Materialism and Human Emancipation*. The article, entitled 'Dialectic, materialism and science', was to be on Della Volpe, Colletti and Timpanaro. This took me back to do extensive work on the whole Marxian tradition, and of course I wanted to write a book on Hegel. I knew I had to come to terms with Hegel. You could say that, to anyone schooled in the analytical tradition, it would have seemed a little odd perhaps to see copious references to dialectic as the key concept that was going to resolve all the problems – the concept about which Marx said he would love to write a couple of pages but never had the time. I wanted to know, for instance, why Marx thought this was the secret to the method of science, when existing critical realism and all the actual texts and references in Marx suggested that both much science and much (perhaps most) of Marx's method could be very well understood in an analytical kind of way, or at least in a way that did not necessitate extensive reference to dialectics. What was I missing? It took me a long time. I did a series of articles on Marx and Marxist philosophy, particularly entries for the *Dictionary of Marxist Thought*. That was in 1983.

I was deeply unsatisfied. Critical realism – transcendental realism and critical naturalism – seemed very neat, the infrastructure was complete, and the pre-existing intellectually hegemonic philosophies had been devastatingly critiqued. At first blush, everything appeared in order, but when one turned to the field of dialectic and Marxist philosophy everything seemed untidy and confused. Subconsciously, I suppose, I wanted to order that in the same kind of way I felt I had ordered the philosophy of science and social science. I wanted to have a framework that would be as simple, if you like, as elegant, as comprehensive, as inclusive. Some of my dictionary entries approximated to this; they seemed to be very inclusive, to be able to situate everyone. But a profound feeling of dissatisfaction remained.

MH: So you were unhappy personally. In your notes for this project, you refer to the 1980s as 'dark days of the left, leading to the spiritual turn'. The grapevine has it by contrast that you were an elegant man about town at the top of his form, and certainly pieces such as the address you gave to the Second Socialist Conference at Chesterfield in 1988 exude confidence, authority and hope, aspiring to help 'win the intellectual high-ground' for a new socialist enlightenment.[3]

RB: Although I might have appeared very confident in my overt transactions with the world, especially the intellectual ones, at a personal level I was not content. In fact I was working harder than ever before. I imagine I was a bit like the eureka guy, unhappy until I had licked the problem. The problem I was working on in the sphere of dialectical and Marxist philosophy was analogous to the isolation of the epistemic fallacy and the critique of actualism in the field of philosophy of science and social science. I was aware that it would be the basis of all the categories and concepts we have for speaking in the negative, and that it had to be *in* reality as well. So although I was actually working on absence and how to understand it from 1980 on, it was only around 1991–2 that I, as it were, saw the light.

The problem I was working on was not simply that of explaining change, because you could very easily explain change in terms of the transformation of structures. So it is not true to say that, using the later terminology, 1M critical realism does not have a concept of change; it does. But the basis of radically irreducible change, the basis of novelty and emergence in nature and a fortiori in the social world, had to be given by a deeper analysis. I was not in a clear state about it. I was unhappy. There were many different clues, many different loose ends. I was reading a great deal and writing a lot.

Moreover, in order to know more about Freud I undertook three years of psychoanalysis in this period, which made me more unhappy. For that I had the slightly sick compensation that it made my psychoanalysts even more unhappy than it made me.

The real problem was that I could not obtain any kind of good intellectual order in the whole field of dialectic. This manifested itself in me in a desire to read and learn more about everything that could cast light on it. I felt I had the practical experience to understand Marx in so far as I had mixed and talked with revolutionaries, visited people in prison, talked about all the questions that revolutionaries are supposed to talk about. But did I really know about the unconscious? For that I had to be analysed. I started a regime of psychoanalysis, basically because I wanted to understand it and one could not really talk about psychoanalysis as a potential science of emancipation without actually having experienced it. This is the unity of theory and practice. I had experienced revolutionary struggle, and in that context I also wanted to experience psychoanalysis. There ensued three years of psychoanalysis with various analysts. I think I should say that the psychoanalyst I knew best on a philosophical basis was a friend of mine, a young trainee who was becoming a psychoanalyst in Edinburgh called David Will. He wrote a very good article on the application of critical realism to psychoanalysis.[4] He said to me, 'Roy, promise me never to be analysed. It will destroy your creativity. Freud was very precious of his creativity, but it was nearly destroyed by analysis.'

MH: When did he tell you that?

RB: About 1977. I was perhaps never very good at listening to advice.

MH: Did he say why it is destructive?

RB: The reason I think he said that was not because of any great revelation you would find out about yourself but because of the method practised in Freudian theory. They tended to have very intensive analysis, and if you are sitting or lying down talking about your parents or your sex life for four or more nights a week for an hour or so, the whole round trip to the psychoanalyst is costing you £40 or even more and taking three hours of your time per day; this process is bound to absorb a lot of your creative energy. And of course I wanted to get to the bottom of things in psychoanalysis as well, I wanted both to be able to use it as a tool and to know more about myself, so I was diligent about it. All this contributed to a sense of malaise, of not really wanting to take up any opportunities that might be there, such as the Leeds chair, until I had finished my intellectual project.

MH: What was the net result of the psychoanalysis?

RB: The end result in 1983 was to make me rather wary about psychoanalysis as a therapeutic technique, a technique of intervention. Had I had a genuine problem rather than just intellectual curiosity I might have had a better experience of it. My admiration for psychoanalysis as an explanatory theory increased if anything during these years, but not as a technique of intervention. I started off with two very bad analysts, one of whom used to sit over me and chain-smoke. Both were obsessed by the phenomenology of my current sexual fantasy life. Then I moved to a male psychoanalyst, who was also a doctor, a consultant. I learnt later that I had played a cricket match with him when I was very young; one of us had batted while the other bowled, and I don't think that conflict had been satisfactorily resolved. And then of course my work was starting to be relatively well known in psychoanalytical journals, and I was better known than he was, so I think there may have been some negative transference there. At the end, I just thought that was enough of that. Other people such as Andrew Collier,[5] Terry Bloomfield and David Will had done quite substantial articles on it from a critical realist sort of perspective. I don't know if this is well known or not in contemporary psychoanalysis, but it is a funny thing, disciplines are a little like places: critical realism could be in fashion for a few years and then go out of fashion.[6] Sussex was a tremendous stronghold of critical realism in the late 1970s and through most of the 1980s but there is virtually no critical realism there now, or so I am told. Similarly psychoanalysis and psychology were strongholds for a while in the same period. And then of course Jacques Lacan became very fashionable with the avant garde, while the work of Melanie Klein and Donald Winnicott and internal relations theory became entrenched within the Freudian mainstream.

After psychoanalysis I went into a bit of humanistic psychology. It was a relief. I had about ten sessions in all. One of these psychologists was very worried about my state of affairs so she sent me back to a psychiatrist, who put me on anti-depressants, or rather tried to put me on them; I thought they were absolutely terrible and soon stopped taking them. I had another encounter with a psychiatrist in 1983. I was about to go to Majorca, but wasn't feeling well, so I went to my GP and got some antibiotics. I very inadvisably drank alcohol when I was on these antibiotics. I passed out. I was at my place in Battersea at the time, alone. When I came to I phoned a friend, who called the ambulance, and I was taken to a hospital, but it was decided that it was too late for me to be pumped out. The next morning I woke up in a ward. I wanted to go home, but I had nothing on except a very flimsy dressing gown, so I could not just leave. I had to get permission from the person in charge of the ward, who told me I had to be seen by a psychiatrist. I had an appointment with a publisher at three that afternoon, the day before I was due to go to Majorca. As it got closer and closer to three I grew more and more concerned. But I was finally seen by two psychiatrists, who asked me why I had tried to kill myself. They had obviously put me down as a suicide case. I told them I had not tried to kill myself, but was very anxious to get out of there. I finally managed to flee from the hospital by about two fifty-five.

MH: How did you get out?

RB: In my thin robe! Luckily there was a heat-wave in London. I got into a taxi, drove to my house, ran in, changed clothes, and managed to keep my appointment. The hospital staff had thought it very odd that I arrived in this very flimsy gown. I remember the psychiatrist describing it as a negligee.

MH: You should have left it on for the publisher.

RB: At several stages in my life doctors have attempted to diagnose me as having depression. The last time was in the early 1990s. I had a GP who insisted on giving me Prozac. He told me he was going to bring me into the twentieth century with this famous anti-depressant. I took it for a couple of days and found my personality was undergoing transformation. So I refused to take it any more. The doctor was absolutely furious. When I told him at my next appointment that I had only taken it for three or four days he stomped out of his surgery, got into his Chelsea tractor and drove off, with all the other patients waiting! I could only think that subconsciously he wanted to control me (he thought I was writing too much). He probably thought that medicine is one field Roy Bhaskar does not know about, yet here he is deciding to be his own doctor. We parted by mutual consent a little bit later. So enough of that detour.

MH: You said in an earlier interview that you wrote *Scientific Realism and Human Emancipation* in 1983, yet as we know it was published in 1986. What accounts for the gap?

RB: When I wrote it I thought it was going to be the first three or four chapters of a larger work on *Dialectics, Materialism and Human Emancipation* (which was eventually published as *Dialectic: The Pulse of Freedom*). However, I was at something of an impasse in my dialectical work, so in 1984–5 it occurred to me that, since it was interesting and important in its own right, it should be published sooner rather than later. It was not easy to find a publisher though. Verso, with whom I had a contract for the book on dialectic, was very resistant. I have already recounted how they sent around Peter Dews to tell me that emergence was an unscientific concept. By this time Perry Anderson and his circle had pretty much adopted the perspectives of analytical philosophy combined with a biologically based materialism, exemplified for example in Gerry Cohen's work on Marx's theory of history and Timpanaro's on materialism,[7] such that you did not really need dialectic or anything very complicated to understand and change the world. But they eventually agreed to publish it, rather reluctantly.

MH: *Scientific Realism and Human Emancipation* is far and away your major published work of these years. For me, it is in some respects to *Dialectic* what *Grundrisse* is to *Capital*. I see it as a kind of prolegomenon to *Dialectic*, or better a *prodrome* in the literal sense, a running towards it, a working through of some of the main issues in that direction, but also a consolidation, a marshalling of energies and resources that 'concentrates its fire' on analytical rather than dialectical philosophy[8] while you seek the key to transposing and elaborating your project in a dialectical register – a kind of analytical laboratory, then, in which you were consciously preparing for the leap into dialectic. Thus, in terms of *Dialectic*'s four-sided dialectic, Chapter 1 focuses on 1M (it justifies and develops transcendental realism); Chapter 2 on 2E (it justifies and develops critical naturalism); Chapter 2.5–2.7 on 3L (it justifies and develops explanatory critique on the terrain of philosophy); and Ch 3 on 4D (it justifies and further develops explanatory critique on the terrain of the sociology of knowledge, engaging in the transformative labour of ideology-critique) – a presentational structure that *Dialectic* itself was to mirror. Extrapolating from this and what you have said in these interviews, is it correct to say that the architectonic of your project went basically as in Table 1?

Table 1 The architectonic of Bhaskar's philosophical project, 1967–94⁹

Ontological–axiological chain / CR as an immanently critical dialectical process	1M Non-Identity / transcendental realism	2E Negativity / (dialectical) critical naturalism	3L Totality / ethics, the theory of explanatory critique (metacritique)	4D Transformative Agency / emancipatory axiology, explanatory critique (metacritique) of philosophical ideologies
1967–79	[PES]; RTS; PN, ch. 1; [EMS]	[PES]; PN, ch. 2; [EMS]	PN, ch. 2, appendix & ch. 4.1; [EMS]	[PES]; PN, chs 3, 4; [EMS]; [PI]
1980–90	SRHE, ch 1; RR, ch. 2; [DM]; [DMHE]	SRHE, ch. 2; RR, ch. 5; [DM]; [DMHE]	SRHE, chs 2.5–2.7; RR, ch. 6; [DM]; [DMHE]	SRHE, ch. 3; RR, chs 3, 4; [DM]; [DMHE]; [PI]; [PU]
1991–94	DPF, ch. 1; PE, chs 2, 3; [DMHE]; [DST]; [HKHM]; [PM]	DPF, ch. 2; PE, chs 4, 5, 6; [DMHE];[DST]; [HKHM]; [PM]	DPF, ch. 3; PE, chs 5.3, 7, 8; [DMHE]; [DST]; [HKHM]; [PM]	DPF, chs 3.7–10, 4; PE, chs 7, 9, 10 & appendix; PIF; [HKHM]; [DMHE]; [DST]; [PM]; [HWP]; [PI]

Note
Square brackets indicate planned books that evolved into others or remain unpublished. Periodisation is in terms of (1) the formation of basic critical realism; (2) the transition from (1) to dialectical critical realism; and (3) the breakthrough to dialectical critical realism and the writing of *Dialectic* and *Plato Etc.* Note that, while the development of the theory of explanatory critique belongs at 3L, the transformative work of its application belongs at 4D.

[DM]	[*Dialectic and Materialism*] (evolved into [DMHE])
[DMHE]	[*Dialectics, Materialism and Human Emancipation*] (evolved into *DPF*)
DPF	*Dialectic: The Pulse of Freedom*
[DST]	[*Dialectical Social Theory*]
[EMS]	*Empiricism and the Metatheory of the Social Sciences* (evolved into *RTS, PN, SRHE*)
[HKHM]	[*Hume, Kant, Hegel, Marx*]
[HWP]	[*Critical History of Western Philosophy*]
PE	*Plato Etc.* (originally entitled *Philosophy and the Dialectic of Emancipation*)
[PES]	[*Some Problems about Explanation in the Social Sciences*] (DPhil thesis; evolved into [EMS])
[PI]	[*Philosophical Ideologies*]
PIF	*Philosophy and the Idea of Freedom*
[PM]	[*The Philosophy of Money*]
PN	*The Possibility of Naturalism*
[PU]	[*Philosophical Underlabouring*]
RR	*Reclaiming Reality*
RTS	*A Realist Theory of Science*
SRHE	*Scientific Realism and Human Emancipation*

RB: I think you are absolutely right about the architectonic. However, one has to remember that the reason why I divided *Scientific Realism and Human Emancipation* up into those chapters was more a legacy of my initial tripartite project, philosophy of science, philosophy of social science and then an explanation of them, a full critique. So the fit is a retrospective one. It is perfect and I agree with it entirely, but it does not represent what I was feeling at the time.

MH: *The Possibility of Naturalism* initiates, it seems to me, an attempt to marry a relational conception of society (later entity relationism as such and in general) with depth-stratification as an alternative to the dialectical couple of ontological dualism and ontological monism/holism, an attempt that you carry forward in *Scientific Realism and Human Emancipation* and through in *Dialectic*. On this conception, the world is both asymmetrically stratified/ differentiated and dynamic/interconnected – both alterity and change are irreducible and external relations are both real and constellationally contained within the internal relationality of open (totalities nested within) Totality; internal relationality does not entail explanatory equality among the aspects related, that is, it is consistent with depth-explanation. In *Scientific Realism and Human Emancipation* this approach to philosophical ontology goes by the names of *integrative pluralism* (IP), also structured pluralism, and *developing* (or dialectical) *integrative pluralism* (DIP). You did not deploy these concepts much thereafter, however. Can you say why?

RB: There is absolutely nothing wrong with these concepts. The idea of developing integrative pluralism leads into the idea of structured and differentiated totality. That is the sort of way I talk in *Dialectic*, and of course that in turn leads into the kind of totality one has in meta-Reality where there are layers of duality within the cosmic envelope or within non-duality and then layers of demi-reality within duality. But they are all distinct concepts. I think the idea of a structured and differentiated totality that is also developing is a permanent legacy. This is very important as against the use of totality in Hegel and in some strands of western Marxism. It is not a reductive or expressive totality, and that is why the point about the different elements not being equally important in an explanatory sense is so crucial. You could say that everything that happens in our world bears the imprint of the fundamental relations of the capitalist mode of production. That is true, but they do so in differential ways. Many of the Marxist critiques of capitalism as a hegemonic totality have viewed it expressively, as explaining what goes on in music or art as much as in the sphere of production. I did not want to go along with that kind of reductionism or expressivism, because you could then apply it to Marx's own work and view all the distinctions that he made as equally important. That of course is not true. Everything is structured, and structured differentially; Marx's work is structured, the social world is structured, everything that happens has its own distinct structure, and what it is cannot be determined a priori on the analysis of one structure, such as capitalism, it always has to be discovered a posteriori on the basis of investigations into the concrete reality you are dealing with. Perhaps there is one thing the idea of developing integrative pluralism has that the simple concept of a structured, differentiated and developing totality does not have, and that is the element of monism. For if it is a developing integrative pluralism it is supposed to apply to everything, and the everything is not theorised as such in *Dialectic*. This is taken up again in meta-Reality in terms of the theme of the priority of unity over conflict and of identity over difference. I think integrative pluralism is an absolutely fine concept.

MH: It is just that it was superseded by others that it developed into.

RB: Yes, that's right.

MH: In *Scientific Realism and Human Emancipation* you give I think the fullest treatment and justification of your conception of philosophy anywhere, as both relative to other social practices and so heteronomous and 'soiled in life',[10] ultimately answerable to the findings of science, yet relatively autonomous in that it proceeds a priori from premises furnished by historical practices (metaphysics α) and conceptual forms associated with such practices (metaphysics β). It is a rich discussion, generating an array of new concepts: metaphysics α and β, the intrinsic and extrinsic aspects of the transitive dimension, the metacritical dimension and metacritique$_1$ and metacritique$_2$, the methodological circle that 'twin-screws' philosophy and science, and axiological standpoint among others. With respect to the last – extra-philosophical practical standpoints and interests that necessarily condition philosophy – you say that philosophy alone can no more justify these 'than boots can climb mountains', such that they present 'an immanent barrier to immanent critique' and one's only recourse in the final analysis is to 'openly take one's stand with science' – not as the only way of knowing but at any rate one with excellent historical credentials.[11] Do you have any further thoughts on this?

RB: Yes. Since writing that, and notwithstanding the qualifications that I made there, I have realised how important it is, if you say anything positive about science or indicate that you are going to take your stand with science, to couple this with a critique of scientism – of pseudo-science, of instrumental, governmental, military-industrial and techno- science. There are many practices in our society that go by the name of science but are not science. I certainly do not want to take my stand with them. Rather, I take my stand with the concept of science, the concept that has been worked out by reflection on some of the great moments in western scientific history, those associated with Galileo, Copernicus, Newton, Kepler, Darwin, Einstein, and so on. That is very different from taking one's stand with practices that masquerade as science. I think it is tremendously important to critique false science, and inadequate and shoddy science.

MH: In Chapter 1.6 of *Scientific Realism and Human Emancipation*, in an exercise in metaphysics α, you obtain an immanent refutation of the conceptual realism of Kuhn and others whereby there is no theory-independent world, such that when our theories change the world changes with them – a position you dub 'subjective superidealism' – by showing that the superidealists cannot sustain the intelligibility of the conceptual transformations and the phenomenon of incommensurability that they themselves draw attention to, whereas transcendental realism can. Do you have anything to add to this critique, or do you rest your case?

RB: I rest my case in respect of Kuhn and Feyerabend, or rather these tendencies within their thought, but of course one has to add to the critique of superidealism in the philosophy of science all the theories of poststructuralism and postmodernism generally and in the philosophy of social science and social theory the new social constructionists. I think one of the weaknesses of *Scientific Realism and Human Emancipation* is that it does not do that. But I was actually doing it in practice in my verbal encounters. I did not really feel confident in writing about poststructuralism and postmodernism until I had dialectic under my belt, and I was aware that I had not adequately metatheorised some of the issues they were dealing with, such as power and the abuse of knowledge. That was to come when I had concepts such as that of master–slave-type relations; and when I had an adequate account of change and difference I could critique the partiality of their accounts.

MH: Am I right in thinking that the whole focus is really on developing your own coherent system through immanent critique, and that you would look to whatever was on offer – Hume, Marx, postmodernism, whatever – in order to achieve this overriding aim?

RB: It wasn't an overriding end in itself. My project was always rooted in some conception of relevance for emancipatory practice. If one could have had just that, then I would not have bothered with the intellectual superstructure. But of course you cannot have it without, among other things, continually underlabouring for it in the particular area I was working in professionally. However, this philosophical critique was in order to satisfy this objective outside philosophy. It was an important part of my conception of philosophy from the very beginning that philosophy exists only in relation to something outside it. You do not have philosophy without philosophers or readers, and they exist as practical, biopsychosocial beings in a social world. The fundamental end for me was always human emancipation, human self-emancipation and self-realisation. I was only really interested in philosophies in so far as they would help or impact upon that project.

MH: *Is* the end of human emancipation outside philosophy?

RB: It is outside philosophy in the sense that the end of human emancipation is to have a society that is eudaimonistic, in which every individual concretely singularised person is in their dharma, is fulfilling their concretely singularised nature. Philosophy is necessary for it in the same way as bread is necessary for it, and music is necessary for it.

MH: But is it really outside? Philosophy, as you say, is 'soiled in life'. It is in a sense refracting the geo-historical process within which the telos of emancipation is inscribed.

RB: Yes. To look at this point in another way, all the categories of philosophy apply to the whole of the world, to the whole of reality.

MH: So it is part of totality. The problem might be mainly terminological. Your formulation in *Scientific Realism and Human Emancipation* speaks of philosophy existing only in relation to something 'other' than rather than 'outside' itself.[12]

RB: Yes, it operates at the highest level of ontology, understanding and situating the world at the highest possible level of abstraction. All the more concrete ways of thinking about the world and the ways of acting in the world have that philosophy in them. You cannot get rid of philosophy in that sense, that is absolutely correct. Philosophy is only one practice among others, and you have to have balance even, or perhaps especially, to be a philosopher.

MH: In the 1989 Postscript to *The Possibility of Naturalism* you wrote in response to a critique by Ted Benton that 'were I to rewrite *The Possibility of Naturalism* today I would stress the way in which the social order is embedded and conditioned by the natural order from which it is emergent and on which it in turn acts back. An ecological orientation to social life is as important as is recognition of our biological being – both are insufficiently elaborated in the book.'[13] In turning in *Scientific Realism and Human Emancipation* to a consideration of the analogies and disanalogies of geo-history and the sociosphere with biology (Chapter 2.3, 'Socio-Evolutionary Concepts, Functional Explanation and Human History') you were presumably seeking to make good this deficit? This links up with a new, I think, insistence that science is not about manipulating and controlling nature, of which it is a part, but about understanding it, and with the new concept of the ecological asymmetry,[14] whereby the world is not made for us, but we for it. Arguably all this was already implicit in the anti-anthropic stance you arrived at in your first book, which you now draw out. And, conversely, implicit in *it* is the non-duality of meta-Reality, is it not?

RB: Yes, absolutely. I think that when I was writing *The Possibility of Naturalism* I was very conscious of the contrast between the social sciences and physics and chemistry. So the resolution of the problem of naturalism was in a way partial.

It was the problem of whether the social and human sciences could ever be like physics and chemistry. But you would also have to ask whether they could be like biology, and you could also ask whether they could be like art or like philosophy itself. And there are very interesting analogies and disanalogies for a range of practices. For instance, I think that transcendental and dialectical arguments play a huge role in social science, so there is an analogy there. On the issue of biology, obviously we are biological beings; as we've seen, you can say we are biopsychosocial mixes. Understanding human beings in that way is important, and that was relatively neglected in *The Possibility of Naturalism*. So this orientation is an important corrective to that, just as the conception of four-planar social being is to the transformational model of social activity.

MH: Do you want to say something about the issue of manipulating and controlling nature as distinct from understanding it?

RB: The overall vision is that the social world, the world I was contrasting with the world of physics and chemistry, is an emergent part of the natural world, particularly of its biological stratum. And that of course was there in my first two books but not theorised. The ecological asymmetry you refer to is very important, because we have to get used to being in the world in accordance with its rhythms. People might say that the whole point about being a human being is that you can rise above the world, why don't we go settle on another planet or another star? But while you are thinking about that, just imagine if something drastic happened, as is happening now of course with our weather system. Imagine if the sun stopped shining. Where would all these projects be? Or if the earth stopped revolving around the sun in exactly the way that it does, or the moon stopped revolving around the earth. We are utterly dependent on nature. It is so important, and of course becomes crucial also at the level of socio-political discourse generally, not just in terms of debates about ecology, but in terms of debates about the nature of reality. The neo-Nietzscheans are inclined to say that history is now whatever we make (of) it. However, they have to accept that there is a reality out there, so that if, say, the neo-cons go in and 'democratise' society in Iraq, making it safe for international corporations, there is of course something, a reality, that is being 'made safe' and that will react back on any neo-Nietzschean project or fantasy. We have to learn from this.

MH: Can you elaborate on what you meant in the last sentence of the following, at the outset of Chapter 2 on 'Critical Naturalism and the Dialectic of Human Emancipation' in *Scientific Realism and Human Emancipation*:

> Emancipation depends upon explanation depends upon emergence. Given the phenomena of emergence, an emancipatory politics (or more generally transformative or therapeutic practice) depends upon a realist science. But, if and only if emergence is real, the development of both

science and politics are up to us. This chapter is intended then as a kind of abbreviated prolegomenon to a natural history of the human species.[15]

Were you consciously thinking of the prolegomenon as a philosophy of geo-history that could furnish the general conceptual framework for a natural history? It is noteworthy, as you would expect in a work preparing for the leap into dialectic, that the concept of (geo-)historicity as the self-reflexive consciousness of the past that can enter into history 'as a material force with an efficacy of its own'[16] comes much more to the fore in *Scientific Realism and Human Emancipation* than in your previous work, together with the related concepts of the presence of the past, process (as 'structure [or thing], considered under the aspect of its story – of formation, reformation and transformation – in time'[17]),[18] historical tendencies$_2$, historical rationality (later dialectical or absolute reason) and so on. On the other hand you argue that the TMSA had already effected 'the geo-historicisation of social theory', which you now underline.

RB: Let me just say that natural history as I understood it, or as I understand it now anyway, includes the rational directionality that in *Dialectic* I was to call the pulse of freedom, and I think this is very important for our present discussion. This is what I meant by historical reason or rationality in *Scientific Realism and Human Emancipation*; dialectical reason is aligned with what I call depth-rationality.[19] I should say that rational directionality is only one of the forces generally at work in history; there are others connected with or seemingly opposed to it. Reflexivity itself, for example, or solidarity, altruism, or empathy; these are all basic tendencies implicated in the rational directionality of history, as is morality, stemming from the altruistic and empathetic. The development of technology is another major force. Then there are other forces, rooted in the heteronomous features of social being, such as oppressive social relations and human greed or selfishness, which are at any time opposed to this telos; so that 'rational directionality' does not necessarily mean that it will always win out in any particular set of circumstances or that it must win out in the end.

MH: I now want to come on to the whole issue of facts and values, explanatory critique and ideology. Although your basic thinking in this complex area was already developed in *The Possibility of Naturalism*, it receives much fuller elaboration in *Scientific Realism and Human Emancipation*. Your claim to have refuted 'Hume's law' by demonstrating that the human sciences are necessarily explanatory critical, effecting transitions from facts to value and theory to practice, is much disputed within critical realism, and in the scientific community generally it is still usually taken as axiomatic that science can have nothing to say about what is morally right and morally wrong; so that, if you are right, this must be seen as perhaps your most radical breakthrough. You have answered the objections a number of times in print,[20] so I do not want to go back over that ground here (unless you want to add anything). As you your-self say in *Reclaiming Reality*, the significance of your demonstration lies less in the formal refutation of Hume's law (important though that is for the valori-sation of critical explanatory social science) or in its delineation of 'the structure of motivating argument for radical political commitment', than in its generalisability from the critique of cognitive ills to other seemingly neces-sary ills conjugating around 'the non-fulfillment of needs, wants, potentiali-ties, interests and aspirations',[21] which together may constitute grounds for emancipatory praxis.

RB: One thing I would stress now is that you do not actually need the full theory of explanatory critique in order to refute Hume's law, because to criticise a belief is implicitly to criticise any action that is informed by it, *ceteris paribus*; once you say no, you are there. That raises the meta-question of why this has not been seen and why the fact–value dichotomy is so widely adhered to.

MH: People say that there are concealed value premises.[22]

RB: But as I have argued right from the outset it is not *necessary* that any value commitment other than commitment to truth enters in, and commitment to truth is a condition of any discourse whatsoever, so it cannot be seized upon as a concealed value premise – it is intrinsic to the concept of a fact. As you say, however, the main point is actually to go on from explanatory critique and from cognitive to non-cognitive ills, and these include the non-satisfaction not only of basic physical needs but more generally of what one needs to fulfil one's dharma, one's concretely singularised potentiality – lack of the tools of one's trade, or of free time, of recognition, respect, and so on, and most impor-tantly of course they embrace oppression, including any violation of self-determination.

   I think some people on the left tend to underestimate the importance of political freedom and self-determination. The wars in Vietnam and now in Iraq and Afghanistan were or are, for the people of those countries, not funda-mentally or primarily about ideology but about self-determination, individual and collective. That is, they are wars against oppression and this matters enor-mously to people. A person cannot be said to be free, even if they are materi-ally well looked after, unless at least some of their life is self-determining, unless they can do something, unless they have projects within that life. So I regard freedom, in the sense of the capacity to act and formulate projects of your own, as just as important as the meeting of physical needs; it is a condi-tion for doing anything else, because if you cannot do that then it does not matter how well basic physical needs are being satisfied, you will not be fully human. It is freedom in this sense that is the overriding concern of *Scientific Realism and Human Emancipation* and *Dialectic*. We need it to call anything that we do our own, that is to attribute it to ourselves; and political self-determination (or the absence of self-determination) still remains probably the single most important cause of war and social conflict generally.

MH: The arguments and discussion in *Scientific Realism and Human Emancipation* in this area are again very rich, laying bare the logic of explanatory critiques in an array of inference schemas, arriving at real definitions of freedom (which is 'irrespective of the arrow's flight, no regarder of the river's flow'[23]) and emancipation, and generating the fundamental concepts of the intrinsic and extrinsic aspects; concrete axiological judgements; transformed, transformative praxis; depth-enquiry and depth-explanation (the possibility of which is transcendentally 'necessary for the unbounded projects and conduct of everyday life'[24]), and so on, and very much anticipating the dialectics of discourse and agency at the heart of *Dialectic*'s emancipatory axiology. What prevented you at that stage from following through to a fuller elaboration of the dialectics of freedom? What was missing?

RB: The simple answer to that is that I had not completed my work on dialectic. This relates back to a question you asked earlier. These were dark days of the left. The point is that the left in Britain did feel it had been hammered in the early 1980s. It was in overwhelming control of the constituency Labour parties and still very strong in the trade unions. I even joined the Labour Party myself for a short period. I knew Tony Benn, and most of my friends were Bennites. In London you had Ken Livingstone's GLC (Greater London Council), to which anyone on the left who had any pretensions of trying to change society tended to gravitate; there were ex-revolutionary Marxists working as advisors to the GLC in one capacity or another. What happened under Thatcher from 1979 was of course that she systematically took on the left in no uncertain terms. She took on the unions, smashed the miners who were the most powerful union and then crushed local government, in London actually abolishing the Greater London Council, so that London had no citywide local government for more than a decade. It was very depressing.

MH: It was the onset, we can see in retrospect, of an epoch of counter-revolution[25] that is only just now showing signs of exhausting itself as it runs up against the limits of the reality principle.

RB: Yes – well, it had begun before, when Denis Healey as Chancellor of the Exchequer instituted savage cuts in 1976 at the request of the International Monetary Fund, not to mention Wilson's decision not to devalue in 1963, which we discussed earlier. From the point of view of the phenomenology of the left it was depressing to see Thatcher winning the war in the Falklands, and instituting more oppressive measures in Ireland and generally. The sale of council houses was a bribe to sections of the working class. Why did they not see that the Labour left were the ones on their side? They did not see it, so these were indeed dark days. And, as we have seen, I myself was personally dissatisfied at this time because of unresolved intellectual problems. In general I did not want to rest on my laurels, I wanted to get to the bottom of the western philosophical tradition. But more immediately I wanted to understand what had gone wrong in the Soviet Union and what if anything had gone wrong in the history of Marxism. More especially, I wanted to understand Marx and in particular why he regarded dialectic as the key to everything. Until I had really got that straight, I could not be very happy or content. That is basically what was missing. Colin Robinson of Verso used to ring me up every couple of months in the late 1980s and early 1990s and ask how I was getting along with my book on dialectic, and I would say it was nearly there. It might have been nearly there in terms of a draft – I was always nearly finishing it – but I had not solved the problem. I did not want to publish it until I had licked the problem.

MH: You argue in *Scientific Realism and Human Emancipation*, as you had already done in *The Possibility of Naturalism*, that in a non-neutral (unjust, asymmetrical) world, social science as explanatory critique is necessarily non-neutral, siding with the oppressed against the oppressors, the oppressed having 'an interest in knowledge which their oppressors lack' and seek to deny them.[26] Of all you have written on emancipation this is the one quote which people most frequently ask me for chapter and verse. It seems to really resonate. What significance would you attach to that?

RB: It is tremendously important that the oppressed have an interest in knowledge that the oppressors lack. We can look at why this is so by thinking about different types of knowledge. The oppressed have an interest in explanatory knowledge of the structures that oppress them. But their oppressors do not need to have that explanatory knowledge and it might be better for them if they do not. The sort of knowledge they need to have is best not called knowledge, but rather information or even data, and that is about how to manipulate events and circumstances and discourses. That kind of knowledge nowadays might be called spin but is perhaps best thought of as information (and dis-information). You can actually develop quite a nice little step diagram or development from the most basic level. This is that of data, which embraces everything you perceive and take in and can describe. The next step or level is information, which is relevant data. This is the epistemic level that is so beloved of people in information technology. OK, it is better than data; the oppressed need information, true, and the oppressors also need and use information, but information is not explanatory knowledge, it is not knowledge of the structures and mechanisms, of the fundamental causes of why things are as information tells us. For that you need, third, explanatory knowledge, preferably explanatory scientific knowledge. And then, fourth, in order to use explanatory and scientific knowledge you need wisdom, which is explanatory knowledge incorporated, in the light of other values, into practice. This is what the oppressed need. It involves many things besides explanatory knowledge, including balance, judgement, discrimination, the wisdom that comes from past practice and experience, and so on. It will be seen that each step – from data to information, from information to explanatory knowledge, and from knowledge to wisdom – involves a huge leap. The knowledge that the oppressed need is explanatory knowledge incorporated into practice. Someone might ask whether, if they just had practical or tacit knowledge, would not that be OK? It might be OK, but it would have to be tacit knowledge of the conditions and causes of their oppression, so it would still be practical knowledge of a structure even if it wasn't discursive.

MH: I think what people perhaps find most arresting about your formulation is the notion that social science, if it does its job properly, is *necessarily* on the side of the oppressed – not from some arbitrary political commitment but as science, from commitment to truth.

RB: It is on their side, if (as you say) it is doing its job properly, in the sense that what it produces is necessarily in their interests.

MH: Because 'some anthropology is the condition of any moral discourse at all', you elaborate a theory of human nature in *Scientific Realism and Human Emancipation*, the elements of which correspond to those of the concrete universal and four-planar social being (which you refer to as the 'social cube' in this book) and on the basis of which you assert the '*existence* of rights (and goods) for all human beings' in virtue of their possession of a core universal nature, manifested in certain species-wide powers and needs 'even though these rights (and goods) can only come to be formulated as demands, recognised as legitimate and exercised as rights under very definite historical conditions'.[27] Alasdair MacIntyre has famously maintained that belief in the existence of such rights is like belief in witches or unicorns.[28] How would you respond to that kind of objection?

RB: In its universal aspect, human nature is an ensemble of potentials and needs (constituted as ensembles of powers and liabilities, tendencies and dispositions) that, while they can only be realised or satisfied in historically specific conditions by concretely singularised people, are not reducible to the conditions of their realisation or satisfaction. Thus all people have the potential to speak languages or to live to the age of a hundred, just as they have needs that must be met in order for them to survive or in order for them to formulate projects. These are all objective facts about human beings, whether you consider all human beings transhistorically as a species, specific classes or groups of human beings, or particular individuals. There is nothing at all subjective about this. The reason why it seems to be subjective is because in the course of time we come to learn more and more about what human potentiality is. Nowadays we tend to take it for granted that disabled people, like everyone else, have a right to be mobile or to have a university education. These are things that only came to be recognised historically. However, the needs and potentials of disabled people, like those of everyone else, have been there all along throughout the course of history. The particular reasons why acceptance or recognition of these rights has come about in recent times do not affect this. I really cannot understand why this confusion is made, and why Alasdair MacIntyre can say such things about the existence of such rights. Is he really wanting to say that the existence of these needs and potentialities is like belief in witches or unicorns? But of course I don't think he would want to say that; it is rather the discourse of rights he is against, as part of an argument against modernity, a discourse in which these needs and potentialities are discussed solely at the level of what society should allow or admit to be owing to particular classes of people and to all people. The fundamental point is that it is wrong to confuse the existence (or not) of such rights, grounded in the needs and potentialities of human beings, their intransitive reality, with the historical relativity of our discourse about such rights, or of our recognition of such rights (our acceptance of them, or not, as rights), or of their satisfaction or realisation (or the degrees and modes of the realisation) in particular geo-historically determinate societies – it is wrong to confound the former with any of the latter.

MH: You want to say that rights exist at the level of the real, not just needs and potentials; rights are grounded in the real?

RB: Yes, a right is the other side of the coin to a potential or need, the realisation or meeting of which is not auto-subversive. Given that freedom is intrinsic to what it is to be a human being, all humans have the right to have it. It might not be realised, but it is real. The genetic structure of a human being is not something I could have accessed before the development of modern biology, but people had it in the seventeenth century or whenever, and a right is exactly like that. It is a bit of intransitive reality that we only start to look at and talk about under certain historical conditions, but it is there all along. One thing that people have said to me is that this idea of human nature and human potentiality is pretty much an open-ended thing, because what are human potentialities? Well, they are open. We do not know what all the potentialities of human beings are, but we do know that there are many potentialities that have been actualised by some human beings and not by others. You can think of it like this. A human being, a group of human beings, or all human beings have potentialities. The first step is to discover or recognise these as capacities, things that in principle they can do. Then the next step is to transform these capacities into capabilities. Thus everyone has the capacity to learn Japanese, but to make that a capability many others things are required: teachers of Japanese, free time and so on, and of course you must have your material needs sufficiently satisfied to do all that. So to transform a capacity into a capability or a concretely singularised ability to speak Japanese is a huge step that depends on social action. The third step, conceptually, is of course the actualisation of the capability in speaking Japanese. So we have capacity → capability → actualisation. The first and second steps, the discovery and recognition of capacities, and their transformation into capabilities as concretely singularised abilities are, generically and specifically, urgent and momentous components of the agenda for the left.

Of course one cannot assume that these powers or potentialities are all good. Just as in a descriptive and explanatory context you have the contrast between a power and a liability, similarly in the ethical sphere you have a contrast between potentialities that are affirming and sustainable and those that are not, which contain internal contradictions. Thus heavy drug-taking or carrying out pre-emptive wars are patently not self-sustainable practices. You can of course carry out a pre-emptive war or take masses of dope but you cannot then also fulfil the other parts of your human potential or realise your concretely singularised nature, your dharma. So you evaluate these in relation to other human powers and needs. Such powers or potentialities are auto-subversive, they deconstruct themselves, not just in theory, but in practicality.

MH: In *Reclaiming Reality* you argue that any distinction between 'basic' human physical needs and 'higher-order psychological (mental) or spiritual needs' is 'crude' because it ignores that the latter needs are 'intrinsic to the way so-called basic needs are met',[29] and you said just a while ago that you regard freedom in the sense of the ability to formulate your own projects as just as important as physical needs. Alison Assiter and Jeff Noonan have a recent paper in *Journal of Critical Realism* in which they uphold the primacy of basic physical needs on the grounds that they are 'constraints of precondition' that 'must be satisfied before any other higher-level project can be pursued at all'.[30] Thus the need for autonomy, to take your example, only becomes possible on the basis of a certain level of satisfaction of basic physical needs. In effect, they argue that basic physical needs are ontologically prior to higher-order needs, in the same way that you argue that love is prior to war. What are your thoughts on this?

RB: I think that their contribution is very welcome because certainly the satisfaction of the needs they specify for food, drinkable water, shelter and a few other things – what they call relative health – is a precondition for any action or project at all. But this is not the only kind of precondition. Freedom in the sense of self-determination is I think just as basic as those physical needs. It corresponds to a different part of our constitution as human beings, not the biological part but the psychosocial part, and we cannot be said to be free unless we are capable of formulating our own projects individually and collectively. So freedom from oppression is a necessary condition also. What one needs is of course a whole set of social conditions – other states of one's psychology can be included within them – that are necessary in order to fulfil the action, in order to have it as a reasonable or meaningful action. Thus a meaningful act presupposes a certain level of recognition, respect, dignity or esteem. It presupposes, moreover, that the particular way in which you want to act is a matter of your well-being or vital interest, say to listen to and play music; this presupposes that you have the right instruments, that there is a society that facilitates people becoming musicians, and so on.

So I am suggesting that there are other universal constraints of precondition, foremost among which are those that are necessary for any action that is one's own, any intentional project. But then when you singularise the universal, build in a whole lot of other projects and put it all in the context of a geo-historical rhythmic, it must be the case that even the specific way in which basic needs are satisfied becomes very important. For example, if you are a vegetarian living in a society that facilitates this and you are suddenly placed in a situation where it is mandatory to eat meat, although your material conditions of survival are guaranteed, this is not enough, you cannot formulate your own project in the way you want to formulate it. This leads us into the whole realm of the relations between the components of concrete being – universality, particular mediations, geo-historical rhythmics and concrete singularity. The way we satisfy our hunger, as Marx stressed, is not any sort of way: there are people who would probably die before they ate a raw animal. The feeling of revulsion that most people would have in doing that is sufficiently great for us to include cooked food of an OK or kosher kind, that is, a kind that the agent feels happy with as part of their conditions for acting and formulating projects. The way we satisfy our basic physical needs is dependent on the way psychological and social needs have developed. There is always an element of singularity and relativity in an assessment of what is crudely physical. The crudely physical is then no longer just physical. Arguably the most horrible thing that has happened to prisoners in Abu Ghraib and elsewhere is sexual taunting and abuse, because it offends their self-identity at a very fundamental level, particularly in the case of Muslims. The American and British guards soon discovered that this is worse for them than any material deprivation. None of this is to say that there are not about two billion people in the world who do not really have enough to survive physically. That is absolutely shocking.

MH: If they had enough to survive physically, but not freedom, that would also be shocking.

RB: It *would* also be shocking, so I completely disagree with their example of slaves: that slaves who are well treated have their humanity in a way that people who are starving do not.[31] But I think this is just the kind of argument that we need to have because it both presupposes the objectivity of needs and potentials and can be developed into an exercise in creative concrete utopian thinking.

By the way, I was using the concept concrete utopianism about this time. I looked in your *Dictionary* and you imply that I introduced it in *Dialectic*.[32] I'm not sure if there were any references to it in *Scientific Realism and Human Emancipation*; it doesn't have an index, perhaps it doesn't come in.

MH: No, I don't think it does. You use it for the first time in *Reclaiming Reality* I think.

RB: But I was using it in discussion in the 1980s before I started using it in print. When I was leading a workshop, say, at the Chesterfield conferences –

MH: What were they?

RB: The Chesterfield conferences were held annually in Tony Benn's constituency from 1987 to 1989. They consisted of gatherings of socialists from all over Britain, mainly inside but also outside the Labour Party. They were organised into and around 'policy workshops'. I was the convenor of the philosophy workshop. This was always one of the more popular workshops, with over 100 participants out of a total of up to 1,000 or more conference-goers. There were some critical realists who participated in the overtly political Chesterfield conferences (such as Doreen Massey) but eschewed the more academic *Realism and the Human Sciences* conferences which were held from 1983 to 1994, before the establishment of the Centre for Critical Realism (CCR), and then the International Association for Critical Realism (IACR) took over their function.

MH: I'll come back to these more academic conferences next time. I think your first reference to concrete utopianism in print is actually in a version of an address you gave to the second Chesterfield conference in 1988.[33]

RB: Right, that figures. At these conferences we would in part be looking at philosophical problems and ideologies through a political and ethical prism. But the point was also to try to see how a Labour government could do things differently. So we would ask the people in the workshop to assume that they had won a majority at an election: so what were they going to do now? And that is the most important question you have to ask because, if you don't ask that question and start preparing for it now, you will be absolutely bankrupt when you get into power – which is more or less what happened to Harold Wilson in 1963, and it would seem is happening to Gordon Brown today. It reminds me of the story of the Brazilian president, Jânio Quadros, who at the end of 1960, just after John F. Kennedy in the United States, won a landslide popular election and then resigned after a few months and went off on a voyage with his advisors to decide what he would do when he was swept back into power by popular acclaim. He never came back. The generals took over. Our aim was to get aspiring left politicians to switch a little bit of their energy away from thinking about how to get into power and put a little bit more into the project of thinking about what they would do when they got into power. It also seemed to me at the time that they would not actually get into power (or at least power as distinct from office) unless they had a plausible concrete utopian vision with which they could inspire the electorate – assuming that they wanted to get into power via parliamentary democracy.

MH: Did you borrow the concept concrete utopia from Ernst Bloch?

RB: It might be a concept that I initially picked up from somewhere else, but I gave it my own meaning. Indeed, I was implicitly using it when I was teaching economics in Oxford in the late 1960s and early 1970s. I had to make sense of what economic theory, more especially neo-classical economic theory, was. I was seeing it as a praxiology, as a way of showing how you could achieve an end with a certain finite set of resources or constraints. What you had to do was formulate your objective function and then economic theory could show you how to optimise or maximise it. These were sound, albeit limited, techniques. However, in economics the ends would typically never be formulated explicitly, dispassionately and neutrally; rather, they were always implicitly to be understood as maximising profit or income or personal pleasure. They were not goals such as maximising the benefit to your customers in a nationalised industry, or fulfilling the wishes of the electorate as revealed at the last election. What one could do in critical economics was counterpose to the implicit maximisation of some egocentric or partial particular interest the explicit satisfaction of some general social benefit. Thus economics tutorials could become or contain exercises in concrete utopianism in their own way. Concrete utopianism was thus in a way with me from a very early stage. Indeed, I have always tried to think in a concrete utopian way in my own personal life, not always successfully.

MH: What do you say to critical realists such as Andrew Collier who reject your utopianism on the grounds that the causal connection adduced in western liberal political theory by thinkers such as Popper, Friedrich von Hayek, and Isaiah Berlin between utopianism, on the one hand, and totalitarianism and the slaughter of millions, on the other, is real, albeit not the main factor in such developments.[34]

RB: If I may say so, Andrew doesn't pay sufficient attention to the adjective 'concrete'. There is no way the revolution is going to happen independently of human agency and ideas, and those actions and ideas are not going to be produced solely as a result of endogenous systemic causes. Emancipation, properly so called, is always self-conscious self-emancipation. Even if the system unlocks the doors of the cell, the prisoner still has to walk out of the door, engage in an emancipatory praxis to be free. And such an emancipatory praxis needs the concrete utopian moment, specifying how the world would, or could, be a better place if and when the constraint or absence that binds the agent is itself absented (or constrained). Concrete utopianism is of course only one of the requirements for emancipatory axiology. What is also needed is explanatory critique and a theory of transition, and all three components are what I came to call in *Dialectic* 'the explanatory critical complex' developing alongside and in unity with a totalising depth praxis oriented to emancipation.

MH: I want to ask you now about the critique of irrealism you begin to develop in *Scientific Realism and Human Emancipation*. Your 'First Steps Towards the Metacritique of Irrealism' (Chapter 1.7), together with Chapter 2.6 'Reason and the Dialectic of Human Emancipation' and Chapter 3, 'The Positivist Illusion: Sketch of a Philosophical Ideology at Work' constitute I think the most adequate philosophical account we have of ideology as false consciousness. This is an area in which you step forward in your most full-bloodedly classical Marxist mode, essaying a proto-explanatory critique of positivism that arrives at its real definition as 'one might say, the house-philosophy of the bourgeoisie' that naturalises and normalises the capitalist social order and 'reflects in an endless hall of mirrors the self image of Bourgeois Man'.[35] Not only is the analysis again extraordinarily rich, spawning concepts such as irrealism, anthroporealism and anthroporealist exchanges, [Tina] compromise formation,[36] the constant conjunction form and the fact form, the Platonic–Aristotelian fault-line, the positivistic illusion (the illusion that there is no illusion) and the speculative illusion, the presence of the past, and subject–object identity theory; but it is exceedingly complex, to the point where, as nowhere else in your oeuvre, you occasionally lose me because anticipated rewards do not match the labour required to follow the intricacies. What drove you to such effort?

RB: What drove me really was the desire, perhaps the need, to explore the full possibilities of an explanatory critique of philosophy structurally. I wanted to see exactly what one could do at a theoretical level in relation to a philosophical ideology. I was also interested at the time in conjunctural analysis of particular episodes in the history of philosophy or the formation of particular figures. My essays on Paul Feyerabend, Gaston Bachelard and Richard Rorty fall into this category.[37] I suppose the fundamental thing was my desire, having done a comprehensive critique of epistemology, at least as applied to the philosophy of science and of social science, to see exactly what the maximum possibilities were in terms of explaining why this had happened structurally. Linguists such as Chomsky, on the one hand, and anthropologists such as Lévi-Strauss, on the other, had shown that human behaviour could be understood as revealing very complex and recondite structures which could however be described very precisely in a logical or mathematical way. I suppose I was imagining that my work might be a prototype for such a structural study of philosophical ideologies. I actually wrote a few more; but I didn't publish them, mainly because the effort did not seem to be worthwhile – and of course I had this problem of dialectic. It seemed to me that, really, what people were interested in were narratives telling a story about how positivism came to be, or how Popper or

Feyerabend or Rorty came to think the things that they did, accounts that were interesting at a human level. Most of the historians I knew, including the Marxist historians, had this view as well. Certainly I felt I was not able to get through to people in this way. I remember that, when I first gave a paper in this area in 1976 at the London School of Economics, the chair asked for questions, and there were none. I was mortified. Then someone did ask a question. But I realised that this work of mine had a sort of 'what-can-you-say-to-that?' effect, which is not what I wanted. I wanted to get people thinking, to start doing their own work differently if they were philosophers or social scientists, and of course acting differently as social agents. But my work on the structural analysis of philosophical ideologies was not having that effect. So I put it aside.

MH: Well, I for one am glad you did this work, not only because it is arguably the best account we have of ideology as false consciousness on the terrain of philosophy and the sociology of knowledge, but because it provides the groundwork for further important theoretical developments. Your analysis in *Scientific Realism and Human Emancipation* ends with the following words:

> Those who would rationally change the world need to re-open the case at all levels, in every science, in each practice, lest they be caught in a trap spun by a spider who knows the web of its problem-field well, knows that another name by which system P[ositivism] goes is that of vulgar (that is, unthinking) materialism.[38]

Am I right in thinking that the 'web' you mention here is the prototype of the web of *maya* in the theory of the demi-real that you later articulated? The analysis in *Scientific Realism and Human Emancipation* explicitly develops a concept of a compromise formation, which becomes necessary to save a theory when it contravenes an axiological necessity, such that you have 'truth in practice combined or held in tension with . . . falsity in theory', as you later summarised;[39] and in 1989, in *Reclaiming Reality*, you mention Tina ('there is no alternative') for the first time,[40] later bringing the two concepts together, in *Dialectic*, in the concept Tina compromise formation. As we know, the demi-real, at the level both of philosophy and of society, can be regarded as a compounding of Tina compromise upon Tina compromise, such that demi-reality is in effect Tina-reality. Also, am I right in thinking that your message about the dangers of getting caught in the web was directed specifically at Marxist unthinking materialism?

RB: Yes, both points are right. 'Unthinking materialism' had become fashionable. I was appalled by the way in which, say, *New left Review* had taken up relatively uncritically, first Galvano Della Volpe and Colletti, and then Timpanaro. Timpanaro was a very basic, almost reductionist materialist. Then of course *New left Review* started paying homage to the empiricists and analytical philosopher figures. You are absolutely right that the web of illusion is *maya*, a concept that goes hand in hand with the concept of *avidya*, which is igno-rance. You must remember that this work was published when I was writing manuscripts about dialectic, including the metacritique of irrealism and the western philosophical system, so it is not surprising that some of what appeared in later works should be present in the earlier one.

MH: You don't actually use the concept of the demi-real yet, but it is just about there when you describe the positivistic illusion as 'half-real'.[41]

RB: You can see the concept in motion. Your analogy with the *Grundrisse* is very flattering, but also apt in this respect.

MH: You deploy the concept of absence frequently in your work from *A Realist Theory of Science* on, and necessarily so in that, inter alia, you are engaging in immanent critique. But in *Scientific Realism and Human Emancipation*, I think for the first time, you explicitly refer to absence as 'causally efficacious'[42] and dramatically illustrate the point by leaving a large blank space under the sec-tion heading 'Ideology in the Metacritical Dimension: Presence of an Absence'.[43] Does this signify a change in your thinking at this stage about the concept of absence and at any rate an intuition that it was the category that could unify critical realist dialectic? This was in 1983, when you wrote the book.

RB: Absolutely right. There was of course an absence in *Scientific Realism and Human Emancipation* itself, which was the lack of a metatheory of absence. There was a metatheory of presence there, but there was not another world worked out, a metatheory of what was not there, and that was to come in *Dialectic*. In a way I was saying look, I cannot say any more at present. I can just show you – show you where I would like to go.

6   The axiology of freedom

Dialectical critical realism
(1986–1994)

MH: We will come on to the entrenchment and institutionalisation of critical
      realism in the 1990s and the wider context and applications of the dialectical
      turn (for example, what went wrong in the Soviet Union) in the next two
      interviews. Today the focus is on the theoretical content of the dialectical
      turn, including its generation and reception. You have indicated that 'it all
      came together' in 1991–2. Can you tell us how, specifically?

RB: To answer this I need to go back to around 1978–9. It then seemed to me obvi-
      ous that, in relation to critical realism's underlabouring for the social sciences,
      the most fundamental body of work was that of Marx and Marxism, from the
      point of view of the science of history at any rate. Patently Marx had not called
      himself a critical realist or even a realist; rather, I had to come to terms with
      his own self-understanding of what he was doing in his method, which
      involved understanding dialectic. So that was my motivation for going into
      dialectic. Quite early on, within a year or so, it became clear to me that
      absence was going to be crucial. But how do you actually talk about absence,
      how do you say or speak the not, which had been declared an impossibility by
      Parmenides and the whole tradition of the metaphysics of presence? That was
      a very difficult problem. In the meantime I wrote dictionary entries in the gen-
      eral area, giving accounts of Marx's method showing how he approximated to
      critical realism, and I think that kind of reconstruction of Marx's method,
      namely as a critical realist, was probably the best that there was to date. But
      these pieces still did not really satisfactorily come to terms with the impor-
      tance for Marx of dialectic. I obviously needed to go into Hegel and Marx's
      relation to Hegel, so I did a great deal of work on this, but still the fundamen-
      tal conceptual problem of saying the not remained unsolved.
          Now I am saying this in hindsight. Obviously I did not go around for thir-
      teen years thinking that I had to crack the problem of saying the not. It was
      rather that there were some things that did not fit. However, in so far as there
      is a key, it is more or less what I say in Chapter 2.1 of *Dialectic*, the section that
      I was now able to write on absence in 1991–2. It started with breaking the link
      between reference and existence. That was the really crucial thing. On page
      40 I say that 'my first objective is to argue, against Plato and Frege, that

reference does not presuppose existence'. I think it is useful to look at the logical infrastructure of that, because the distinctions that I refer to there, following R. M. Hare, between the phrastic, the neustic and the tropic, enabled me to see that actually you have the not or the negation at all three levels, and that we need to be able to understand in particular that the negation of a proposition at the level of its phrastic or ontic content is not the same as negation at the level of the neustic, which is saying no. I also say elsewhere in the book that I had previously been focusing on absence as essential to change and depth, which of course it is, but had been overlooking that there are also simpler forms of absence, such as a void in space–time.[1] At any rate, you have a clear distinction, which I was analysing in terms of absence, between the not at the level of the phrastic (non-being) and at the level of the neustic (negation or denial); so you could deny a positive or negative ontic content, you could deny a presence or an absence. And then of course something else that had been confused in the literature was the nature of fictional discourse, at the level of what Hare called the tropic. The non-existence of Hamlet is not the same as the non-existence of caloric or phlogiston. This gives you three distinct levels of negation. The non-existence of Hamlet involves negation at the level of the tropic, the non-existence of caloric involves negation at the level of the neustic in the transitive dimension, and non-existence or absence simpliciter involves negation at the level of the phrastic in the intransitive dimension.

The clear demarcation of these three levels was the key to unlocking the problem of the not. In particular, it revealed absence ontologically, absence at the level of the phrastic or ontic, what I call the de-ontic. This then enabled me to simplify Hegel's dialectic, and I think at the end of Chapter 1 there is quite a nice account of the simple logistics of the Hegelian dialectic which proceeds by the rectification of incompleteness – and incompleteness is of course an absence. I think I could put this all much more simply now, but that was the essence of my treatment of what Marx called the rational kernel of Hegelian dialectic. Then of course the mystical shell followed very straightforwardly from that, because it was the oblivion or forgetting or undoing of absence in Hegel, the forgetting that it was actually a negativity. It was always sequestered at a very early stage in his systematic dialectics. In the *Science of Logic* becoming is sublated for Hegel in determinate being. Moreover, once I had the logical apparatus of the three levels I could of course focus on determinate absence. The realm of negation was not limited to things that existed at a more abstract level than determinate being. It included determinate absences, determinate non-beings as well as beings, and of course in real life almost all of the uses of dialectic are specific, they are about determinate absences. So the mystical shell then became ontological monovalence, the assumption of a purely positive account of being. So now I was making sense of Marx's intuition that Hegel was both really important, because he gave an account of the fundamental way in which knowledge, in particular scientific knowledge, progresses; and at the same time (in the last instance) an apologist for the status quo, because of his reinstatement of the positive, his ontological monovalence. Then I began to see philosophy as such as a response to threatening change, a way of unconsciously and aporetically normalising the existing order of things. So I now had many of the fundamental elements of the logical infrastructure of the book. It all stemmed from seeing that you can have absence as well as presence in being, and that you can talk about this: you can assert absence just as you can also deny presence (or for that matter affirm or posit a fiction). You can, after all, say the not.

MH: How does that connect up with your earlier work? After all, absence is fundamental to *A Realist Theory of Science*.

RB: Of course, if you think about it, absence and change are the essence of my account of the transitive dimension, because you only talk about something like epistemological relativity in the context of change, that is what makes knowledge relative. But this does not mean that I had an adequate account of absence or change, in fact I did not go into it.

MH: And then of course, in the intransitive dimension, the domain of the real and the possible might be absent from the level of the actual, but this was not conceptualised in terms of absence.

RB: It should have been. Once you have ontology separated from epistemology, it is easy to see that the notion that the whole domain of ontology is filled with positive existences without any non-existences or absences, which are necessary for change, is an absurd superstition. You could present critical realism through to the dialectical stage much more simply than I have done. It all follows from the distinction between knowledge and its objects, the situation of the domain of ontology. Just as *A Realist Theory of Science* is structured around the theme of ontology and the distinctiveness of epistemology from ontology, so *Dialectic* is structured around the theme of absence. I say that alethia is equally important, so that is another theme, but absence and alethia stand to dialectical critical realism somewhat like the transitive/intransitive and real/actual distinctions stand to first-level or basic critical realism, and they are all pretty simple, if fundamental, concepts.

MH: You set yourself three closely related aims in *Dialectic*: the dialectical enrichment and deepening of critical realism; the development of the dialectics of freedom – of a general theory of dialectic capable of furnishing a metatheory for the social sciences on the basis of which they can play a significant emancipatory role; and the outline of the elements of a totalising critique of western philosophy. That is an extraordinarily ambitious agenda that must have required a stupendous and sustained concentration of powers to address. I have heard tell that you were totally exhausted when you finished. On the other hand, the work is positively exuberant conceptually, and you have sung high praises in a number of places to the angel of creative work. How would you describe your experience of writing this book?

RB: Well, it does cover a long period of time, from 1979 through to 1993. If I restrict myself to the period between 1991 and 1993, I think I felt isolated – certainly intellectually – in my creative work. Undoubtedly there was more than an iota of what can only be described as alienation there.

MH: Isolated in a way you had not felt before?

RB: Yes, intellectually isolated. It is difficult to say to what extent this is endemic to any creative work while you are doing it, because obviously it is very important, particularly when it is a completely new idea, not to release it prematurely while it is still in a vulnerable form.

MH: You were re-working pre-existing materials of your own, various manuscripts?

RB: Yes, working through the same sort of content. At the same time, there was a kind of separation phenomenologically, and even alienation, from the community in general. But there was also a feeling that, even if I was alienated in the immediate context in which I was writing the book, I was nevertheless in touch and in resonance with what was happening in the wider society, including intellectual society. I kept in touch through activities such as the *Realism and the Human Sciences* conferences[2] and weekly trips to Oxford to do teaching. I often stayed there a couple of days attending conferences and also carrying on writing (I'm actually talking about the whole period now). But whereas in *A Realist Theory of Science* I was among other things bringing together the best insights of the anti-deductive and anti-monistic traditions and there were many philosophers of science who were already moving towards my position, in the case of *Dialectic* I felt I was more or less out on my own. There was a discussion in Sartre's *Critique of Dialectical Reason* that was useful as far as it went, and then there were helpful clues in Marx, but you could not get very far with Engels's dialectics of nature. I had more or less to do it for myself. Of course, I was helped by the fact that it was a development of basic critical realism and this was being gradually taken up around the world. At this time critical realists were still finding it difficult to get their work published. So the work of keeping in touch with critical realists personally and attending conferences and seminars was even more important for me than perhaps it is today (though of course it is always important) and through that work I kept in touch with what was happening in the wider academy and the wider world. I continued to be politically active as well. But it was all definitely secondary to my intellectual work. I was probably very far from the picture one might have of the organic intellectual rooted in concrete struggles. The hero or heroine of the book I was writing is someone who lives the unity of theory and practice. Well, of course, I tried to live it, but in a very removed way. I think most of this was inevitable really, given the lack of immediate antecedents or precursors of what I was trying to say.

MH: Your intuitions were borne out by events. When the book came out, it was basically regarded by many in the critical realist world as impossibly and unnecessarily difficult, so that must have reinforced your sense of isolation. That is the way with very original works, initially. Anyhow, it did not exhaust you?

RB: I think I was exhausted when I finished it. But I immediately decided to write a simplified form of it, which was *Plato Etc.* I wrote that in 1993–4 and then in the second half of 1994 I had one cold after another. I was trying to write something on the philosophy of money and also to complete *Philosophical Ideologies*, but I just could not do it because I was always getting ill. Then I went to Cyprus for a holiday. I will tell you about that next time, because I had an experience there that leads on to the spiritual turn.

MH: Your father died during this period. How were you affected by that?

RB: Of course, I was upset by his death in 1991, I think it was probably about February. But I did not have the same sort of malaise I had after my mother's death.

MH: I understand he didn't leave you a penny.

RB: My father made it very clear to both me and my brother from very early on that there was no way he was going to leave any money to us.

MH: That's a very unusual thing to do.

RB: I know, and when my mother died, I think he had managed to ensure that her assets or share of their joint assets went to him. So nothing actually came from either of my parents.

MH: While he was alive you were receiving assistance from him?

RB: No. There was no assistance from him other than help with the Mini and then the sports car when I was at Oxford and a deposit for my first flat in Edinburgh.

MH: You had a house in Islington when I first met you. How did you manage to buy that without a full income?

RB: I will tell you. In 1978 I bought a flat in Edinburgh for a few thousand pounds, my father assisting with the deposit. At the same time Hilary's father had given us, as a wedding present, a house in Herefordshire which cost about

£1,000. On those two bases in 1979 I bought a flat with a slight mortgage in Mayford Road in Battersea. Then I moved from one place to the next. The Mayford Road flat was about £10,000. It was sold a couple of years later for £25,000 and then, with the help of a mortgage, a house in Battersea was purchased for £40,000. Then by the same sort of step up this house, in Balfern Street, was exchanged for another in Battersea, in Altenburg Gardens. Then the house in Islington cost much less than the Altenburg Gardens house was sold for; this was in 1995. I was a beneficiary of the property boom. Hilary's father left myself and Hilary a small legacy, most of which was pretty soon consumed. As you know, *Scientific Realism and Human Emancipation* was dedicated to Andrew Wainwright, and that was actually partly a way of saying thank you to that family. Andrew Wainwright was the third of the children of Hilary's father. He had committed suicide at about the age of nineteen or twenty by setting fire to himself. He was a very lovely person who was unable to live up to his understanding of his parents' conception of himself – I am not attributing blame. According to his understanding, his parents wanted him to become something like a chartered accountant or lawyer, but he did not shine at academic studies. Rather he was excellent, kind and caring with people; he probably would have liked to be in some kind of voluntary service for the rest of his life, as a kind of generalised carer and poet. He was very interesting to talk with. But as soon as he committed suicide his parents took the line that he was schizophrenic; it was something caused by chemical reactions in his brain. They denied a Langian explanation of it, which I would have been inclined to give. Of course, this dispute goes on today within psychiatry.

MH: Before we leave the business of writing *Dialectic* too far behind, can you say something about the diagrams. They are quite extraordinary, some of them distil an argument ranging across 2,000 years onto a single page.

RB: When I was working on my DPhil thesis and gearing up to writing *A Realist Theory of Science* I had the feeling that, really, the truth oughtn't to be that complicated, you ought to be able to say it on, if not the back of an envelope, then at least on a single page. This caused me to write smaller and smaller, and I had the feeling that if there was anything wrong, if there was a mistake, or even some crossing out on the page, then this was or at least might be a sign of some imperfection in the argument. I soon realised that this was obsessive. But I still had the basic idea that you ought to be able to summarise or diagrammatise a complex argument in a simple way. So I decided to represent many of the arguments and discursive structures in diagrams.

MH: Did they come before or after their written form, or simultaneously?

RB: Many came after. It was a way of summarising and perhaps internally checking whether what I had written made sense. It was not of course peculiar to *Dialectic*, only more prevalent – there are many representations of complex arguments diagrammatically in the earlier books, especially in *A Realist Theory of Science* and *Scientific Realism and Human Emancipation*. The diagrams are also a way of overcoming the linearity of the text. Dialectic in particular is obviously not simply linear, you are dealing with totality and there are a whole number of possibilities and directions that a dialectic movement might go in, and sometimes one wants them all together. You yourself make a similar use of tables in *Dictionary of Critical Realism*. Even a table helps to surmount the linearity of the text. It does not say first go from here to there, it presents a spread.

MH: So it was mainly in the writing that you mapped new conceptual space. The diagrams for the most part just registered and perhaps clarified what you had done, like my tables (which in their basic form accordingly preceded my own writing). Coming now to the text of *Dialectic*, its presentational dialectics correspond loosely to the stadia of the causal-axiological chain (MELD). Chapter 1 deals with critical realism, Hegelian dialectic, and the problems of philosophy – the material that is to be worked on/with and developed or transformed (1M non-identity); Chapter 2 expounds dialectic as the logic of absence (2E negativity); Chapter 3 presents the system of dialectical critical realism and the totalising dialectic of freedom (3L totality, the domain of ethics); and Chapter 4 engages in the transformative labour of the metacritique of western philosophical irrealism (4D). Rather than attempt to work through the myriad complex issues they raise, I think it best to concentrate on those that have proved particularly difficult or controversial. First, since I have just mentioned it, even after they are well into the book for the first or even second time, many people have difficulty grasping what MELD is, and why it is necessary to think in terms of 1M, 2E, 3L and 4D – it seems so complex. How would you begin to explain this to relative novices?

RB: The simplest way to answer this is to think of basic critical realism as opening up the whole domain of ontology and dialectic as deepening that ontology by supplying concepts and exploring domains that were only presupposed at the first level. One way to see this deepening of ontology is in terms of what I have called the 1M to 7Z/A schema. You move through, first, the domain of 1M non-identity, which is also a domain of structure. Why is the starting point characterised as non-identity? Because all the basic distinctions within transcendental realism turn on non-identity relations. The object is not the same as the knowledge of the object, this is the transitive/intransitive distinction; then you have the distinction between the domains of the real, actual and empirical. All these involve non-identity relations, and that supplies the logical infrastructure of basic critical realism. It is true that emergence also plays an important part in it, but it is not yet theorised very fully, just as the spatio-temporality of social structures is part of the architectonic of critical naturalism, but is not yet explicitly theorised. So you can think of the movement of dialectic as opening up, finding it necessary to unravel, deeper levels of ontology. 2E is the realm that is opened up by absence, but it includes the whole world of process, negation, and transformation. So while at 1M you think being as non-identity and structure, at 2E you think it as process. Then at a third, deeper level, 3L, you think being as a whole, so critiquing ontological extensionalism by seeing internal relations between the different parts of being, not just external connections. And then at a fourth level, 4D, which is obviously already present in an under-elaborated way in critical naturalism and indeed in transcendental realism, you think being as incorporating trans-formative praxis, agentive agency or intentional causality that effects material changes in the world. Then at the time of the spiritual turn I saw that it was necessary to have three further levels: at 5A you think being as spiritual or as incorporating self-reflexive human praxis; at 6R you think it as (re-) enchanted or as meaningful and valuable in itself; and then at 7A/Z you think being as non-duality, more generally as one. The first four steps (MELD if you abstract from the numerals) are the crucial ones for understanding what I later called the world of duality, including specifically the world of demi-reality. They are perfectly adequate for understanding that world, but not nec-essarily for bringing about the changes we want, which require the further deepening of ontology in the last three steps.

MH: We will come on to them in subsequent interviews. People also experience serious difficulties with the key unifying concept of absence. They say that an absence, qua pure negativity, cannot by definition possess any causal powers[3] and they are uncomfortable with the notion of the ontological priority of absence. Even those who cannot gainsay your arguments for ontological pri-ority within at any rate the world as we know it, that is, one containing both absence and presence, seem much happier with the notion that absence and presence are somehow on a par.[4]

RB: There are two basic arguments or considerations that suggest that absence is logically prior to presence. The first is that you can coherently imagine or con-ceive of a world without presence, but not of a world without absence: there is no internal contradiction in the idea of a complete void, of there not having been anything. That is the way in which I argue, using a number of subsidiary arguments: it is impossible to conceive of a world without gaps, spaces, and boundaries, or at least some of those things, or without changes, including in particular the human changes that we bring about in our agentive agency. That is the first argument, there could not be a world without absence. The second argument is that if one wants to think about the beginning or the end of such a world, if you want to ask causal questions about the coming into or going out of being of such a world, then this must be from and to a void. The beginning must be from a void and the end must be to nothing. The beginning would have to be some sort of radical autogenesis, the coming into being of the universe has to be out of nothing. I think that is logically absolutely correct. If you go into stories of creation, they have great difficulty in explaining what happened before God created the universe. The most consistent ones try to picture some way in which the universe comes into being when the creator creates it. Often this involves obscure sexual imagery, a god or a goddess fertilising themselves. But does the god or goddess have a beginning in time, or does it create time? There is a footnote in *Dialectic* about contemporary cosmological theory,[5] and I think, whichever of those routes you take, they are going to involve the idea of a world in which there was no positive being and no positive presence, in which there was just absence.

MH: That footnote itself seems to reject the notion that something can come out of nothing.

RB: Yes, I think that is right. I think this sort of thing has to be decided in the context of scientific theory.

MH: It does not seem scientifically possible.

RB: No it does not.

MH: Some recent speculative cosmological theory does purport to show, although perhaps not very convincingly, that the universe or multiverse could have originated from absolutely nothing in accordance with the laws of physics.[6] The other thing people say is that in working out what must logically be the case – that is, that you could not have a purely positive world but you could have just nothing – you are logicising being.[7]

RB: I don't know about that. We are talking about something, so we are in the realm of discourse. Just think about a world without absences. It is literally inconceivable. How could you identify anything except by reference to what it is not; by reference, if you like, physically, socially or conceptually, to its space? So I cannot see that it makes any sense to talk about logicising being. This is a discourse about being.

MH: If the argument for the priority of absence logicises being, then all transcendental argumentation logicises being, because it works out what logically must be the case relatively or absolutely independently of human being.

RB: And of course you are not supposing this is why it is the case, you are not saying the reason why it is the case is because of a logical proposition, it is just a question of whether it can be the case or not. How could you begin to explain an absolute beginning except in terms of something that conceptually involved the coming into being of something out of nothing?

MH: Your current position on this then, is it correct to say, is that although it seems to go against a great deal of science, it must be the case that there was a radical autogenesis out of nothing?

RB: Outside our universe I think there were other universes, but outside any possible universe it would have to be so. I do not actually think there was ever a time in which there was absolutely nothing, but that is to take objection to the whole hypothesis of the Big Bang. I think there might be modes of absence that we do not fully comprehend and degrees of absence that we cannot think about conceptually, and the beginnings of the multiverse might be a case, if you like, of something less absent coming out of something more absent or a deeper level of absence. I would like to have the time to go into that in relation to current scientific thinking and disputes.

MH: That would be fascinating; there have been some very interesting and pertinent recent developments in cosmology. I now want to ask about the dialectics of nature. You arrive at a real definition of dialectic as 'the axiology of freedom – or as *absenting absences*, or, applied recursively, as *absenting constraints on absenting absences*',[8] thereby retotalising the diffraction of dialectic under the sign of absence. Where does this leave the dialectics of nature?

RB: There are a number of things I want to say about this. First, I think the Engelsian formula for the dialectics of nature in terms of the transformation of quality into quantity, the unity of opposites, and the negation of the negation is very limited. That is the first thing. I do try to situate it in *Dialectic*, and I am not saying it is not important. The second thing is that the dialectics of nature and the whole discussion about them should presuppose a resolution of the problem of naturalism of the kind I achieved in *The Possibility of Naturalism*, but then deepen it so as to incorporate a conception of four-planar social being, as in *Scientific Realism and Human Emancipation*. And from within this standpoint, then, one has to say two things. First, dialectics or dialectical movements cannot exhaust the study of change. There are non-dialectical movements and changes in the social and natural world, of which the most important is probably the entropic transformation of a structure into its elements. This is not the resolution of a problem-field but its proliferation – which in a way is a moment within dialectics. Moreover, one cannot assume that there is always going to be a negentropic outcome to changes such as that. Entropy stands alongside dialectic as the two great possibilities. But there are other, subsidiary possibilities, and in *Dialectic* I canvass some of them in relation to Hegel.[9] So dialectics does not incorporate the whole of the study of change. Second, the extent to which dialectics applies in the natural world always depends on specific dialectical laws, so there is no one answer to it. Contradictions, it seems patently obvious, exist in nature, and the emergence of human beings out of nature or of primate animals in biological evolution is something that involves dialectic. Indeed, if you look at the sweep of biological history, you could also recast the theory of evolution in a dialectical way – by arguing that a species that survived, as distinct from one that did not, did so by managing in its history – in its evolution – to liberate itself from some constraints. It was absenting an absence, getting rid of a constraint. This is not to presuppose any purpose or teleology, and that was Darwin's point, but nevertheless it still involves movement towards greater order and complexity, and in a way towards greater self-determination or possibilities of self-determination and, we could say (at least in the domain of human life), greater volition. Here you are going pretty far into the dialectical thicket, though of course it does not make any sense to talk about assertorically imperatival sensitised solidarity or the fiduciary nature of the expressively veracious remark when you are referring to animal existence.

MH: Can we apply that to inorganic nature, as a real developmental tendency?

RB: This is very interesting because inorganic nature had to evolve and the dream of the alchemists, in a peculiar way, must have been realised at one point in the natural history of the cosmos – gold, or at least its possibility, must have been formed from more basic elements or their atomic and subatomic constituents. Of course, quasi-alchemical processes would not have resulted just in gold, and they would have issued from hydrogen and helium or some mix of basic elements, but you would have had to have the transformation of one element or its components into another. And you could recast this in dialectical terms.

MH: Not in terms of the extended definition I have just cited – 'the absenting of constraints on absenting absences', or the axiology of freedom. You can extend this to the biosphere, as you have just pointed out, but for inorganic nature you need the abbreviated version, just 'absenting absences'.

RB: That is the most basic one, because absenting absences in the human sphere means eliminating, transcending or transforming constraints – absenting the ill or the constraint that plagues you. It is just much richer, much more immediate, in the social world, whereas what you would be doing in the natural world, given that inorganic nature has not by and large been understood dialectically by scientists, is imposing as it were a schema on it. How important it is to think human action in terms of dialectical categories! Human intentional action is always dialectical, it is always eliminating a want or trying to relieve a need; whenever you are producing a material change in your environment because you want to get rid of – eliminate, absent – something in that environment that is constraining you or that constrains you in some way. The dialectical transposition of human actions is of course a prolegomenon to the dialectical transposition of human and social problems. That is the way you have to situate them to make sense of them philosophically, at least from the point of view of praxis.

MH: When you talk of emergence in nature you speak of 'a quantum leap . . . of (one feels like saying) the materialised imagination — or even, with Hegel, reason . . . This is matter as creative, as autopoietic.'[10] So there is a sense in which you seem to be connecting the dialectics of nature up with the dialectics of human geo-history, by indicating that the latter is implicit as possibility in the former.

RB: This is right. Perhaps we will talk about this when we come on to meta-Reality. There is a way of looking at the natural world as already implicitly containing our consciousness of it; and of seeing all the possibilities of development and self-awareness that can at the moment, as far as we know, only be instantiated in the human world, as already enfolded in the organic, and beneath and before that the inorganic, world – because the organic world came from somewhere.

MH: To have a dialectic that embraces the whole of being presupposes system-building; as Hegel put it, since what is concretely true is so only as totality, the thought that seeks to grasp it must take the shape of a system.[11] But system-building in philosophy is still much out of fashion, and among critical realists Andrew Collier,[12] for one, has expressed doubts as to whether it is desirable or even possible on the grounds that our knowledge of being is necessarily fragmented or partial.

RB: Yes, our knowledge is necessarily partial, but you are going to organise your understanding of being anyway, willy nilly: if you do not accept the dialectical critical realist way of organising being, then you are going to be accepting a poststructuralist or empiricist or some other vision, some framework or schematism is unavoidable. What is the typical empiricist response to being? It is that the world is partial and fragmented, atomistic. This objection is manifesting the assumption that everything is at bottom fragmented. This is also one of the refrains of poststructuralism with its critique of grand narratives. The critique of grand narratives is of course itself a grand narrative, the grand narrative that you cannot tell a story, any story, that would gainsay the grand narrative or myth that there is no story. Similarly, any story here, in response to this kind of objection, that attempts to see being as a whole – attempts a systematic analysis of our most basic concepts for ontology – is only implicitly defending what is already there, because there is no way of thinking about absence and change, for example, without invoking a category of causality of some sort or another.

MH: My next question concerns the ethical inflection of absence. As I point out in *Dictionary of Critical Realism*, the ancient Greek word on which deontology, the study of moral duty, is formed – *dein* (vb) or *deon* (n.) – has two basic meanings which coincide with the two you derive for absence, which allow you to unify ethics with the theory of being-becoming, that is, constraint and absence simpliciter, or more fully (1) a bind, fastening, or fetter and (2) want, lack, or need.[13] Were you aware of this at the time of writing?

RB: Thank you for telling me that. I think it is very indicative.

MH: Perhaps you were drawing out what was already implicit in the etymology.

RB: Or perhaps I made a certain move using the language at my disposal. And the roots of that language derive from a time in which the distinction I am trying to draw now was also drawn.

MH: Where did the Greeks who made the distinction get the insight? Perhaps the real connection here is praxis, which supplies your main premises and a form of which the ancient Greeks were of course engaging in.

RB: I would have to look into that. You talk in your excellent dictionary entry about the etymology of alethia, the original concept meaning the undoing of oblivion, and it does fit very well with what I say about alethic truth.[14]

MH: Let us move on to alethia, then, and the theory of the truth tetrapolity. You say that next to sustaining an adequate account of negativity, the second great discovery you would like to claim in *Dialectic* is that of 'a genuinely ontological notion of truth: alethia – the truth of things, as distinct from propositions'.[15] Alethia is but one, albeit the most important, moment in the theory of the truth tetrapolity, which some view as 'simply a list' or 'aggregation'[16] of different meanings of the concept of truth. I would like you first of all to comment on that.

RB: I do not think the four components of the truth tetrapolity are just a list, because they are related in terms of a dialectical deepening of truth. This has four stages, each presupposing the next. First there is truth as normative-fiduciary, or the trust-me-you-can-act-on-it sense of truth. That is a very early and primitive stage in the dialectic. Although you need not use them in a uni-linear way, in science that might be the stage of subjective conviction – but it is more than just 'I believe this, you should believe it too'. Second, there is truth as adequating or warrantedly assertible. Here the claim is that this proposition is adequate for the description of reality for this moment in our epistemic enquiries, and this of course brings out much of what the correspondence theory of truth intends. Third, there is truth in an expressive-referential sense, in which you say this is how the world is. At this level, truth is a duality that both expresses and refers to the world; it is not the dualism you get in correspondence theories whereby the world is out there and our language in here, it is just simply the way you express in discourse the nature of being. You have now found a way of expressing what being is that is the best possible way you could have and is a deepening and refinement of the adequating concept. However in the dialectic of science you eventually get to the point where you have the real reason for something. The truth of the proposition that this is water is that it is constituted by molecules of H_2O. When you get to this level, especially if you can in turn give an account of the constitution of hydrogen and oxygen, there is no disputing about the proposition, because you have the real reason why water must be the way it is. I do not think this tetrapolity is simply a list, because what we see here is how the components are related in a progression, a notional temporal process, and how they are also systematically related in various ways.

MH: They map on to 1M–4D.

RB: Absolutely. The second thing I want to say is that most of the objections to alethic truth, or misunderstandings of it, fail to take into account that in the domain of alethia we are talking about the truth of things, not propositions. Now I want to distinguish here three levels: the level of ontology as such; the level of truth or epistemologically mediated ontology; and at the level of the ontic, the objects of specific epistemic enquiries. First and most basically, there is the level of ontology as such, the whole domain of ontology, of being and reality. Then there is the level of truth that in its ontological aspect is ontology given the possibility of language, of human practice; so it is epistemologically mediated or tied to the possibility of human practice. That is the domain of alethic truth. At a third level you have the domain of the ontic, and this is where you are talking about a further division within ontology that consists in the intransitive objects of specific epistemic enquiries. Most of the critics of alethia fail to see that you cannot collapse it to the purely epistemic level or even further; it is not just an ontic, it is a deeper level of ontology. It presupposes ontological stratification, that is absolutely true, but you have to be careful here: if there were a world without human beings, you would still have ontological stratification even though you did not have truths; if you could take us humans away, you would have deep strata but you would not have alethic truth, because you only have the concept in relation to what we mentioned earlier, the undoing of oblivion – it does not make sense to speak of nature being oblivious of itself: nature does not disguise itself from itself. So this is ontological stratification from the point of view of the possibility of human practice. And that is a deeper level – the level of objective truth – than the level of epistemology, that is, the level at which we have a transitive/intransitive differentiation and at which we have specific enquiries with specific intransitive objects, and at which you begin to see the sense of the other aspects of truth. In considering ontological and alethic truth we make the mistake of tying ontology, not to the possibility of human practice, but to specific cognitive enquiries.

MH: The concepts of ontological and alethic truth would seem to have affinities with Hegel's concept of the Idea as 'the *adequate Notion*, that which is objectively *true*, or the *true as such*', a concept in which '*being* has attained the significance of *truth*' and which expresses the real reason for everything actual.[17] To what extent are you indebted to Hegel here?

RB: In Hegel there is a positive and a negative. The real reason is, on the one hand, thrown up by the process of reality itself, that is to say it is immanent in reality; this is the positive point. But, on the other hand, it is ultimately and only a (process of) thought; this is the negative point, betraying Hegel's continuing commitment to the principle of identity or realised idealism, and thus to the epistemic fallacy.

MH: Is alethia in any way, other than etymologically, related to Heidegger's concept of *alētheia*?

RB: In Heidegger the alethic truth, what is undone in the 'undoing of oblivion', is always ultimately a truth about ourselves, whereas for me alethic truth has no such anthropocentric connotations. What we are oblivious to include truths about the objective, existentially intransitive world in which we live and of which we are a small and temporally ephemeral part. Human being, *Dasein*, is inscribed within a greater being, to which we also pertain – and just because of this, knowledge of the alethic truth of things, including ourselves, can help us become free, indeed is a necessary condition for our liberation. Of course, it is true that, at the level of meta-Reality, we have a philosophy of identity or unity again, but it is a differentiated and developing identity, in which there are still and always an other, an outside, that which is existentially intransitive, to our embodied personalities, though our ground-states and the cosmic envelope may be one.

MH: You have already partly answered this next question. Probably the majority of critical realists accept that truth is in the final analysis ontological and alethic, such that the world imposes its truth on us rather than the other way around. Quite a few do not, however, holding that truth is an exclusively epistemological notion and that one gains nothing by extending it to ontology. If *x* is the generative mechanism of *y*, one gains nothing by adding that *x* is the truth of *y*. But one stands to lose something: fallibilism and anti-absolutism;[18] a few seem to think alethia leads straight to God, so some Marxists simply ignore it.[19]

RB: To think about *x* being the truth of *y* is to think about it being a real reason or dialectical ground for *y*, and that is also to be able to show why *y* occurs. It is very important to see that this does not gainsay fallibilism or anti-absolutism, because of course one's account of the real grounds or reasons for something is fallible, but the grounds themselves are not, so you have to understand the real grounds as being ontological. Fallibilism does not apply to ontology, it refers to something within the epistemological or transitive dimension.

MH: That is why some want to keep truth as an exclusively epistemological concept.

RB: There *is* something infallible. What is infallible is the real grounds for something, the real reason why it happens, and that ontological notion is very important: it is one of the meanings of truth – that is my claim – one of the components of a full analysis of truth to the effect that our accounts of it are fallible. Ontological 'infallibilism' is necessary for epistemic fallibilism. If you were to have alethia in isolation from the dialectic of truth, or from the broader dialectic of scientific discovery I sketch in *A Realist Theory of Science* as later elaborated in the epistemological dialectic, you might well ask what it really adds. But once you have a sense of the movement of human knowledge, that what you are really trying to do in science or any process of learning or discovery is to move from one level of structure to a deeper level of structure, it can be seen that alethia brings out what you are actually trying to do. For when you have reached the alethic level, when you have attained alethic knowledge or knowledge of the alethic truth of something – and it is always relative – you then move on to the alethia of that alethic knowledge. An account of critical realism that leaves this out might not be disastrous for your practice, but it would be impoverished. It is not so difficult to understand. Particularly when you go into the ethical realm and then some of the developments of the alethic strand within *Dialectic*, the basic notion of alethia can be seen to be actually very like the notion of absence. It depends on simple distinctions, really, between the level of human-independent ontology, the level of an ontology that relates to or is tied conceptually to human practice, and the level of ontology in which you are talking about the specific content of particular enquiries. Like the distinction between the phrastic, the neustic and the tropic, it is not so difficult to understand.

MH: Some have difficulty with the notion that alethia is developing and dynamic – emergent, 'the stratified form' of referential detachment;[20] and conversely with the concept of emergent falsity and related concepts: the alethic truth of falsity, which might itself be false.[21] I say relatedly because falsity as well as truth is here being taken as ontological, though I do not think you had yet begun to speak of (real) false being(s) as such, as you do later.[22]

RB: If you think of alethia as being the real reason or dialectical grounds for something then these grounds are in time-space, particularly, but not only, in the social world. Because alethic truth is the real reason for things insofar as humans have encountered it in their practice, it can be transformed in its intransitive aspect and our knowledge of it is also undergoing a process of transformation. So the structural grounds, the dialectical grounds, the real reasons for things are developing and dynamic. We tend to view causes in a very static way, but a cause, as a generative mechanism of a structure, is the mode of operation of that structure. If you turn to the social realm, you can say that the dialectical ground for the collapse of Northern Rock is a certain property of capitalism at a certain stage in its development. That is the alethia of the collapse of Northern Rock. But for a Marxist capitalism itself is false and potentially historically transient. You could argue that the real reason why women in the nineteenth century had such little influence in the body politic was in part because they were denied the vote and so excluded from political participation. That would be a dialectic ground that was false in itself but was also transformed in history. When using the new notion of alethia in the sociosphere one still has to retain the basic conceptual machinery of critical realism, but in the context of an understanding that one is talking about a real ground or a real reason for something that is in history and is itself subject to critique and transformation, to geo-historical change.

MH: Can you explain the relation between alethic truth, the reality principle, and axiological necessity? We have begun to see them at work in the previous interview in the constitution of Tina compromise formations. Am I right in thinking that, though there might be subtle differences, ultimately they are the same thing?

RB: You are basically right, they are essentially the same thing. However they can also be seen as different perspectives on the same thing. If we refer back to what I was saying about the different declensions of ontology, then within the level of ontology related to human practice, that is, the level at which you talk about alethic truth, the most objective of these three concepts is the concept of alethic truth, and the most subjective is the concept of axiological necessity. You can talk about the alethic truth of something that happens at a certain level without thinking of human practice in a concrete way, whereas when you talk about axiological necessity it is always from the point of view of some specific practice: you are looking at the way in which alethic truth, the truth of things, imposes itself on your praxis. And then in between the two you have something like the reality principle, which I think I do not use very much and which refers to practices in general in the sense in which Freud wants to talk about this.

MH: You use alethia much more frequently, but the reality principle does make its presence felt in the text, as indeed it should. I now want to come on to ethics via discussion of the relation of dialectical critical realism to Marxism. I think it is true to say that Marxists, like most critical realists as such (although this seems to be changing), have a higher opinion of basic than of dialectical critical realism, valuing in particular the emergentist stratified and differentiated ontology that the former articulates and viewing the latter as unnecessary or at any rate unnecessarily complicated on the grounds that first-wave critical realism is already dialectical.[23] On the face of it, there is something of a paradox here, since it is dialectic that Marx held to be 'a scandal and abomination to the bourgeoisie', as you remind us in the quote from Marx you give pride of place alongside ones from Plato and Hegel at the beginning of *Dialectic*. Marxists by and large seem to like your materialist diffraction of dialectic, initiated by Marx, and also explanatory critiques, and leading on from that some value the dialectics of freedom highly, but a number of other things or perceptions seem to have them really worried, especially it would seem Marxists who see materialism as going together with atheism. First, they are concerned that your dialectic intends to englobe and supersede Marxism, that is, transcend or (essentially preservatively) sublate it, to which they respond by attempting to show that Marxian dialectic can sublate dialectical critical realism, in that it can in particular better handle the dialectics of nature and provides a conceptual toolkit that more adequately guards against slippage into irrealist 'idealism and/or godism'.[24]

RB: It is not intended to supersede Marxism; rather, it operates at a different level. What I am trying to do in relation to Marxism is to bring out the most fundamental categories it needs in order to understand a subject-matter that is intrinsically dialectical, and so it is at a more basic or abstract level than Marxian dialectic. Were I writing a book on the unfinished business of Marxism at a substantive level then obviously it would have to be much more concrete and specific. The examples I give in *Dialectic* are exactly that, exemplifications. In relation to my alleged intention to englobe, I think englobing is the wrong metaphor for what a philosophical discourse is trying to do. If you think of being as a sort of dynamic pyramid, at the top you have being as such; then the categories of basic or first-level critical realism, such as structure, and so on; and then what dialectical critical realism does is go from there to a set of categories necessary to think process and change as such; and then come the categories that are necessary to think specifically historical changes, for instance, using a substantive theory of history such as historical materialism. Dialectical critical realism provides the most abstract concepts for understanding being and therefore the most abstract concepts for a critique of developments within Marxism. It provides a critique of anti-Marxism, and I think on the whole my intention, certainly at the time of writing *Dialectic*, was to support the science of history Marx had opened up.

MH: Yes, that is underlabouring. But you can see how the idea arises because you do say such things as dialectical critical realism claims to sublate previous dialectics.

RB: That's right, it means dialectics at that level. It claims to sublate, for example, Marx's comments on dialectic by bringing out their rational essence, and getting rid of what is not essential. It claims to be able to show why Marx found it so difficult to say what was so good about Hegel by critiquing the sin of ontological monovalence as a founding error of the whole history of irrealism and by situating Marx's own work at a level that is more specific, showing how it was that he was unable to do justice philosophically even to the levels that are addressed by basic critical realism. That is why, if you are a Marxist, you need basic critical realism and also, I am suggesting, dialectical critical realism.

MH: Another concern of some Marxists is that dialectical critical realist ethics are idealist in the sense of articulating mere ideals, not real tendencies, that is, they are unanchored in the concrete tendencies of actual geo-history,[25] and that this paves the way to the alleged outright idealism and spiritualism of the books of the spiritual turn. Your powers are evidently in sad decline in *Dialectic*,[26] you begin to 'go off the rails'[27] and you are yourself guilty of 'the speculative illusion'.[28] As you know, Alex Callinicos attributes this at least in part to your deployment of transcendental arguments, albeit from historically relative premises. The best way to stay on the tracks of Marxist materialism and atheism is to read one's metaphysics off from science, as Marx and Engels of *The German Ideology* were prone to do, and venture a few cautious conjectures.[29]

RB: I think it is really important to see rational directionality as one of many real tendencies that operate in a particular situation, but as a very important one that takes us from any action or even any remark all the way through to something like Marx's vision of the ideal society, which I call eudaimonia, a society in which the free development of each is a condition of the free development of all. Rational directionality is, if you like, the logical underpinning of a real tendency operating in history that is the throwing off of constraints or action oriented towards throwing them off. It is currently very fashionable to say that this does not happen. But how, in that case, do you begin to make sense of at least part of what is happening in Afghanistan or Iraq except in terms of self-determination and the struggle to throw off constraints imposed by the imposition of alien rule? As I argued in relation to needs, it is difficult not to see self-determination or the desire for self-determination as absolutely basic in human life.

MH: Relatedly people claim that your dialectics of freedom are contextualised socio-substantively by a concept of generalised master–slave-type (or $power_2$) relations that is too abstract and generalised to be of much use in 'unravelling the complex relational determinations of the various axes of social power'[30] and that downplays the central explanatory importance of class. Thus you wrongly criticise Marx for being 'fixated on the wage-labour/capital relation at the expense of the totality of master–slave relations'[31] – which is taken to imply that you yourself do not think that class is 'arguably the explanatorily most important . . . of master–slave-type relations'.[32] Moreover, focusing on the master–slave trope, it is claimed, obscures the fact that under capitalism $power_2$ is an epiphenomenon of a form of $power_1$ – control over resources – and thus leaves $power_2$ without an explanation and plays an ideological, reproductive role.[33]

RB: The first point that I would want to make is that $power_2$ refers to at least two planes of what I call four-planar social being: not only the plane of social interactions, but the plane of social structures sui generis, so that I use the concept of power$_2$ to refer to the structures of exploitation, domination and oppression, including of course the structures intrinsic to capitalism. I just do not think you can get away with translating everything back to power$_1$. Structural domination and oppression is an indisputable fact, it needs to be registered as such. Otherwise I can agree with Andrew Collier that the imposition of differential control over certain kinds of resources, for example the means of labour, is indeed a fundamental act.

MH: That would seem to make control over resources a form of power$_2$.

RB: Power$_1$ and power$_2$ are mutually interdependent. Whenever you have an instance of power$_2$ either at the structural or at a more personalised level it is also an instance of power$_1$: power$_1$ includes, but does not entail, power$_2$. Typically in the kind of domain we are talking about many instances of power$_1$ will also be instances of power$_2$. But the reason why it is important to have the notion of power$_1$ distinct from power$_2$ is because, of course, not all power is bad, that is not all instances of it. Transformative capacity is an essential part of freedom. So it is absolutely vital to have a conception of transformative capacity and thus of power$_1$. This relates to the concept of power as causal powers. On the other hand, the concept of power as domination, power$_2$, is just too prevalent to forget about, and it applies at both these levels. I find it somewhat difficult to understand what that debate is about really.

MH: What do you make of the issue of 'fixation'?[34]

RB: It is evident to me that in addition to class oppression and our understanding of it there are other modes of oppression. These have to be theorised in their own right even if at the end of the day you can come to some sort of synchronic explanatory reduction of them in terms of class oppression – and I say 'even if' because I do not think that is possible. Either way, they still have to be theorised in their own right and are still going to form an important constituent of any conjuncture in which you act. I am saying that Marxists have to accept the plurality of the forms of oppression.

MH: Is this compatible with the notion of a hierarchy of causes?

RB: Class oppression colours all the others, and is the most important, or at any rate a very important, causal factor in explaining them.

MH: Finally, and relatedly, some Marxists claim that your dialectic is headed towards voluntarism and the downplaying of structural constraints, and ignores that people are not essentially free (or god-like) but rather essentially both free and unfree; hence your eudaimonia is idealistic and utopian or perfectionist in a pejorative sense and plainly unachievable.[35]

RB: People are both free and unfree, as the objection says, but it overlooks that these things are not on the same logical level. People are actually slaves but really free. What people want to do is to deconstrain themselves, to remove constraints in their environment or in themselves on the achievement of what they want, and so to become free in actuality, or more free than they were. So understood dynamically the two things are not on the same logical level. Understood statically one would not know what a society was like in which there was no freedom or nobody was in any respect free; it would be a society in which there was no intentional action. But the converse is possible to imagine: a society that is eudaimonistic, in which the constraints have been removed, or rather the constraints at the level of the demi-real have been removed, because there will always be challenges (and so duality) in the world. So freedom is analytical or essential to human action and to human being in a way that unfreedom is not.

MH: In his forthcoming book on your dialectic, Alan Norrie has characterised its ethics as 'constellational' and 'cumulative', by which I take him to mean roughly that, while ethics on your account is embedded within the geo-historical process and subject to extrinsic structuring, it is also, in virtue of what you have called 'the deep content of the judgement form and the latent immanent teleology of praxis',[36] intrinsically critical of actually existing morality, such that moral alethia, like alethic truth as such, is dynamic and developing?[37] Can you comment on this? The key notion underpinning cumulation is of course something we have already touched on, that of the tendential rational directionality of geo-history towards the moral object/ive of the species, that is, the pulse of freedom, which is dialectic itself. Marxist critical realists such as Sean Creaven welcome this thesis as rehabilitating in philosophy and social theory a concept of progressive if uneven and contingent social development that they see at the heart of Marx's social theory,[38] but some other commentators close to critical realism, for example Radha D'Souza, view any such notion as irredeemably contaminated with residues of Eurocentrism, colonialism and imperialism.[39] What is the way forward here?

RB: We are in the sphere of practical reasoning, and what we have to understand when we are talking about ethics is that it is always action-guiding, on the one hand, but on the other it always exists in relation to some actually existing morality and some concrete situation or set of circumstances. In this sense it is always within history and always potentially involves explanatory critiques of actual existing morality. So you could say that it is always critical. As action-guiding, I argue that the moral alethia of the species is universal concretely singularised human flourishing in nature, but also that the ethical thing to do will always be something that is specific to our different concretely singu-larised natures, rhythmics and circumstances, and actionable in that context. That does not mean that one cannot have a general theory of it. What I attempt to do is to bring out a theoretical infrastructure at the centre of which is what I call the ethical tetrapolity, in which one moves from the solidarity implicit in what I call the expressively veracious remark to the content of explanatory critical theories – what we need to do, what needs to happen in the world to resolve the ill that is afflicting us – through the totalising depth-praxis necessary to remove the constraints, to the pulse that is movement in the direction of universal human emancipation or eudaimonia. That brings out the directionality of ethics, but any particular judgement or any particular moral stance is always going to be very specific.

MH: What do you say about the perceived Eurocentrism of rational directionality, its possible affinity with 'the idea of progress' and theories of modernisation and social evolution that provide a rationale for imperialism?

RB: Let us look at the higher levels of freedom I distinguish: emancipation from specific ills through to autonomy or self-determination, through to well-being, through to flourishing, through to universal flourishing or eudaimonia. They all encompass colonial rebellion, the suffragettes' revolt, the revolt of the oppressed, the revolt of the periphery, and so on. It is very Eurocentric of people to say that this is western – to imagine that, say, Islamic people today are not concerned about liberty. I find that an extraordinary idea, indeed a quasi-Eurocentric conceit. They are concerned about liberty under the declension of self-determination, of freedom from arbitrary arrest, or freedom to practice their religion in the way they want to, and so on. This is what we are all striving for. The struggle for freedom comes from people wherever they are, there is nothing Eurocentric about it. What Radha says is mediated by a certain kind of post-modernist and poststructuralist perception of narratives and grand narratives. It is correct to say that what I am essaying is a grand narrative, it is not correct to say that this work is in any way Eurocentric. The fundamental basis of this could have been developed in critical engagement with Chinese or Indian or Indigenous philosophy, and I would very much like to complete it in that way. The philosophical tradition that denies the pulse of freedom and is being artic-ulated here is irrealism. It is basically oppressive illusion, and perhaps delusion.

MH: Let us turn to your critique of irrealism or non-transcendental realism, then, your totalising metacritique of western philosophy. It is geared around the 'unholy trinity' of ontological monovalence, the epistemic fallacy and 'primal squeeze' on empirically controlled theory and natural necessity. Since primal squeeze is generated by the epistemic fallacy, mediated by actualism, the trinity reduces to a pair, and the question arises as to which is the more primordial and fundamental error. When you explicitly weigh them in the balance, you award primacy to ontological monovalence, but some of your formulations seem to suggest otherwise. Thus western philosophy is historically determined by rationalist criteriology generated by ontological monovalence↔monism/reductionism but structurally dominated by empiricist ontology generated by the epistemic fallacy↔fundamentalism, and this structural domination comes into its own in the modernist epoch via the mediation of 'the great subjectiviser',[40] Descartes, ensuring the triumph of empiricism; and as we know some postmodernist philosophy runs a critique of the philosophy of presence. So the balance seems to be tipped towards the epistemic fallacy in the philosophical discourse of modernity.

RB: I think if you go back to ancient Greek times there is something that needs to be said in favour of the epistemic fallacy already being there. The Greeks implicitly assume a kind of exact correspondence or homology between the world and what they say, between logos, our speech, and the world – that the world is what is sayable. That of course takes them very close to the epistemic fallacy. On the other hand, against that, they did explicitly thematise ontology and properties of being, they were aware of other cultures that had different views and were upfront about it, so they were not so far away from the fundamental themes of basic or first-level critical realism. However the thing that they really wanted to do was to give a rational account of the world and their place in it that did away with the spectre of instability and change – that would normalise Athens at a certain time in its history or, going back before that, Pythagorean or other early Greek conceptions of what the world ought to be like. The whole motivation here was the ruling out of absence and change, it was about ontological monovalence. If you read Plato this is clear: change is just a form of difference, and difference is a useful and acceptable category for thinking the world. This history is continuous, going right through to the rise of modernity. It is then overlaid by, first, the dispute between rationalists and empiricists and then by the trap of Humean empiricism or its Kantian version in which the epistemic fallacy and the impossibility of talking about the world becomes, as I characterise it, structurally dominant. Now you could not talk about change for the added reason that you cannot talk about the world, so forget about change: if you cannot talk about it, it does not happen. Some critical realists, maybe Alan Norrie, seem to think that some of the poststructuralists can have a coherent concept of change, but I do not really see it. Postmodernism in general is an important corrective to modernism, but to thematise difference alongside dialectical universality is better. We have to get rid of any abstract universality and then thematise difference in a way that allows us to see that it actually presupposes all the levels of the concrete universal. Similarly, we have to analyse change and difference to make it clear that they are fundamentally different things.

MH: Underlying the fear of change must have been not just a desire to preserve the status quo, but ultimately fear of death. You say in *Dialectic* that you can dialectically detach the fear of death and discard it as obsolete way of thinking.[41] Why could they not have learnt to do that?

RB: Once you accept emergence and disemergence, in other words birth and death, coming into being and passing out of being at any level of being, then you have change as fundamental. To get rid of death in some way might appeal to some philosophers as members of a relatively privileged elite. But the fundamental thing that philosophers have been doing for rulers is provide an account of the world that would show how the order that the (and their) rulers wanted to establish was going to be eternal, could not and would not be changed. You can see this in our own times. The neo-conservative idea of an American century is only a step away from the idea of the thousand-year Reich: what exists now is going to be always. Once you situate death as fundamentally disturbing, then you are half way to all the other changes, the transformations that might occur in your world. Children do not behave the way you behave, and that is unsettling. Then what do you have? What the philosophers thought they had was the notion of consciousness as universal and infinite. Of course the content of their thought, what it is talking about, does have a universal aspect, but their understanding at any moment of time is itself going to be transient. You have to understand thought in both its aspects, as potentially making a claim about all magnetic bodies (or whatever) and as itself transient – as transient as the bodies it is talking about. There is no way of getting rid of change, and no way of getting rid of the fear of change except by embracing change.

MH: Any major philosophical treatise on dialectic has to settle accounts critically with Hegel and Marx, which *Dialectic* essays. I heard you say soon after *From East to West* came out that you had been too hard on Hegel. Why so? Would you say the same of Marx?

RB: I probably was a little too hard on Hegel in the sense that what he had done was something pretty enormous, that is, bring out the generative role of absence, such that the basic form of a dialectical learning process is very roughly (and suitably reconstructed) as he said it is. But of course where he erred was in proceeding to eliminate the absence – the absence he had discovered – by various intellectual sleights of hand. I was very concerned that it should not be eliminated, so I concentrated on the negative side of Hegel, especially because I then wanted to go on more positively as it were to evaluate Marx as founding a science of history. If this project was to be sustained I had to be very hard on the Hegelian and other residues in Marx; in order to sustain Marx's intuitions and innovations, I had to be critical of much of the content of what Marx said. My main concern was not so much to be hermeneutically accurate to Marx as to clear the ground for the unfinished business of Marxism: historical materialism and the critique of political economy. I proceeded from the point of view that Marx had started something, but that Marxists have not well understood what he started; Marx had set an agenda, raising many important questions and it is the job of Marxists, as successors of Marx, to work on and develop this agenda. The reason why I was hard on Hegel is thus probably because I wanted to be hard on Marx, and the reason I wanted to be hard on Marx was to clear the ground for an understanding of contemporary developments and the lack of them. This is very important, and what I would like to do in one of the succeeding sessions, as I have not written about it anywhere in much detail so far, is to talk about the fate of actually existing socialism: what happened and what went wrong there.

MH: I will make a point of asking you. In *Dialectic* and *Plato Etc.* you claim to have solved most of the textbook problems of western philosophy. In *Dictionary of Critical Realism* I wrote:

> This has been taken for hubris, but clearly, if the problems have been generated within and in virtue of an irrealist *problematic*, and in particular, in virtue of the absence of (adequate) concepts of ontology and alethic truth at 1M, of absence at 2E, of totality at 3L and of agentive agency at 4D (such that the problems of philosophy are unified by the absence of the concept of absence . . .), remedy of these lacks should make their resolution, in theory, possible. The real problem with Bhaskar's claim is perhaps that in professional philosophy, as Popper has noted, 'nothing seems less wanted than a simple solution to an age-old philosophical problem', and the basis for *this* very probably lies in what the paradox-ridden condition of philosophy reflects in the sociosphere . . . . The *problematicity* of philosophy is almost an article of faith, and, since philosophical problems are 'supervenient on life', provides an important diagnostic clue to social problems.[42]

Would you want to qualify or add anything to that sort of defence against the charge of hubris?

RB: Intellectually, either the existing textbook problems of philosophy have been solved or they have not. What someone who claims that this is hubris has to do is to show how my solutions fail. Of course, it is quite possible that some of these problems will not have been resolved, but someone has to show that, and so far no-one has. That is the intellectual answer. What you then have to do is ask why people think that the problems of philosophy have not been resolved, but that just takes us into the realm of the diagnostic: what does its problematicity tell us about (1) philosophy and (2) the social context in which philosophy subsists or flourishes? If philosophy is understood only as a discipline that is entirely aporetic – that exists only in these problem-fields – then of course philosophers will go out of business once their problems have been resolved. However, I think there is another future for philosophers: conceptually articulating proposals for better futures. Let them be underlabourers for and in relation to concrete utopian enterprises, the other and better worlds that our world implicitly contains.[43] As for what the problematicity tells us about the social order, this is where the platinum plate of Hegelian dialectic is so important. What it basically tells us is that, if you take a specific ideology like that of poststructuralism, its position that there are no grounds, no deep structures, is a kind of oblivion – alethic untruth – of the fundamental facts of our societal existence, which remain under the dominance of the deep structures of capitalism. Poststructuralism is there as an accompanying ideology: capitalism does not exist, nor does the pulse of freedom. What exists is the surface, what you have really got, and since that is all that exists, it will always be there in one form or another. This is rather like assuming that you yourself as an embodied being are going to be immortal. That is the kind of thing the problems of philosophy point to. They all have their roots in the characteristic errors of irrealism – the epistemic fallacy, ontological monovalence, ontological extensionalism and the denegation of intentional causality – errors that are underpinned ultimately by fear of change manifesting itself in the normally unconscious desire to maintain or affirm the status quo.

MH: Which brings us nicely to my next question: philosophy, you say, must in the long run be consistent with the findings of science.[44] How does *Dialectic* stand in relation to the findings of modern science? Would you want to rewrite anything today?

RB: I think it stands up pretty well really. Today I would want to say more about technology, particularly information technology. I would also want to do a critique of grand theories of everything, which are very fashionable in physics and popular cosmology, and of biological reductionism, which is pervasive. Although I lay the conceptual groundwork for it, I do not explicitly critique the new fundamentalism associated with bourgeois triumphalism, which is a market fundamentalism predicated on the success of the revolution of 1989. Obviously I did not foresee the extent to which religious fundamentalism would arise, but I think it too fits very nicely into the schema, as the dialectical counterpart of market fundamentalism. Also I would probably want to thematise in a more systematic and perhaps dramatic way the ecological crisis, but I do think most of my work reads pretty well in that respect, because I have been aware of it from the 1970s.

MH: Far more so than your earlier work, *Dialectic* has largely been ignored by mainstream philosophers. What do you see as the main reasons for this and do you expect it to continue? Under what conditions would *Dialectic* come into its own?

RB: This is an interesting question. I can begin to answer it by reference to the three aims I set myself in *Dialectic*. These were, as you've mentioned, the dialectical enrichment of critical realism; the development of a general theory of dialectic, including Hegelian dialectic as the special case; and the elements of a totalising critique of western philosophy.

   In reference to the first aim, I think you can practise critical realism up to a point without reference to the categories of dialectic, but then you will be sticking mainly to the first level of ontology, overlooking the potential benefits of the deepening of this ontology in the ways I have indicated. As critical realist research into concrete and applied topics develops, researchers will feel the necessity to deepen their understanding of the structures that they are analysing or situating and of the actions that they are exploring in their research process, and they will begin to make conscious use of dialectical notions. Of course, they do this spontaneously anyhow, they think contradiction and negativity. Many people have pointed out to me that it is not as if I discovered contradiction, which of course is true. But there is a problem about using the concept of contradiction. If it comes at too crucial a point in your analysis and promises to give rise to a radical social theory, you are going to have philosophers stomping on you, telling you that you cannot think the negative or contradiction. The one thing that drove Rom Harré apoplectic about my work was the fact that I defended absence and negation; he said Kant had shown that to be impossible. Once you are confronted by such a philosopher you have to defend yourself, and that is where *Dialectic* can play an essential role by providing a philosophical rationale for thinking the not. But of course then it is not just a question of using a category, you want to know all its implications and ramifications, you want to come to self-consciousness in your research about that category, and that might allow you to explore the way in which your first-level constructions can be thought in a supplementary or second-level way such that you can see intentional action in terms of the remedying of lacks or absences. You get a new spin on the same subject-matter that increases the number of ontological options you have available as tools to think that subject-matter. So I think this process is inevitable but slow.

Turning to the second motivation of *Dialectic*, the general theory of dialectic, I think people will slowly start to use Hegel and Marx more readily when they realise that dialectical categories can be defended or given an adequate rationale philosophically. In relation to my third motivation, the totalising critique of western philosophy, getting into this probably does require special conditions. There is evidence that, as moments of far-reaching change or revolutionary rupture approach, people become intensely and more openly engaged in reflection on the most basic things, all the things that are normally taken for granted. Thus Lenin wrote *The State and Revolution* in 1916–17 and he did all his dialectical philosophy then. The interest in Marxism and also critical realism soared in South Africa during the struggle that ended Apartheid. Another example is provided by an episode at the time of the publication of my critique of Rorty, *Philosophy and the Idea of Freedom*.[45] This occurred soon after the fall of the Berlin Wall – it was still being dismantled – and the book's launch was one of two meetings in the Institute of Contemporary Arts held next to each other and simultaneously. One was a debate about my book between myself and Jonathan Rée, since Rorty had declined to come; and next door there was a discussion of the fall of the Berlin Wall, which I would have been interested to go to myself. The room I was in was packed out, there were a couple of hundred people there, and in the room next door there were only a handful. It was a revolutionary moment in history, but what people wanted to talk about was Rorty and how to understand

reality. If you have a view of categorial error in reality as very deep and pervasive, then you can see that what we have to do is transform the categories of
social life. There was a rationale to what might appear as topical madness in
the imbalance between the meetings that day.

MH: One last question. In the Introduction to *Dialectic* and the 1998 Preface to
The Possibility of Naturalism you announced five forthcoming books: *Plato Etc.*;
Hume, Kant, Hegel, Marx; *Dialectical Social Theory*; *Totality and Transcendence*
and *The Philosophy of Money*.[46] You brought only one of these (*Plato Etc.*) to
publication, though the *Totality and Transcendence* manuscript presumably
went into the making of the books of the spiritual turn. I take it that the others were, so to speak, victims of the drive to the spiritual turn. You said last
time that you gave up writing *Philosophical Ideologies*, which was near completion, to pursue the new line of thought, and clearly after the publication of
From East to West you would have focused on elaborating the philosophy of
meta-Reality. Do you now intend to complete and publish any of the other
books you announced?

RB: I do not think I will write a book on Kant, Hegel and Marx, although I would
love to engage in a more detailed hermeneutics of those thinkers. I would also
love to do more work on the philosophy of money. The project of *Totality and
Transcendence* was taken up into the meta-Reality books. I now think
Dialectical Social Theory would have to be done at a level of concreteness I was
not envisaging at the time. It would have to be on a specific area, for example,
peace, and I have elements of a draft text that concerns itself with problems of
incommensurability, not only in peace negotiations about human conflicts,
but between cultures and civilisations. So that is one way of concretising
dialectical social theory. Another is through thematising the character of
applied critical realism, which I have been working on for the last several years.
And then finally there is a question of whether you can make the categories
much more specific and concrete than they are in, say, *Dialectic*. The category
of education in that work, for example, is a very broad one encompassing the
learning process not just in schools and universities but in life as a whole. But
you can also develop it further at the level of the philosophy and sociology of
education, which is something I am doing now at the Institute of Education.

MH: It is interesting you say you would like to do a more detailed hermeneutic of
Kant, Hegel and Marx. You have done only one book like that, the one on
Rorty, and certainly critical realists often say they wish you would engage
other philosophers in more detail. I have always taken it that you operate at a
much more abstract level, going for the really pivotal aporiai and lacunae in a
thinker's thought, and so are not particularly interested in the detail as such.
But you are saying this is not the case, you are interested in the detail –

RB: It is just that I have not had the time.

7 The spiritual turn

Transcendental dialectical critical realism (1994–2000)

MH: Before we come on to the spiritual turn, I want to ask you about critical realism as a movement in the period leading up to it. The 1990s saw the entrenchment of critical realism in a wide array of areas of study within the academy around the globe, the inauguration of a major critical realism book series with Routledge and the emergence of critical realist organisational forms, in the establishment of which you played a leading role: the Centre for Critical Realism (CCR) in 1996, and the International Association for Critical Realism (IACR) in 1997, together with the IACR newsletter *Alethia* (1998), which grew into the peer-reviewed *Journal of Critical Realism* early in the new century. A series of *Realism and the Human Sciences* conferences in the 1980s and 1990s was followed by the first of the ongoing IACR international conferences in 1997. Some commentators seem to think that there is something inappropriately evangelical or distasteful about a philosophy and social theory assuming organisational forms. How would you respond to that?

RB: I think the idea that it cannot or does not need to organise is very naive. There is no way of propagating a standpoint in the present world other than by doing things like writing books and getting these books distributed. Of course, if the academy had been spontaneously receptive to critical realism we could just have used the organisational forms of the academy, but it was not. In the late 1970s, more so in the early 1980s, I was very concerned that people who were taking up critical realism or themes from my work were finding it very difficult to get their work published. At times I felt as if critical realism was in real danger of being suffocated in the academy. I think that is true of all revolutionary new ideas; obviously they meet with resistance. This of course eased once critical realists started getting chairs in the academy; however there was still the danger that the radical thrust in critical realism would be submerged. Early in the 1980s we set up conferences on *Realism and the Human Sciences* where we could gather for three or four days, and these were like an oasis for the early critical realists. They were characterised by friendliness – a good, higher level of friendliness – commitment to truth and working through the arguments. They were very rewarding experiences for everyone. They were self-organised and there is no way that any philosophy, whether it is critical realism or a part of the established order, can reproduce itself except in a socially organised form. The same motivation lay behind the establishment of the Centre for Critical Realism and the other semi-independent institutions. So I think this is a socially naive objection.

MH: In our last interview you referred to an experience you had in Cyprus in 1994 that marked the inception of the spiritual turn. Can you begin our discussion of the spiritual turn by telling us something about it?

RB: What happened is that I went to Cyprus on Boxing Day for a holiday. *Dialectic* and *Plato Etc.* had come out, but I had not been able to complete the follow-up, *Philosophical Ideologies* – which was annoying. I was feeling physically run down. When I arrived in Cyprus I thought this is really great, I can swim and be with nature, and enjoy myself. The second day in Cyprus I caught another cold, a bad cold, and I went to see a local doctor, or rather I think my hotel called the local doctor because I had a temperature. He gave me antibiotics yet again, and said no swimming. So I thought just my luck, and was feeling really fed up. No swimming, no drinking because of the antibiotics – what could I do? I was staying in the Hotel Annabelle in Paphos, and they were advertising aromatherapy. So I thought why not, let's try alternative medicine. The person who was doing the aromatherapy said what you really need is Reiki. So she gave me Reiki, and it opened up a new world of experience to me. Reiki is a form of hands-on healing that originated in Japan in the early twentieth century. In the 1990s it was quite common to find Reiki practitioners in, for example, hairdressers; it was something you could get on the High Street. So I had Reiki, and this was a revelation to me. It occurred to me that everything I had been doing referred to the world of external objects and material things, whereas Reiki (at least in the hands of the practitioner, an English woman living in Cyprus) put me in touch again with a deep inner world: what was happening, as it were in myself, behind – or rather in the deep uncharted interior of – the world of physical bodies and material objects. And then the next thing I discovered was that the Reiki practitioner's husband was a teacher of transcendental meditation. So I did a course in that too. This reawakened me to things that I had been vaguely familiar with in my youth, and again I found this a very moving experience. I decided to undertake a systematic investigation into the forms, practical and theoretical, of what could be called eastern mysticism. Reiki did not last. Meditation is something profound. I am sure that personal contact is very important in forms of healing, so there is a rational kernel to the hands-on healing of the Reiki. For whatever reason, I soon found my energy levels returning. I interpreted this as my higher self telling me that there was no point in writing another book on the themes or topics I had explored up to now, that I had to do something else. So I gave up writing *Philosophical Ideologies* to try to explore this alternative world that I had forgotten about or repressed. The whole area of eastern culture and mysticism was a huge absence in my experience of life, and so in a practical way I wanted to discover what it was all about; and that was the beginning of my spiritual turn.

MH: What you've said implies that this experience was – to use the terms of your later writings – an experience of transcendence, of non-duality, of union or identity, and to a considerable extent a case of East meeting West, or the 'undoing of oblivion' in relation to the Indian side of your self. To what extent did the earlier theorisation of an adequate account of negativity – and specifically, of the moment of absolute transcendence or creativity ex nihilo in the process of scientific discovery,[1] and of ultimata for science – feed into this experience, and had East already made an input into that? Your first major work of the spiritual turn, *From East to West: Odyssey of a Soul* (2000), seems to give grounds for inferring that the experience was a religious one (that is, of God or the ultimate or absolute),[2] whereas previously your position from your late teens on had been agnostic or atheist.

RB: I think the first thing to do is to situate this particular moment in terms of the method and the process of development of critical realism. Throughout I had adopted an approach of immanent critique. This consisted in going into a subject-matter and exploring the internal contradictions and aporiai that might lead to a metacritique, in the first instance to the identification of an absence that was causing all those problems. You can see this, to put it in terms of MELD, in the revindication of ontology at 1M, the thematisation of negativity and absence at 2E, the situation of internal relations at 3L and the demonstration of the causality of transformative praxis at 4D. All these things were in a sense taboo in the dominant traditions at the time, ontology was taboo, negativity was taboo, the internality of relations between at least externally related things was taboo, as was intentional causality and a host of other notions necessary for the intelligibility of transformative praxis. What I tried to do, and critical realism tries to do, is to bring these hitherto tabooed topics that were causing the intellectual problems in an area reflexively into self-consciousness, that is, into the discursive domain, so that we could then say the previously unsayable, think the previously unthinkable, and hence restore coherence to the hitherto aporetic subject-matter.

One thing that had been troubling me for some time, but especially from the early 1990s, was the fact that there were colleagues and friends of mine, some of whom were committed to critical realism, who were deeply religious but were, so to speak, in the closet. They would not, and felt they could not, talk about their religiosity. And of course this perception was further deepened when I went again to India to speak as a philosopher around the turn of the millennium, because the academics I encountered there were in their private lives deeply religious but in their public intellectual lives professed a kind of atheism. There was thus a profound contradiction within their beliefs, more generally a contradiction in their theory and practice. One of the things that I wanted to do in the spiritual turn was to make the unsayable sayable, and in initiating discourse about spirituality as taboo, in starting to talk about it, I took it that we would be enhancing the overall rationality of critical realism. I'll say something about the discussions I had with these religious fellow critical realists later, but one thing I think is very important to register here is the fact that for me religion was not the same thing as spirituality. Indeed, even at the time of the spiritual turn I did not hold any deep or specific religious convictions. Conversely, there was an element or moment of spirituality that I had always recognised even in my most militant and atheist days. I still retained the memory of the experience of moments of transcendence in my youth and I had a kind of naive feeling that at some point it might connect up with my intellectual project.

MH: Does that still apply today – not having deep religious as distinct from spiritual convictions?

RB: I do not have any specific religious convictions. Or rather, I would say that I subscribe to something like Shankara's higher truth. All religions are paths to the absolute, but none are strictly necessary; nor is it necessary to have a religion as such, if one has, for instance, the secular spirituality situated by the philosophy of meta-Reality. From this metacritical perspective, of course, many secularists and atheists implicitly have a religion, or absolute, or sense of ultimate concerns, that imparts coherence, identity and form to their understandings and practice.

MH: How did the spiritual turn tie in initially with your project to rethink (the deficiencies of) the theory and practice of the left and of 'actually existing socialism'?

RB: One of my motivations – the most important motivation – for the spiritual turn was actually to strengthen the cultural resources of the left. I think that what I wanted to do, at the formal level, was to critique the one-dimensional practices of actually existing socialism, by which I mean the practice not only of Soviet communism but also of the social democrats in the West, and one-dimensional in the sense of four-planar social being. The project of constructing socialism had been seen essentially as a project of transformation on only one of the planes of social being, that is, the plane of social structure. In the case of our material transactions with nature, we had ecological degradations presided over by actually existing socialism in one form or another as great as anything by unfettered capitalism. The quality of inter-personal interactions under Stalinism was perhaps not as bad as under fascism, but it was at least comparable, so that books could be written assimilating fascism and the practices of communism to the same paradigm. And, of course, understanding of and work on the stratification of the embodied personality were virtually non-existent in the practice of socialism. This was despite Marx's injunction in the third thesis on Feuerbach that the educators – those who would usher in a new society – must themselves be educated, that is, must educate themselves.

That was one aspect of the formal change I wanted to bring about. Another – and this ties in more directly and immediately with the spiritual turn – involved the idea that our conceptual resources were too weak. This was a problem particularly about the West, because western civilisation and science had been oriented to the understanding and mastery of the world external to us. Within the East, in practices that you find in South and Southeast Asia, especially in the Indian subcontinent but also in Taoism and to some extent Confucianism in China, Japan, and Korea, in the whole region east of – wherever the East starts –

MH: East of Istanbul?

RB: The Middle East is really part of the West in many respects. But anyway, in India, China and the civilisations that grew up from them, there was some understanding of the inner world. The experience I had in Cyprus, or the sort of experiences that began in Cyprus, led me to refocus on this. I had the sense of a kind of revelation when I realised that, just as the internal structure of an atom is spacious and comparable in size, in terms of relative distances, to the internal structure of the universe, so what we ourselves have inside in the inner world (which is of course a metaphor but still one with a great deal of literal bite) is an extraordinary realm waiting to be plumbed as the physical world had been plumbed by western civilisation. I felt very strongly that the only way one could come into a really authentic understanding of a domain of phenomena was not just by studying and understanding it abstractly but by going into it and experiencing it. This was one aspect of the unity of theory and practice, and of course I had already started to do this in the 1980s when I spent three or four years in not very successful psychoanalysis. So when I arrived back in England from Cyprus I gradually, but in a methodical way, attempted to get as much experience as I could of what struck me as potentially deep aspects of the cultural traditions of the East. So I attended classes on meditation, but also on tai chi, Reiki, feng shui and the like, and this was an important part of the overall experience. In order to do those courses and have these experiences, I adopted a standpoint of innocence. This is rather like the standpoint of immanent critique. When you go into a subject-matter, the point is not to apply some external findings that have been produced elsewhere, but to generate a critique as a result of an immanent resolution of the aporiai and contradictions within the subject-matter. So that meant that I went into these experiences with a certain degree of innocence. This can be understood in a double sense: first, I did not have preconceptions and, second, I was just going into them and in the moment of the experience suspending my critical faculties. It struck me that this inner world I had discovered did contain a spiritual element, but that the religious element in it was a contingent one, not a necessary part of it, so that it was possible to have a secular spirituality – an intuition that I saw the necessity to develop in the philosophy of meta-Reality. I also felt that it would be wrong to identify the inner and the spiritual, because the inner also contains an emotional life which is something other than the spiritual. However, the spiritual was certainly not just to be identified with the religious, let alone with any one form of religiosity.

MH: You mentioned discussions you had with deeply religious critical realist colleagues. At what stage did you have these discussions, with whom, and can you give us something of their flavour and importance for your intellectual trajectory at this time?

RB: They were with Maggie Archer, Andrew Collier and Doug Porpora. I think they started in 1998, by which time I had thoroughly immersed myself in reading and experiencing as much as I could of this terrain. Maggie and Doug are Catholics and Andrew had a Church of England background. I had one-on-one discussions with each of them, and we also discussed as a group in meetings over long weekends at my house in Suffolk (where I was living at the time). We talked about a whole range of things, but mainly about how critical realism might make talk about God and religion and more generally spirituality intellectually respectable, how it might bring them into the discursive domain. We decided to write a book together, and this eventually led to the publication of *Transcendence: Critical Realism and God* a few years later.[3] However, for a number of reasons I decided in the end not to lend my name to it. Perhaps I did not at the time fully share my friends' commitment to making religion as such, as distinct from spirituality, respectable. However, for me the exact point of tension, or the most important one, can be brought out in relation to the 'Twelve Propositions on Transcendence, Critical Realism and God' that I formulated as a summary of our discussions in 1999. These were discussed at a weekend in Suffolk and then debated with a number of other critical realists at a seminar in London which included Maggie and Andrew;[4] and I included a further developed version of them in *From East to West*, in the section 'Twelve Steps to Heaven'.[5]

  The most important of these propositions was the first one. This applied the critical realist 'holy trinity' of the compatibility of ontological realism, epistemological relativism and judgemental rationality to the topic of God. Basically the vision was that God or the absolute (in my later terminology the cosmic envelope) could be an object, ontologically, which could be said to exist or not exist and could be understood in different ways. I was saying that the different religions understand this object in different ways and also that this understanding can be seen as a form of manifestation of the object or, to put it in an ontologically stronger way, that the object itself is manifesting itself differently to different people. If the absolute is manifesting to people in different religious traditions in different ways, that gives you an immediate tolerance for other religions. The stumbling block is of course that most people who profess a particular religion feel that they have the unique, the only way to God: this is the only way that God can be described, and if your description is different you are not actually describing God. So in a way it was probably the alleged uniqueness of Christianity that was the stumbling block for me – a position that we can call *uniquism*. We did not actually discuss that – my position was more or less assumed in practice – but when it came to the writing of the book I felt that a Christian slant or interpretation was being put on things, whereas it was my aspiration to be neutral.

I firmly believed that the distinction Shankara introduced between the higher truth and the ordinary truth, which I sketched in our first interview, is very relevant here. The higher truth, known to the esoteric, sees all religions as so many different paths to the absolute; the ordinary truth, which is what the masses believe, proclaims a monopoly of truth. The higher truth is actually present as a lived reality in most of the major religious traditions and practices: in Judaism you have Kaballah; in Christianity you had the mystics and latterly you have the varieties of liberation and some liberal, postmodern and (recently) critical realist theology, and so on; in Islam you have Sufism, which tries to incorporate the best insights from, for example, Hinduism, Buddhism and Christianity; and in India you have the paths sketched out by the Vedantic mystics, and by Buddha and Krishna, all of which were differentiated from popular religion. So Shankara's distinction is there in actuality, but of course it has to be acknowledged that we can no longer afford to accept that it is permanent. The time for the higher truth to become the ordinary truth has arrived; and so we have to understand that, although on the 'holy trinity' of critical realism I must give rational grounds for the beliefs I have, and I might be able to say that my path is the best path for me, it does not necessarily follow that it is the best path for you, or him, or her. For other people have their own rhythmics, and might have very good reasons for preferring another path to the absolute. These considerations ground religious diversity in a way that contradicts the formal teachings of most religions and yet is implicitly practised by their higher saints and teachers.

MH: This was a bone of contention between you and the other discussants?

RB: They did not accept my interpretation, and do not now. It was brought home to me recently that for some critical realist Christians uniquism is the limit to the acceptance of meta-Reality; and of course uniquism is what lies behind 'the clash of civilisations' in its religious form. To the Christian right in America there is no way Islam can be seen as an alternative path to God, and similarly for the Sunni or Shia masses and their imams, there is no other way.

MH: How important for you positively, in terms of moving forward and developing your own position, were the discussions with Andrew, Doug and Maggie?

RB: To discuss these topics with people who were close colleagues and friends was very important and meant that I was not completely isolated intellectually.

The limits to this were inscribed in differential interpretations of what follows from the application of the 'holy trinity' of critical realism in the first of the 'Twelve Propositions' (which were going to be the first chapter of our book). Really, it is very difficult and perhaps impossible to have a uniquist interpretation of these and it is also impossible to justify the interpretation they subsequently put forward. Three main things should follow from a critical realist approach to God. First, the compatibility of alternative descriptions with judgmental rationality. Second, the co-implication of immanence and transcendence, of the divine already within us and the divine outside us that transcends all human beings. On critical realist premises, if God is real, God must be both ingredient in people and unsaturated by them, providing only their highest-order conditions of possibility. Third, a solution to the notional problem of evil. Although God might be ingredient in and everywhere sustaining the world, it cannot be the case that God exhausts it, because of course you have emergence. God or the absolute is responsible for higher selves or souls or ground-states, but not for the actions of heteronomous human beings. If you put this in the context of four-planar social being, as we did in our discussions, you can isolate some interesting analogues of evil on all the four planes. So in the case of the social structural plane you have the phenomenon of 'structural sin'.

MH: Did Maggie contribute that concept?[6]

RB: Yes, but these ideas were also part of the theoretical infrastructure of transcendental dialectical critical realism.

MH: It comes out of the Catholic tradition.[7]

RB: Yes, in particular the work and concerns of the liberation theologians. You could thus formulate a programme for emancipatory action that was very strong, meshing in with the eschatological project in a religious sense of becoming an ever better vehicle for God's purpose: a programme of universal self-realisation, whereby you progressively eliminated the heteronomies both in yourself and your praxis and in society.

   Of course the next step – and an equally important reason why I did not lend my name to *Transcendence* – was that it became obvious to me that spirituality, which had been clearly situated in *From East to West* as a presupposition both of religious and of emancipatory projects, was also a presupposition of everyday life. This was tremendously important, because it means that there is no necessary connection between spirituality and religiosity, that the ways in which religion is practised are not just distorted manifestations of spirituality, and that you can have a completely secular spirituality – which is what is attempted in the philosophy of meta-Reality.

MH: Can you summarise why you did not go ahead with co-authoring *Transcendence*?

RB: There were two reasons. First, the position of the other authors was too uniquist in relation to Christianity. Second, it was too religious and not sufficiently secular, and this is something the extended periods I spent in India in 1999–2002 helped me to understand. More about that next time.

MH: Can we pursue a little more what you were saying about the implications of the spiritual turn for rethinking the left, and vice versa? Your interest in where the left had gone wrong did not of course come out of the blue, and the dialectics of *Dialectic* had already entrained an analysis in terms of substitutionism, elitism and commandism, cognitive triumphalism, and so on. How did the two sources of critique in the dialectical and spiritual turns link up?

RB: If you go back to actually existing socialism in the form of Soviet communism, it is obvious that there was no attempt to transfer power to the immediate producers, the agents involved in the labour process. Instead, power was transferred from one set of commanders, roughly the capitalist class and their agents, to another, the commanders of the party state. This was if you like the first failing, that actually existing socialism did not even try to do the socialist thing. Then, as I have already pointed out, there was no attempt to act on any plane of social being other than at the level of social structure, except in the early days of the revolution when, in the intense energy of what Lenin had called 'the carnival of the oppressed', new initiatives and ways of doing things did flourish and there was an extraordinary dynamism. I am not trying to put the Soviet Union down, because its very existence enabled gains to be made elsewhere. In the South, it was there as an alternative source of inspiration and support for people who were looking for a different road from the capitalist one. In the West, we had Keynesianism and the welfare state, the improved position of women, and greater degrees of racial equality all as a result, at least in part, of its direct or indirect presence; the danger is that with it gone we will see further reversals on these fronts. But internally its project was only to transform social structure, and hence things on the other planes of social being were left as they were. While the other planes are also massively important, most fundamentally from the point of view of this argument (we are talking about the spiritual turn), there was no orientation towards the self-transformation or self-realisation of the nature of human beings, and this is very odd in view of the fact that Marx had formulated a vision of society in which the free development of each would be the condition of the free development of all. When I was reflecting on this aphorism during the experientially investigative moment of the spiritual turn, it occurred to me that this involves an absence of ego because, if your development is as important to me as my own, this means that I cannot have an ego that privileges myself over you. And not only you, but that person there doing the hoovering[8] – her development is as important as mine – and I cannot place myself above her in any way: everyone's flourishing and development is equally important. But this is very similar to the injunctions of, say, Mahayana Buddhism, with its battle against the ego or the privileging of one's own standpoint. So the affinity between Marx's Marxism and Mahayana and other forms of Buddhism was very clear. This is how I began to understand spirituality as a presupposition of emancipatory projects as such. When I studied it further and began to see it as a presupposition of everyday life, this was in no sense to weaken that thesis, but to reveal spirituality as a tremendous taken-for-granted and unthematised resource underlying everything we do.

MH: I now come to the specific contents of your first book of the spiritual turn. Contrary to what is probably the majority opinion within critical realism today, I think *From East to West* is in some ways a really important work, though I have reservations about a few things. It was initially greeted with considerable hostility and consternation, including (as you know) by myself, though I changed my assessment after a while.[9] I think the main problem was that many people saw you as operating within a tradition of ontological, epistemological and practical materialism from a position within the European Enlightenment and received a rude shock when you espoused views that seemed at odds with that tradition as they understood it: the ideas of an immortal soul and God, the primacy of spirituality understood as self-reflexivity and self-change, an allegedly inflated view of the role of ideas in history, and so on, not to mention flirtation with what some have called 'New Age spiritualism'.[10] Let me list the areas in which I think this new philosophy (dubbed 'transcendental dialectical critical realism' because it *further* transcendentalises [dialectical] critical realism) makes a valuable contribution (all of which involve clarification and development, sometimes radical, of pre-existing positions), some of which I will then come on to seriatim: dispositional and categorial realism (1M); life as a dialectical learning process, the dialectics of co-presence, the deployment of dialectic to provide diagnostic clues to social and human problems and ills, the concepts of transcendence and creativity (2E); the account of the self and self-realisation, the theory of ideology/alienation and the demi-real (3L); thematisation of spontaneous right-action as a basic human capacity (4D); the thesis of the primacy of self- or subject-referentiality or self-reflexivity in social change (what you were later to designate 5A or fifth aspect: the spirituality presupposed by emancipatory projects); and the way in which *From East to West* brings to a culmination the drive in your philosophy to help effect nothing less than a paradigm shift from the outlook of the bourgeois enlightenment to an outlook fitting for a post-slave order, a eudaimonian enlightenment. I think it is a grave mistake, in short, to dismiss the book just because one does not like its discourse about God and so on. And whatever one might think of its 'novella' section, which recounts the odyssey of the Bhaskarian soul on its way to enlightenment over fifteen lives, there are some real gems to be discovered for those who persist; for example, the paean to the teacher–student relationship as a model for the kind of relationships that must supersede the master–slave order – a relation between equals in which all learn and which 'does not abolish but universalises essentially unilateral progressive development'.[11] It is noteworthy too, in relation to the more personal thematics of the present book, that the soul in a number of lives is a busy 'Bumblebee', and that, taken as a whole, the lives are clearly an important record of your own authentic spiritual experience over the years.

That is my general position on the book. Here is my first question. *From East to West* attempts to synthesise the dualism of East and West, whereas the philosophy of meta-Reality seeks to transcend it. Synthesis – which leaves the original dichotomy intact – is not really in character with your philosophy, with its drive to transcendence in ever more complete conceptual totalities. Why was it a synthesis that you attempted in *From East to West* and not a transcendence?

RB: If you look at any process of resolution of an aporia or rectification of an absence, what normally happens as you try to work your way to a new transcending concept such as gravity or relative space–time is that you borrow a concept from a pre-existing field and then attempt to mesh or mix it in with the aporetic or otherwise inadequate conceptual field. Thus the first moment is where you try to synthesise, to hold the two together; it is the moment of model-building if you like. You can, of course, do it theoretically just by imaging that the world is as postulated in some other domain, and you have the model there as abstracted, but when you come to the point, when you actually want to revolutionise your field, you have to put it into the field in some way. And this is the moment of the coexistence of positive contraries, when both cannot be true, and when you realise that you must now move on to their transcendence.

MH: So there are two phases, presumably corresponding to the σ (sigma) and τ (tau) transforms in your epistemological dialectic?[12]

RB: Yes. The moment of transcendence is when the positive contraries are held as a memory, as negative sub-contraries, and you redescribe the terrain. But I think the first moment is always synthesis if it actually involves the presence of another field and cannot be done solely by internal resolution (which in general it cannot).

MH: This means that transcendental dialectical critical realism is going to be transitional and not one of the main moments in the development of the system, on a par with basic critical realism, dialectical critical realism and meta-Reality – as Seo MinGyu has recently argued.[13]

RB: That is absolutely right. Transcendental dialectical critical realism is, if you like, a half-way house at which there is a conception of the absolute and a conception of the interconnectivity involved, but it is not yet adequately theorised because it is not comprehensive. It seems to exclude those who define themselves as agnostic or atheist, and there is no reason to do that. Most importantly, it leaves out everyday life. This means that, when I am talking about the absolute as immanent in human beings, many people probably have the feeling: 'The absolute present in me? Me?!' Indeed, in *From East to West* I treat the whole subject-matter in rather reverential terms, as if you might perhaps have a moment of transcendence in your life if you are lucky; whereas I would now say that you cannot live without it and that its occurrence is commonplace and routine. I suppose if I had done something analogous to *From East to West* in the case of *Dialectic* I would have published the results of my investigations in that area in about 1991. But I did not. In the case of the spiritual turn, there was such a taboo, so many blind spots in the discursive domain, that I felt the need to give the topic an airing at an earlier stage. Also I was in a process of personal experience and deepening, and I could not be certain where it would all end.

MH: But if your main concern was with spirituality, why did you first need to talk about religion and God? I should perhaps say for our readers that *From East to West* thematises God as the ultimate categorial structure and ingredient pure dispositionality of the cosmos. Whatever the merits of your case for the reality of God – and as an agnostic about God I have no objection personally to people referring to the dispositional and categorial ultimata of the cosmos, if there be such, as God – putting forward the case seems problematic in terms of your attempt to address the question of what is wrong on the left, because the new philosophy (transcendental dialectical critical realism), as you say, could not aspire to command the assent of atheists and agnostics, who were given to understand that their unbelief alienated part of their being. This is a point the philosophy of meta-Reality, with its appeal, via the concepts of the cosmic envelope and the ground-state, to 'those of all faiths and no faith', seems to concede, although it does still acknowledge 'god' and the divine.

RB: This relates to the general point about synthesis and transcendence. More specifically, there is a blind spot about spirituality, especially in the West, and an even bigger blind spot about the possibility of a secular spirituality, so the only way you could start talking about spirituality, at least it seemed to me at the time, was to talk about religion. At some time in the future it might be possible to talk about spirituality without talking about religion, but it wasn't then. I would say similarly that I could not have arrived at transcendental realism except via an immanent critique of transcendental idealism. Religion hegemonises the concept of spirituality, so in order to see the possibility of a non-religious secular spirituality you have to go via it.

MH: We must have an open mind about religious spirituality.

RB: Of course we must be tolerant of it. The cosmologists of such secularism have in turn to account for the totality of human experience, and no doubt they will.

MH: In your previous work you had elaborated both dispositional realism and categorial realism without naming them as such; I personally have no quarrel with them – I accept them as fundamental – only with some of the uses to which you now put them. The issue I want to take up in regard to dispositional realism concerns the soul, construed as a disposition or set of dispositions at the level of the real, and reincarnation. The nub of your argument for reincarnation seems to be that on ubiquity determinism it is impossible to explain differences in intellectual attainment (emergent intentional states) except on the assumption that they stem (at least in part) from past lives – there are insufficient causes and consequences in a person's lifetime to explain such differences. So we can account for Einstein's genius and its impact, for example, only by presupposing that he had a soul that both pre-existed and post-existed his embodied personality, a soul that developed over a whole series of lives, including lives after Einstein's death. But surely there are strong rival explanatory hypotheses here (a fortuitous coming together of conditions to nurture a genius, the resonance of ideas with the material conditions that made their emergence possible), such that the deduction fails, or at any rate the matter must remain an open question. I would want to argue that the dialectics of learning processes do not necessarily presuppose any continuant other than that of social relations and forms as established by the transformational model of social activity. Does not your position actually land you, despite your overt anti-dualism, in some kind of spirit/matter dualism here (what Andrew Collier has referred to as a Gnostic tendency in your work),[14] and indeed, since the soul constellationally contains the mind, mind-body dualism? In a subsequent book you suggest that if 'the physical basis of our embodied being' were destroyed there is no reason to suppose that beings with minds and feelings 'could not survive without that basis'.[15] But this is just what the mainstream critical realist reading of synchronic emergent powers materialism (SEPM) denies; it is of course a possibility SEPM allows for, but only on pain of SEPM reducing to 'a species of dualistic interactionism'.[16] What do you say to those critical realists who, like Garry Potter, hold that espousal of reincarnation damages or discredits critical realism?[17]

RB: This has a number of aspects. First, we are all familiar from contemporary physics with the idea of action at a spatio-temporal distance. There need therefore be no continuant between lives. L2 can resume the challenges of L1, even if they are spatio-temporally discrete, and indeed, distant. Something like this is close to a standard Buddhist view of reincarnation. Moreover, it is implicit in the Christian idea of the resurrection of the body.

Second, the idea of the post-existence, as distinct from pre-existence, of feelings and thoughts, does not seem to me to be too difficult. It is clearly established (as a possibility) by SEPM, once the emergence of feelings and thoughts is conceded. One could imagine the post-existence of these phenomena, until perhaps they gradually fade away (without the urgency imposed by the physical). This gives us the post-existence of feelings and thoughts, on the one hand, and the pre-existence of non-embodied possibilities, on the other.

Third, what are these possibilities possibilities of? They may be conceived as the possibilities of individual, concretely singularised psychic beings or as the possibilities of larger or smaller entities. The idea of the pre-existence of non-embodied possibilities as possibilities (powers and liabilities) of the species – that is, of humanity as such – allows us to understand the Mahayana Buddhist idea of *dharmakaya* as involving the taking up and discharge of the karma of others, in the first place by the enlightened or self-realised one, the Bodhisattva, the one who has no karma of his/her own.

Fourth, what of the idea of the coming together of a fortuitous combination of circumstances as a sufficient explanation of agency? What this leaves out is precisely the subjective side of our agency, and in particular the contribution of the ground-state. The response to a situation can be more or less evolved, and more or less inspired, more or less released from the rebound of karma, the residues and recoils of the heteronomously informed intentional causality of the past; and the evolution of a psychic being, of a reincarnated one, may consist in the process of the shedding of such heteronomies, and with it, progressive liberation from the inherited causality of the past.

Together, considerations such as these allow us to sketch out some of the components of a theory that would situate the possibility of reincarnation. There is need for their further development, elaboration and integration, which perhaps I will be able to undertake one day.

MH: I now want to ask you about categorial realism. *From East to West* develops and sharpens up the view, based on your earlier work, that the categories are real: both the social and the natural world are precategorised in the intransitive dimension independently of any account of their categorisation in the transitive dimension. If valid, categories are constitutive of reality; if invalid, they miscategorise it and are in part constitutive of (social) reality, though dependent on valid categories. This position is absolutely fundamental to your critique of irrealism and your theory of the demi-real, hence to the dialectics of self-realisation, but some critical realists have problems with it on the grounds that categories are, they hold, essentially ideational or semiotic, hence pertain exclusively to the epistemic order, except where, as in the case of the social world, they are partly constitutive of being. This of course relates to our earlier discussion of alethic truth. What is the way forward here?

RB: I want to make two points in response to this, first about categories in general, then about alethic truth. If you have a conception of there being just one world, then the categories refer to the most abstract generic features of this world, for example, causality. From a generically realist standpoint, you either have to say that causal laws are real, but there is no such thing as causality, which does not make sense; or else you have to say that both the category of causality and the category of a causal law apply to reality. You then have to say that the categories are constitutive of reality in exactly the same way as the referent of any other description, however abstract or concrete, is part of the world. It is just that the categories are very abstract, that is, their referent is constituted by vast swathes of being. So you are not required to defend categorial relativism.

We can deepen this argument by referring to ontological and alethic truth which, as we have seen, is reality tied to the possibility of human language and practices. Once you can defend an ontological deployment of truth you can understand that it applies even when you are operating at the expressive-referential level of truth. At the expressive-referential level, where you just have the world expressed in language, you can then make sense of the way in which the truths of the world impose themselves on the projects of human beings, rather than that human beings impose their truths on the world. The neo-Nietzschean project of the neo-conservatives around George Bush to produce an American century comes with claims that reality and facts are old-fashioned and have been superseded, and furthermore, if you are strong enough, if you are a Nietzschean superpower, you can invent any world you want; so we have the idea that the American dream can be imposed on the rest of the world. This presupposes the abolition of intransitivity. But of course it does not abolish intransitivity in practice, and we can see that the truths impose themselves – the truth in Iraq, the truth of Afghanistan, is imposing itself, and so is the truth of global warming. This is a dramatic way of talking about reality: from the point of view of our practices. It reinforces the case for categorial realism, but without being essential to it. This is important when we come on to the theory of the demi-real, because I want to say that categorial error is there in our practices. The wage-form, for example, as Marx demonstrated, embodies a huge category mistake, and that has disastrous effects, as do illusions generally.

MH: Why do you think this is so strongly resisted by some critical realists?

RB: All you need to get there is the idea that you cannot be a consistent critical realist without being a categorial realist and it is absurd to regard causal laws as real without regarding causality as real. The reason why critical realists naively slip into the contrary way of thinking is because the western philosophical tradition – well, especially from Kant, and including Popper in recent times – has always regarded the categories as ways of classifying the world, rather than being in the world itself. The same chain of argument would say that Ohm's law, for example, is a way of talking about the world and not in the world itself. Some would say global warming is just a way of talking about the world, so we do not have to worry or do anything about it; this is the line put out about global warming.

MH: I asked you last time why you were saying round about the time of the publication of *From East to West* that you had been too hard on Hegel in *Dialectic*.

A re-reading of *From East to West* reminds me that you draw heavily on Hegel in a range of positive ways in this work. It is Hegel's demonstration of the diagnostic value of philosophy in relation to social problems (what you call his 'platinum plate') that gives you a clue to the fundamental malaise of master–slave-type social orders: the irrealist categorial structure of philosophy (involving alienation from reality in thought) accurately reflects an irrealist (false or inadequate) categorial structure of society (involving alienation from reality in our social practices and in our selves, both inner and outer). It is Hegel's 'golden nugget' – the dialectics of co-presence – that then assists you in thinking the reality of a true categorial structure underlying/underpinning and occluded by the (emergent) irrealist ones, such that (necessary) autonomous orders of determination are co-present with and sustain (unnecessary) heteronomous ones that occlude them – which leads straight on to the theory of the demi-real and to a re-casting of the dialectic of freedom as a dialectic of shedding or disemergence. And it is Hegelian dialectic as a learning process (the 'rational kernel') involving the absenting of absences (incompletenesses) that informs the dialectic of desire for freedom (which now transmutes into a dialectic of freedom from desire as constituted in the demi-real), as well as the more contentious but phenomenologically interesting account of the odyssey of a soul in the novella section. Even Hegel's 'mystical shell' – his ultimate ontological monovalence – plays a crucial role, negatively, as the absence of the concept of absence that underpins irrealist categorial structures. And the overall structure of your dialectic as geo-historical process is now clearly similar to Hegel's (though of course it is not original to him but has roots deep in the Judaeo-Christian tradition): from an original undifferentiated unity to diremption followed by a return to a fuller, more richly differentiated unity, in which diremption based on ignorance and error is necessary for eventual enlightenment. You even speak of the drive to 'complete' totalities,[18] whereas previously you would perhaps have spoken of 'more complete', such that one wonders whether you yourself are not closing geo-history down in some sense in eudaimonia. What are your thoughts on all this today? Does the notion, cardinal to your critique of modernity, that desire as we experience it in the demi-real is itself a fundamental constraint on human happiness in that it is a bad infinite, rooted in alienation, come from Hegel or is it of more eastern provenance, or both?

RB: I think Hegel was very important – we stand on his shoulders – but as I indicated last time I don't really agree that I was too hard on him. What is important to register is that the critique of Hegel – the critique of ontological monovalence – stands in full in the spiritual turn. When you say that my position ends up looking somewhat like Hegel's because of a similar model of geo-historical directionality, you have to bear in mind that some such model is going to be there if you talk about alienation, because there is something essential to yourself that is not now part of yourself. One of Hegel's errors was to assume that he restored the self, the path of the self, in his dialectical

idealism; but he did not, he transfigured reality without resolving the contradictions within it. The position of *From East to West*, by contrast, is that the
overcoming of alienation is to be achieved by the praxis of universal self-
realisation, understood to embrace all four planes of social being. In relation
to desire, what it is important to see – and perhaps this book is not all that clear
on it – is that desire, like challenge or contradiction, is something that is fundamental to the world of duality as part of the structure of intentional action,
and what the vision here is trying to do is get rid of the dominance of desire and
greed in our life, the dominance of motifs from the world of duality in a dualistic form. So I am not saying that desire has to be abolished, but that it has to
be constellationally contained within emergent practices informed by and
oriented to unconditional love and universal self-realisation.

MH: I think one of the profoundest contributions of *From East to West* – but of
course it presupposes much else – is the theory of the demi-real as an emergent
level of reality comprising a web (*maya*) of ignorance (*avidya*), informed by
categorial error and illusion, underpinned by insecurity rooted in desire/fear or
attachment, and deriving ultimately from alienation from our true selves; a
level of reality that is '(1) *irrealist* in character (i.e. not realist); (2) *demi-real* in
truth-value (i.e. false), but (3) *real* in causal aefficacy (and hence being),
although dependently so'[19] and that includes social practices such as the wage-
form and the illusion that we have egos; a level of reality that we accordingly
have to shed in order to be free or self-realised. Although it builds on the
theory of the Tina syndrome, such that (as we have noted before) demi-
reality *is* Tina-reality generalised, many critical realists do not much like the
theory: they are uncomfortable with the alleged implication that we only
inhabit some sort of half-world, and they are also concerned that you might be
explaining the heteronomous structures that constrain us by philosophical
mistakes in the manner of historical idealism. Am I right in sourcing your use
of 'demi' here to the connotation it has in Hegel of 'irrational existent' as well
as to the more conventional meaning of 'halved or curtailed'?[20] And are you
being historically idealist here?

RB: We do live in a half-world. It is a world in which we have potentials that we
cannot fulfil. I plead guilty to that. We are living very fractured forms of a life
that we could live, and the world could, even now, be a world of plenty –
poverty could be abolished – but we live in the midst of poverty.

MH: There is a sense in which we do not just live in a half-world. You are not saying we are completely cut off from the rest of reality.

RB: The demi-real world has as its condition of possibility relative reality and then
a stratum of absolute reality; that is what we are enjoined to become aware of
in the philosophy of meta-Reality. But in the world of the demi-real it is as if
we are seeing everything in a terrible smog, and the metaphor of a half-world,

or for us a half-existence, accurately describes the situation. Once the smog lifts – once we get rid of demi-reality – we will be able to see that the world is actually far richer than we ever thought.

MH: What about 'irrational existent'? Does it connect up with Hegel?

RB: In a way it does, and in a way it does not. I cannot really remember why I thought of using the notion of 'demi-', I think I probably toyed with 'semi-'.

MH: You do comment on Hegel's thematisation of 'demi-', including thinking of women as 'demi-'[21]; and leading on from that you dub the Hegelian present, which is irrational because it is constellationally closed, the 'demi-present', and deploy the concept of the 'demi-actual' to refer to that part of actuality Hegel's system cannot rationally explain.[22]

RB: Yes, that is right. This is the aporia of Krug's pen. Krug said to Hegel, in effect, 'You can explain the rational state, but can you explain my pen? If you cannot explain my pen you are not so clever.' So Hegel said that what he was trying to do was to explain (to put it in my terms) the contours of actuality; and that the way these contours pan themselves out, how they are inhabited, is not a question for philosophy but for the empirical sciences. But I think that Hegel's use of 'demi-' is different from my use of 'demi-', which is more germane to talk about a half-world. I am not saying that when we have a eudaimonistic society we will be able to explain the position of pens or anything like that.

MH: Yet from a eudaimonian perspective, demi-reality as a whole is an irrational existent.

RB: It is an irrational existent, but the bar is not set by some particular philosophical account; the bar is set by the nature of human being, its potentiality as we know it.

MH: Along with creativity (transcendence) (2E), *From East to West* identifies freedom (1M), love (3L) and spontaneous right-action (4D) as basic human capacities pertaining to our essential selves. It is the 4D concept that *From East to West* introduces for the first time, although the related concept of *unconditional* love is also new. As I think of it, spontaneous right-action is that sort of action in which careful or mindful action consistent with our essential selves (to take a very simple example, learning to ride a bicycle) passes over into carefree or spontaneous action (just riding). How does the normative aspect enter in?

RB: Spontaneous right-action has to be seen in the context of a dialectic of learning. In our life we learn or acquire properties that we then manifest in a spontaneous way. When you learn French, for example, at first you have to think about it a lot. As you become better at it you stop using rote sentences and learn to play with French for yourself, but it is still something you have to think about. Then there comes a moment, typically when you are in France, or talking with French-speaking people, when you can just do it spontaneously without having to think about it; it is now in-built into your essential being. And that is how we learn to do anything. An important theme I take up, particularly in the meta-Reality books, is the idea that mind, or rather thought, gets in the way of right-action and that in general if you are placed in a situation in which you have to do something courageous or noble, if you think about whether to do it, rather than just doing it, you will often end up giving yourself reasons for not doing it, rationalising inaction.

MH: This relates to your critique of the discursive intellect, which we will come on to next time.

RB: Another theme is that basically we know what to do and what is right. Of course, we could if necessary stop and think about it and argue the pros and cons, but when we pass that stage we just do it. The capacity for spontaneous right-action has become coiled into our being at the level of the transcendentally real self or ground-state; we have actually built specific capacities into our ground-states. That is why we just do it, and why you get people who are heroes who say: 'There is nothing special about what I did, I just did it – anyone would do it.' It is true that anyone could do it, but many people do not. And that is either because the process of making the right-action a part of our being such that it just flows has not been accomplished or because, although we have it, we have allowed something to interfere with it. This is all part of an attempt to begin to see the role of the transcendental qualities of human beings, and to bring into full view the huge domain in which we do not do things instrumentally or contractually – the domain of caring and unconditional love, reciprocity and solidarity, and creativity, in which we actually embody some of the teachings of Christ and other great religious teachers, but which is occluded and thwarted by the smog of the demi-real.

MH: How does this relate to the problem of radical evil? It is possible to 'just be' a fascist, spontaneously roaming around the streets and kicking people –

RB: It is impossible. That is to say, I do not think it is possible to be living and to be completely detached from your alethic self. This would be, for example, to be without the capacity to be creative, or to be trustworthy. How could you, for instance, use or understand language, without *trusting* that others would continue to use words in ways that you could rely on – or at least retaining the hope or belief that this would or could once again be so? And you would be relying on the spontaneous right-action of others.

MH: As I see it, the thesis of the primacy of self- or subject-referentiality, of self-change, is grounded ultimately in the axiological commitment implicit in human praxis to universal autonomy or free flourishing already argued for in *Dialectic*, which of course you now explicitly link to the transcendentally real self. It states that only we can act on the world, no-one can do it for us (and we must act – the axiological imperative – such that 'the action I perform is mine, not yours'), and all social change is also self-change. We have been over this ground in an interview a few years ago.[23] Can you say again why this conception is not individualist and voluntarist?

RB: The most important thing to realise is that there is no way of acting on the world immediately except through your own action. There is no way of doing something without *you* doing something. The re-orientation of spirituality and our received notion of it that *From East to West* and the meta-Reality books are trying to effect is one in which we are continually engaged in the world. But as spiritual beings we do not act as isolated individuals, we act to abolish inequities, master–slave relations and so on, to abolish injustice and oppression wherever we see it, so that we are continually extending the scope of the expression of the ground-state quality of unconditional love, for example. We engage with others in concrete utopian exercises, in thinking creatively about how we can use resources such that they are more fulfilling to us. The stress on self-referentiality makes a virtue of the necessary and, one is tempted to add, the obvious – but unfortunately it is not so obvious. Once you realise that you have to do something to do anything at all then you might pay some attention to the you, the agent, because you will better do things in the world the clearer you are, and clarity presupposes that you are not split. If you have a project in life that is inconsistent with your ground-state, you are going to be split because you cannot get rid of your dharma which, if you like, is trying to tell you what you should do in your life. If you are not in your dharma you will be split, and in the case of the great majority of people the world itself splits them because it removes them from the possibility of their dharma.

Of course, this only becomes a real contradiction or a problem if in some sense you have a choice as to what to do. It is within a framework of choice that western philosophy and morality always situates the problem. If you have a choice, the answer is that you must choose your self-realisation or a project that entails it. If you do not have a choice, you are just going to be staying alive, and one of the things about physical corporeality that is important to note is that we cannot get away from the idea of staying alive; this is something that just in virtue of being a human being we want to do, to preserve ourselves. I do not think we can get rid of that, but in any case it is tautologically obvious that if you have to struggle to stay alive physically then that is going to be the supreme objective in your life. And my claim is that we can all have survival easily, even today if there were more social justice, and then the predicament of only the few in the West would be generalised and there would be a notional choice for everyone as to what to do in their life. And where you have that choice then you should always orient it to make yourself a better agent. If you think of self-realisation as making yourself a better agent for performing acts in the social world, then it does not have the individualistic and narcissistic connotations that are sometimes read into it.

MH: In forming the view that it is individualist and voluntarist, people I think overlook that transcendental dialectical critical realism, like meta-Reality, presupposes the whole of the rest of the system and the emphasis you place there on collective transformative praxis and struggle. It is just that you are focusing on this area that has been neglected.

RB: Absolutely. It had been taken for granted, presumed. But of course, what we saw in the case of actually existing socialism is that we cannot presume it, we have to engage in conscious practices of self-change.

MH: One notes in *From East to West* an increased urgency in your warnings of the possibility of ecological catastrophe, which you had begun issuing far ahead of most other commentators. A leading environmentalist has recently power-fully articulated the view that, if we are to avert catastrophe, we must abandon 'growth fetishism' and consumerism but that this would involve a well-nigh impossible 'psychological transition'. Profligate consumption defines who we are, it is profoundly embedded in 'manufactured selves that we fear relinquishing . . . more than we fear the consequences of climate change'.[24] Is this a line of thought that underlies, at least in part, the emphasis on the primacy of self-referentiality? Does it mean that we all have to get into, inter alia, turning off our electrical appliances, taking fewer plane trips, and so on, in order to save the planet?

RB: Yes. But that alone will not save the planet, we have to act on the other planes. In particular, it requires a profound change in social structure as well, such that we have a simpler form of society in one respect yet also a richer, deeper and more complex one in other respects. But we can go into that when we discuss meta-Reality.

MH: Yes, I want to ask you next time about the relation of meta-Reality to deep ecology. An Indian friend of mine recounts having had a copy of *From East to West* lying about in her home in Mumbai and one of her Indian guests came across it and asked, 'Why are you reading this Brahminical nonsense?' She explained that the red rose is a Brahmin symbol. Is there any connection with the rose on the cover of *From East to West* and Brahminism?

RB: No. I did not know that. No such connection was intended; and I was not aware of any such symbolism – certainly, if it exists, it is not very well known. However, the thrust of the observation is anti-Brahminism, because the big conflict in Indian religion and philosophy was between the Brahmins, who were the priests and the highest caste, and by and large upholders of the status quo and, if you like, the sadhus, the seekers or sages and travelling teachers, who emphasised self-realisation for everyone through their own practices. Although I have a Brahmin background on my father's side, I have always been on the side of the sadhus or seekers.

8   The philosophy of unity-in-difference
Meta-Reality (2000–2002)

MH: You started calling yourself Ram Roy Bhaskar again at about the time the meta-Reality books came out. This suggests that you were feeling a new level of being at home with the Indian side of yourself. We talked about this last time in the context of the experience of 1994, but can you bring us up to date in the context of meta-Reality? The discourse of the philosophy of meta-Reality is of course congruent in important respects with eastern philosophy, and you seem to have been immediately at home in it. Re-visiting it, it struck me as an extraordinary efflatus on a par with the creative multiplication of concepts in *Dialectic* (and at least as difficult to get on top of!). Yet it is almost as though you had always been in that element.

RB: I think there are three aspects to this question. The first concerns the whole issue of secularism. In 1999 I went to India for the first time in a long while, and as a philosopher – the trip had been set up for me as a philosopher. During the period I wrote *From East to West* and the meta-Reality books I made five or six trips to India. I was there lecturing and doing workshops in all the major cities and regions for about a third of the time, perhaps even more. So I was spending time in India again, and it was brought home very clearly to me that there was a problem in talking about God. I probably would have experienced this anyway in the West, but the problem was not so much hostility to, as a lack of any level of intellectual seriousness about, talking about God. It was clear that my audience had very different conceptions of God, and most of these were exclusive. They wanted to know, for example, was my God the same as their God, in which case was he Allah, or was he Brahman or some other Indian god? And so on. Most people in my audiences interpreted God in an exclusive way, in the sense that my God cannot possibly be the same as your God. So in order to talk about the absolute I had to move to a more mutual or secular way of talking about it. Of course, this was something I was very happy to do because, although the focus in *From East to West* had been very much on God or the absolute as a presupposition of all religious practices (including, I might add, Indigenous religious practices, although I did not explicitly discuss them), it was also clear to me at the time of writing that what I was talking about was in fact a presupposition of all emancipatory practices. I remember, when I drew up a prospectus for some lectures I was invited to give at Rabindranath Tagore university in Kolkata on comparative religion and spirituality, called the Radhakrishnan lectures in honour of the erstwhile President of India, I was very explicit that all forms of materialism and atheism are on a par with religion in so far as they posit, explicitly or implicitly, some sort of absolute. By the time *From East to West* was published I was very interested to see how the conceptions of transcendental dialectical critical realism, which were to become sharpened into those of meta-Reality, functioned not just as presuppositions of emancipatory projects but of ordinary life. As I indicated last time, this was for me a stunning revelation. At the same time I wanted to preserve the critical realist orientation to science, and it seemed to me that to cast everything in a secular way would make it easier to look at the implications of science, including fundamental physics, for spirituality. There was no intention of course to collapse philosophy at this level to science, but by not talking about God one preserved that opening. God became the cosmic envelope and, as the god within, the ground-state. What I wanted to do was to make spirituality compatible with secularism.

MH: You do still talk about god with a small 'g'. It will perhaps be perceived as not such a big change really.

RB: While I was in India – the question is about the Indian side of my identity – there were very bad riots of a sort that had not been seen since 1947. Muslims in Gujrat, in Gandhi's home state, were killed, and there was a widespread sense of a tinderbox waiting to explode. The whole question of secularisation was very prominent, and it was brought home to me that secularity is an important principle to uphold. So that was one kind of effect that the Indian trips had on me.

In the second place, it struck me that Hinduism, Buddhism and other religions within the Indian context had a long and distinguished pedigree that was certainly as good as the pedigree of western Christianity. The six schools of Indian philosophy – an extraordinarily complex structure – stretch back several thousand years to the time of the classical Greeks. Arguably the kind of developments in Indian philosophy at that time were superior to those of the Greeks. There were also remarkable parallels, and I do not think you can say that Indian philosophy owed much to the Greeks, although you cannot rule out the possibility of various borrowings, and direct or indirect influences. But here I was on a terrain where Indian philosophy was at least as good as Anglo-Saxon or European philosophy, and that of course made it easier for me to acknowledge openly as it were the Indian side of my identity. In fact, I became a kind of ambassador for Indian philosophy. I found myself in a difficult situation with Indian intellectuals on those lecture trips because most really did not want to talk about Indian philosophy in any way and indeed some of them were very ignorant of it; and I thought it part of my duty to call their attention to the great heritage they were in denial of.

In the third place, the Indian trips started me thinking and writing systematically about the philosophical discourse of modernity. A number of people had asked me to talk on modernity and modernisation; and globalisation, which was seen as inevitable to India's modernisation, was a hot intellectual topic. Although I confined my written reflections at the time to western modernity, I also started to think about situating and critiquing the philosophical discourse of European modernity, including critical realism, within the context of other possible modernities. This involves going back roughly to 1000 BCE and what Max Weber and others have called the axial age and the axial revolution. Somewhere between 1000 and 500 BCE a multi-faceted revolution seems to have occurred in various different parts of the world simultaneously. First, there was sufficient surplus there to allow a class of intellectuals enough leisure-time for philosophical reflection. A certain amount of leisure-time is clearly necessary for a tradition of intellectual reflection to be set in train. Of course, it was unequal, as it is in our society. If the necessary work were more equitably distributed we would now be in an era of universal or generalised leisure-time, such that everyone could be an intellectual and indeed an organic intellectual. But at least there was a stratum of intellectuals. Second, there was a switch in the relation between the towns and the countryside, with the countryside basically feeding the towns. Relatedly, you had the development of the early empires and standing armies, and of money in the form of coin to pay for these. Hand in hand with this went a growing cosmopolitanism that fed into intellectual discussion, when the following kind of question started to be asked: given the past practices in our community, and given the practices of other peoples and cities we know about, what should we do, and how are we to justify it? So we have the beginnings of a sustained reflexivity associated in Greece with Pythagoras, Socrates, Plato and the like; in China with Lao-Tse and Confucius; in India with Buddha; and so on. What I would like to do is to situate western modernity within a longer and wider geo-history, a longer and wider profile or rhythmic of axiality. This leaves of course the question of all those peoples and societies – commonly known today as Indigenous peoples or First Nations – that did not experience an axial revolution or its effects, and did not develop a written culture or a characteristic philosophical mode of enquiry. We need to do much more research on that. We have the modern societies, the axial societies and then the Indigenous societies. I think in many ways the Indigenous societies were just as sophisticated, but they had a different form of sophistication if you like.

MH: So India acts as a stimulus to your bringing systematically together all the strands of the critique of the philosophical discourse of modernity you had been developing from the outset of your career. But it also brings you to see things you had not seen before. You now see the need to put it in a much bigger picture.

RB: It would be nice to do that. To bring this home, there are passages in *Dialectic* where I talk about the co-presence of different times and levels of development. You cannot go to any Indian city without immediately noticing this. Modern cars are co-present with buffaloes, elephants, and cows strolling across the road, and twenty-first century joggers à la Jane Fonda weave in and out of processions enacting ancient rituals. This was a stimulus to reflection on modernity, and modernity is up front in the meta-Reality books.

MH: I understand there was an unfortunate sequel to the experience of 1994, in that you fell in with people whose company turned out to have problematic consequences for you in some respects. Can you tell us something about this? I take it that you trusted certain people only to discover that your trust was radically misplaced?

RB: I have already indicated how, during the experientially investigative phase of the spiritual turn from 1994 to 2000, I adopted a certain standpoint of innocence, and I have related this to the practice of immanent critique. With the benefit of hindsight I can see that, in entering into circles where the kind of topics I was interested in were accepted as a matter of course, I practised a degree of suspension of my critical faculties that I subsequently came to regret. Some suspension is absolutely indispensable for such a project, but my suspension was definitely too all encompassing. This led me to depart from a principle of balance and discrimination that I believe should guide us. It was very much part of an attempt to embrace something fully.

  Now in revindicating ontology in *A Realist Theory of Science* I had wanted to keep my distance from the past history of ontology, the baggage of ontology, and so invented the neologisms transitive dimension and intransitive dimension. Similarly, what meta-Reality did was belatedly provide the neologistic structure in terms of which I could talk about issues that had been talked about in terms of God, the soul, spirit and so on. Before that, in trying to normalise or regularise discourse about God, I was at the sort of epistemic half-way house we talked about in Chapter 7, corresponding to the σ (sigma), as distinct from the τ (tau), transform in the epistemological dialectic from dialectical critical realism to the philosophy of meta-Reality, en route to my final or settled position, which is very much as meta-Reality sketches it out. In *From East to West* I talked enthusiastically about God, and all the experiences that I had and that I have had throughout my life are there as authentic experiences. I made no attempt to deny them or other people's religious experiences, rather I embraced them and said in effect: 'Here is a framework where we can put experiences from different religious paradigms together.' If you go into a new domain a certain degree of trust is absolutely necessary. But as you say some trust was misplaced. I would recommend to anyone going into a new area that they think of the area as a room: take your critical faculties into the room, and whilst you are listening to everyone switch them off, but have them there with you – don't leave them outside the door.

MH: In practical terms it had severe effects on your trajectory in the sense that, since it left you impoverished financially, you had to return to the concrete via employment opportunities that presented themselves in Scandinavia. So paradoxically it ended up inhibiting the elaboration of meta-Reality in the sense that you could not devote much energy to it, and a number of books you announced never saw the light of day.[1]

RB: Absolutely. But it could also be said that the turn to the concrete was anyway necessary.

MH: Yes, we'll talk about that turn next time.

RB: I would of course still love to do those books, but probably in another form.

MH: We have discussed the genealogy of the idea of meta-Reality to a considerable extent in previous interviews: how it was anticipated by various themes from *A Realist Theory of Science* on – the thematisation of depth-stratification, of both a relative and an absolute moment of transcendence in science as indispensable to discovery, of the co-presence of the false with good scientific practice and of false with true categorisations of reality, of ultimata for science, and so on; the role of the experience of 1994; and the arguments concerning the spiritual presuppositions of emancipatory projects entraining transcendental dialectical critical realism. Pursuing this line further, can you elaborate a little how the philosophy of meta-Reality differs from transcendental dialectical critical realism and why it was developmentally necessary? In our last interview you indicated agreement with Seo MinGyu that transcendental dialectical critical realism is a mediating stage between dialectical critical realism and the philosophy of meta-Reality in the development of your thought rather than an independent stage in its own right,[2] and you've just referred to it as an epistemic half-way house. On this interpretation, and if the theory of explanatory critique is seen as transitional to dialectic,[3] the development of your system falls into three main stages: (basic or first-level or -wave) critical realism (transcendental realism, critical naturalism, explanatory critique); dialectical critical realism (including transcendental dialectical critical realism); and the philosophy of meta-Reality. Were you aware at the time of elaborating the new philosophy that the turn to spirituality and non-duality was part of a wider movement on roughly similar lines on an international scale and oriented, like yours, to 'articulating ways of transforming our transformative praxis in the world'[4] – it was 'in the air' such that today notions such as 'spiritual internationalism', 'progressive-rational spirituality for global society' and 'reconnecting transcendence with a militant materialism' are starting to become buzz words?[5] Would you agree that the movement from non-identity to identity was necessary for the 'completion' of your system, and in particular for carrying through its anti-anthropic intent?[6]

RB: I think the fundamental difference between transcendental dialectical critical realism and meta-Reality is the one I have already indicated: in meta-Reality spirituality was now seen as something that is a presupposition not just of religious or more generally emancipatory practices, but of everyday life. Thus I now saw the kind of reciprocity you have in, say, the golden rule as a presupposition of all commercial transactions and indeed everything we do. I saw the solidarity involved in ordinary care as having a direct analogue in the solidarity expressed immediately in ordinary understanding, which is an empathic putting yourself in the place of the other; we all do this easily and automatically. The transcendental identity and identification that is so difficult in meditation and prayer is very easy and routine when we are reading a newspaper or watching television: if we are not in transcendental identification with what we are reading or watching, we have to go back a step or two. I saw that the kind of unconditional love and solidarity involved in parenting a child is present in every workplace in which we spontaneously attend to the ills of our colleagues and spontaneously work together. All of this suggested a level of praxis that is hidden, a hidden substratum to social life. There is an esoteric sociology in everyday life, the sort of things we do routinely and unconditionally but which do not count.

MH: Not hidden so much as just not noticed.

RB: Unrecognised. The extraordinary thing about this is that in this realm we are very creative, spontaneously and unconditionally loving, with many of the attributes of a good society, the sort of society in which the free development of each is the condition of the free development of all. Certainly there is not an ego. There is no sense in these spontaneous roles and acts of privileging your own health or wealth or well-being at the expense of the person you are solidarising with. This is a wonderful realm of possibility which philosophy and the social sciences have not taken account of. This sphere has qualities that are in many cases directly opposite to what it underpins. Acts of exploitation and greed are actually underpinned by and presuppose unselfish and spontaneous trust and altruism. The horror of war presupposes all the peaceful acts necessary to keep it going. What it seemed to me we needed to do was to recognise and empower this unrecognised world, in some cases hidden, in some cases just unrecognised; and liberate it by getting rid of the oppressive superstructures.

So what we have here is a very general pattern or logic of emancipatory discourse pertaining to all emancipatory projects which can, for instance, be exactly exemplified in the structure of Marx's critique of capitalism and more generally in his dialectic of the productive powers of the species and social relations of production. There is an essential level, then another level emergent on it, which is useful for the development and flourishing of the basic or essential level up to a point, after which the secondary or superstructural level acts so as to constrain the development of the primary level, or at least its negative outweighs its positive effect. The point then becomes to disengage or dis-emerge the emergent level; to shed it, releasing the powers and the potentiality of the hidden or unrecognised, but essential, realm. One consequence of this of course is that at the essential level, the level of creative praxis, eudaimonistic society is already here as a capacity which is exercised and partially actualised. We do not actually have to transform human nature radically. All we have to do is recognise the eudaimonian person inside us, the elements of non-egoistic action that are always there, and necessarily there, in every human being, and shed the rest on all four planes of social being. This means that utopia, concretely understood, is not so far off, in fact it is here; the actual finished state is relatively far off because it involves the shedding of all those heteronomous orders of determination.

MH: Which of course entails an enormous amount of hard work and struggle.

RB: Yes, but at least the programme starts here. So what I was doing in meta-Reality was uncovering the most basic ground for the emancipatory projects I had been talking about since my earliest writings.

MH: Andrew Collier has criticised this theory of shedding as 'the nutcracker model of human liberation', involving the view that 'there is a good and free being fully formed inside each evil and enslaved one, just waiting to get out'.[7] Do you want to comment on that?

RB: Shedding is a necessary, but not a sufficient, condition for emancipation. A transformative moment is involved along with the shedding. This specifies the transformation of capacities into capabilities, or of abstract powers into concrete ones. Of course, for their effective exercise and realisation there must also be the satisfaction of a whole host of social, and arguably natural, conditions. Their satisfaction too requires in general a labour of transformation. However, it is important to hold on to the point that what is released after the shedding are the powers of human beings, possibilities of the ground-state which, as such, were possessed all along. These powers, as capacities, are gradually and arduously unfolded, as capabilities, into the actuality of the embodied personality.

MH: Did you feel that what you were doing was part of an incipient wider movement?

RB: The honest answer is not really. Of course, I knew that Derrida had in his last years started talking about God, but I could not see anything very interesting there – he started talking about Marx at the same time – and I knew that Habermas had as well, and so on, but I wasn't really aware that I was part of a wider movement. I was of course aware that there were people such as Rabbi Lerner, and it was obvious to me that there would be connections between a radical left politics and some form of spirituality but I did not feel part of a wider movement.

The final question here is about the movement from non-identity to identity being necessary for the completion of my system. I agree with that. Unless I had achieved identity the result would have been aporetic. But it is very important to remember, first, that the identity is nothing like the identity of subject–object identity theory or identity-thinking. Rather, it is the sort of identity that is involved in transcendental identification in consciousness, which actually preserves the non-identity of the elements that are in transcendental unity or identification. Second, that the identities we are talking about here are not atomistic or punctual, they are rich, differentiated and developing. Think about standing or sitting in front of a beautiful picture in an art gallery and being lost in appreciation of it. The deeper your appreciation, the more you will notice all the specificities. You do not just sit there in a passive, inert way. Your involvement is active, your consciousness is a rich, developing and differentiating one. Or take a Shakespearean play. Every time you read it or go to see it you might find that your understanding of it develops.

I should also say something about my alleged anti-anthropic intent. Although anti-anthropism is a theme in all my work, it was not part of my intent: it was a result or a consequence of what I did. When I was writing *A Realist Theory of Science* I did not think, 'I must think of a way to dethrone human beings', and similarly when I arrived at the formulations of meta-Reality I did not think, 'This will put man in his place.'

MH: So it just names a result of your enquiries and we can see only in retrospect that it issues in a really consistent and unifying theme in your system overall?

RB: Yes. And it is certainly a good hermeneutic exercise to trace it.

MH: On a more specific genealogical point, Philip Tew claims to have originated the concept of 'meta-realism' in discussion with you and others at the first IACR conference at Essex in 1997.[8] Is that how you see it – that is, Tew came up with the idea and you ran with it – or were you already thinking along those lines?

RB: I hope this involves no disrespect, but I am afraid that I don't have any recollection of that conversation or of the persons involved. It is interesting, but I do not think that can possibly have been the case; it cannot even have been that I unconsciously did it, because I hit upon the idea of meta-Reality very late, towards the end of 2001 or even early 2002. Otherwise it would have found its way into *From East to West*. When I coined it I wanted a way of describing the new development other than as a form of critical realism; my concern, at any rate initially, was to avoid embarrassing and causing consternation among other critical realists. I thought, well, let's call the whole pre-existing system critical realism and see that as a jumping off point for what I am saying now. I actually see it as continuous with what I have said in the past, but I cannot assume that other people will, and that is why I wanted a different name for it.

MH: So the actual concept arrives late, but presumably you had been thinking along these lines earlier, at least in general terms. The basic idea is implicit in, for example, David Bohm's distinction between the implicate or enfolded and the explicated or unfolded order,[9] and of course the perception of an underlying non-dual order, though not expressed in exactly those terms, is common in literature and art, not to say in philosophy outside of the tradition of irrealism, and in religion.

RB: I would definitely say Bohm was an influence, in the sense that I read him. And an ally. I would put the actual coining of the concept of meta-Reality on a par with the coining of the concept of transcendental realism. I arrived at the distinctions between the transitive and the intransitive dimensions and the domains of the real, the actual and the empirical long before the concept of transcendental realism, even though I had been consciously using transcendental arguments and reading everything I could lay my hands on by and about Kant. The concept of transcendental realism does not actually come into what I wrote before *A Realist Theory of Science*. Then it occurred to me that I needed a name for it.

MH: Why did you give the 'Reality' in 'meta-Reality' a capital R?

RB: It is partly stylistic. I prefer 'meta-Reality', but I am tolerant about 'meta-reality' and, in some cases (e.g. titles), Meta-Reality. When it is not a title, I think that meta-Reality signifies that we are talking about a level, aspect or component of reality, that is, it is qualifying the kind of reality that is being referred to or discussed, so that the 'Reality' in 'meta-Reality' functions as, in effect, a proper noun.

MH: Minimally stated, the philosophy of meta-Reality holds that the dualistic world we inhabit, as best described by (dialectical) critical realism, is ultimately sustained and powered by non-duality as the ground or ground-state of being, as the mode of constitution (reproduction/transformation) of everyday life via transcendence, and as the fine structure or deep interior of beings. These modes of non-duality correspond to 1M–3L in the MELD schema, and by extension (from 2E) 4D – so non-duality underpins the whole of being as understood by critical realism (relative reality or the world of becoming), and the whole point of the new philosophy is 'to re-ground the relative in the absolute, . . . re-connect and re-unite our embodied personalities with our ground-states from which, so to speak, they have cut loose'.[10] We arrive at the eudaimonistic society by shedding heteronomous orders of determination and becoming who we already essentially are. How are these propositions established? You address the issue of justification globally at a number of places, and it is of course vital to be clear about what the main lines are. As I see it the argumentation, like that for the priority of absence in *Dialectic*, is multi-pronged and complex, certainly nothing like the 'short, quick' transcendental arguments Alex Callinicos claims you are prone to make do with already in *Dialectic*.[11] You yourself summarise them in terms either of how they relate to the two stadia of meta-Reality, enchantment (6R) and non-duality (7A/Z)[12] or of the main themes of meta-Reality as a whole.[13] To take the latter approach, you suggest that the argumentation comprises (1) objective and (2) subjective considerations and (3) the unity of these in an argument that meta-Reality is a necessary condition for any being at all. (1) shows, by immanent critique and extension (by transcendental argument) of critical realism, that the world of non-identity or duality and dualism studied by critical realism is unilaterally dependent on (has as its condition of possibility) a world of identity or non-duality and that critical realism's own emancipatory project, along with all other such projects, secular and spiritual, presupposes such a world together with the possibility of shedding the dualistic master–slave social order that is dependent on it. (2) By subjective, I take it you mean (transcendental) arguments taking as their premise aspects of human intentionality, in particular successful action and fulfilled intentionality. (3) needs no further comment here, other than to mention the fundamental point establishing the ontological, epistemological and logical priority of non-duality over duality: interrelation or interconnection 'always presupposes some prior or encompassing identity or identification, otherwise there would be no grounds for declaring the non-identical elements distinct'; dualistic understandings of being always involve mis-identification and truth is most basically the revelation of identity.[14] The fundamental procedure overall is the transcendental analysis familiar from your earlier work, including metacritique of the philosophical discourse of modernity, supplemented by phenomenological analysis, reductios and so on. And the arguments map on to each other or are cumulative, such that, for example, the cycle of the human creative process thematised under (2) mirrors that of the cycle of the cosmic creative process articulated under (3).

RB: What you say about the objective considerations is fine, I agree with that. But the subjective considerations don't really involve transcendental arguments; rather, they suggest a very practical route to meta-Reality. I think the best way of articulating the objective considerations is in terms of the three main ways in which non-duality underpins the dual world we inhabit, which I summarise in the Preface to *From Science to Emancipation*: as mode of its constitution; as its basis or ground; and as its fine structure or deep interior. Mode of constitution refers to the sense in which the non-dual is a necessary condition for the reproduction and transformation of any social form, for all social action and life. Without transcendental agency you do not have agency at all. The argument is along the lines that, unless you could act in a non-dual way, unless transcendental agency is real, you could not perform any act at all: if you always thought about how to do what you were going to do, you would never get round to doing it. The transcendental self is established in the same sort of way. It doesn't matter how fractured or split you are, you still have a sense of yourself being fractured or split, so you still have a sense of yourself as a transcendentally real being. Similarly with transcendental identification in consciousness: we could not have a conversation with our worst enemy unless we could understand what they are saying; it would not be a conversation. The second objective consideration is that meta-Reality underpins duality as its ground or basis. You could not do anything at all without possessing the primitive qualities of the ground-state.

MH: Am I right in assuming that, while it is your term of art, the concept of the ground-state derives from quantum field theory, where I understand it refers to the quantum state with the lowest possible energy (the vacuum state)?

RB: The ground-state is the state that is present in all other states, the state that all other states presuppose. It is something like an absolute zero of consciousness, or as you say, the vacuum state of quantum field theory. As present in the concrete actions of the embodied personality, the more heteronomous that personality is, the more noise or interference its causality will suffer and, consequently, the more mediated its aefficacy will be. However, its aefficacy and our energy will be at a maximum, not a minimum, when there is no such interference. Basic will, creativity and unconditional love and the capacity for spontaneous right-action, these all provide an essential basis for the world of relative and demi-reality. A meta-Real dimension is thus the essential but unrecognised or hidden substratum of all other aspects of social life, as peace is essential for war. Then the third objective consideration is that everything has a deep interior. This does not really involve transcendental argument and immanent critique, but rather phenomenological experience. The argument is basically that if you go into anything sufficiently deeply you will find qualities that can only be described in terms of the void or the Buddha-nature, a level of pure bliss or some other property such as that. If I am trying to understand someone else, on the one hand I have to go into their deep interior at the level of the ground-state, and on the other my reception will be best when I am in my own ground-state; so you have a ground-state in unity with another ground-state. This could be a paradigm or model of what you want to achieve in a peace negotiation, because everyone wants to negotiate with their enemy when their enemy is at their most just and merciful. This would be the standard or norm, but of course it is also the standard or norm for all the other kinds of human action, including our own parenting of ourselves. And it provides a paradigm of a good social structure: one that does not embody structural sin, that does not prevent us from being consistent with our ground-state or mediate or obscure it. It is just like the basic concept of reality – you cannot get away from it; or like the concept of a causal law as a structure or operation of a mechanism that is pulling you to the ground. There is no way you can get around, or get out of, or bypass the level of meta-Reality.

The subjective considerations are practical arguments. The basis of these is that unless someone is at one with their ground-state their intentionality is going to be split, because their intentionality is always going to be at least partly directed by or coming from the ground-state. They are going to be unhappy in some way.

MH: But the argument presupposes the reality of the ground-state.

RB: That's right, it's a practical argument. It is not a transcendental argument, it is an ad hominem argument that says, 'Look, just try it in practice, and see for yourself. You will be split.' This has a resonance with the sort of thing Buddha was saying: if you are a human being at least set yourself an objective you can achieve, and what you can achieve is realisation or enlightenment, as he put it. If you do not achieve that, you cannot satisfactorily achieve all these other things you want to achieve; in popular parlance that would be because there is a bit of you that is unhappy with them in so far as they conflict with your ground-state, because you won't be satisfying the urgings of your ground-state. If you are not at all in touch with your higher self – whether or not you believe you have a higher self is not really relevant – this argument will not impress you, but your higher self will still have some, however remote, aefficacy on the totality of what you do. So this subjective argument is practical, it concerns what you might do in practice; it ties in with what I have said about being being as not just a question of thinking, you actually have to do.

Then the third line of argument is the unity of the objective and subjective considerations, in which you might come to see the sort of cosmological, including social, considerations born from the objective arguments as in resonance with the structure of your own action and the necessary structure in your action.

MH: In his critical assessment of meta-Reality, Jamie Morgan[15] focuses on the objective considerations, and within that the experience of transcendental identification in consciousness, agency and teamwork, which he regards as 'the basis from which the system is constructed' (somewhat confusingly dubbing it 'the Archimedean point').[16] He argues that the inference to non-duality is only one of a number of plausible interpretations, and in particular that it might equally be the case that (1), as neuroscience suggests, 'material changes to the structure of the brain . . . *emerge synchronically* with the ability described',[17] conferring powers of simulation and imagination: for example, the emergent power of propriaception could explain our sense that we are part of our own frame of perceptual reference,[18] which you use as part of your overall argument for meta-Reality; and (2) the special sense of connectivity experienced in prayer, meditation, and so on could be a mistake or mis-identification (a possibility you yourself take on board[19]). Assuming that one accepts this, how would it affect the overall case for meta-Reality? Do you agree that there needs to be serious engagement with neuroscience on the issue?

RB: 'Material changes to the structure of the brain . . . emerge synchronically with the ability described': that is right, the material structure of the brain confers a power; whether we exercise it or not is up to us. I would not deny that for everything we can do in the world as we know it there is a material basis. And of course we need science that takes into account all these other phenomena. In terms of engaging with neuroscience: yes, there would be something wrong if neuroscience came out with a finding that disproves or discredits this.

MH: If neuroscience were to find that there is no conceivable way that transcendental identification occurs –

RB: The question is does it occur or not? If it occurs without a conceivable basis, I am afraid empirically I would have to take its occurrence as real, and I hope that neuroscience would take on board that the phenomena we are talking about are real. Whether the philosophical apparatus I construct for it is a good way of situating it or not, there is a real level of phenomena that I am talking about and we can talk about, under the rubric of transcendental agency or not. If neuroscience comes along and says it does not believe in these phenomena then it is not really being scientific. But supposing that what neuroscience shows is that these phenomena are not what they appear to be, then that is perfectly possible: it is perfectly possible that this could be a level of illusion. However, what you would have to do to justify that position would be to show how in that case agency is possible, or understanding, or team-work or all the practical instances of it that Freud and especially Jung, pointed to – in, for instance, what Jung called synchronicity – all of which are very common and widespread in ordinary life. Neuroscience would have to situate the possibility of agency without an element of non-duality; it would have to explain how despite the absence of that element action was still possible. It is perfectly conceivable that it should do so, but that is what it would have to do, and it is very difficult to imagine it actually doing it. It is not very plausible as an exhaustive approach to this domain of phenomena because, when the neuroscientist had actually achieved some sort of explanatory reduction of the field and been awarded a Nobel prize, the whole domain of intentionalistic phenomena that has its own level of reality, its own emergent powers, would still be there as the level at which we operate, at which our social life and our language operates. Unless the reduction were to miraculously transform human beings such that they no longer took pleasure in a challenge successfully met or a struggle won, it would be a very hollow victory: it would not *be* a victory, it would not have done justice to the phenomena.
      Having said that, everything that meta-Reality says should ultimately be compatible with the findings of neuroscience and any other kind of science,

and of course neuroscience is very important here in investigating phenomena such as telepathy. Meta-Reality also is supposed to underlabour for the sciences. It does this in the first instance for what I call the esoteric sociology of everyday life. But there are other elements to it: for example, the understanding of the deep stratification of our embodied personalities. That is a huge research project. How memory and how the past is locked in. How we think of other people. Is it like a series of concentric circles, with ourselves in the centre and our nearest and dearest ones very close to us and then the species as a whole in a much remoter position and other species further out still, and so on? Or is it perhaps the case that you cannot generalise because we are all concrete singularities: to some people their cat or dog is the most important thing in their lives, because it does not answer back.

MH: You say in the *Preface* to *Meta-Reality*:

> Perhaps it is best not to call the philosophy of meta-Reality a realism, as realism connotes the idea of a split or opposition between a world and its description, that is, insofar as the very concept of realism is itself dualistic. So I prefer to think of it as describing being but oriented to being which does not think being, and which in fact engages as much a polemic against thought, and the ego, and the products of thought and the ego, as it does against subject–object duality as such. So it is not really even a system of thought, but an intervention in the discursive process which is designed to enable agents to reflexively situate their own non-dual being in the context of their growth and development in the dual realm and their struggles in the dualistic realm which dominates and screens or occludes not only the relative world of duality but the absolute non-dual world on which it entirely reposes. So this could be said to be a philosophy of truth, rather than reality (insofar as reality is affected and so to speak contaminated by duality and thus – in our present epoch – dualism). Hence the 'meta': it is the ground and truth of reality.[20]

Is the formulation, 'a philosophy of truth rather than reality', one you want to stick with? How would you say the shift of focus registered in this passage from 'thinking being' to, as you put it a few pages earlier, '*being being*, . . . or rather a *becoming of our being*, the becoming or realisation of ourselves, self-realisation'[21] relates to and/or improves on the thematisation of absolute reason in *Dialectic* – the unity or coherence of theory and practice in practice entrained by the dialectics of freedom – as the overcoming of alienation?

RB: In the meta-Real moment our physical being and other aspects of the physical world and all the dimensions of the world of duality are preserved. In a way you could say that they are suspended in the moment of direct identification in consciousness. But they are still there. Understanding that what meta-Reality describes is the most basic and essential level of human beings and, so I argue, all being, you can set yourself the task of always being in a state where you can be in your ground-state, which means eliminating from yourself the heteronomous levels and orders of determination that are a part of what you are in your relative embodied personality. When you reach that point we could say that you are self-realised, but you can also think of self-realisation as progress or movement towards that state. Now when you are self-realised there will still be lots of things outside you, you will still be outside them, you will not know everything, and you will not be able to see everything, so there will still be many challenges for your own personal growth. Even more importantly, to be such a person means that you will be very creative and you will be imbued with compassion and love for the rest of creation, and particularly that part of creation that is close to you, your society, so you will be an agent in the social world, seeking to transform it. You will be a non-dual being in a sea of duality with the goal of absolute or dialectical reason, which is the unity or coherence of theory and practice in practice, so that you are not split. You will have made yourself maximally apt to be an agent of dialectical or absolute reason. You will be the best possible agent for eliminating heteronomies in the social world, in other people, in our social relations and our transactions with nature.

MH: Overcoming alienation.

RB: Yes, but there will still be a huge task there. So this is the answer to the question, how do the two stand to each other. In realising yourself, you will be being or rather becoming the being that is yourself. You will have minimised the theory–practice contradictions and alienations in your own practice and life and will be the most effective agent of dialectical or absolute reason.

MH: How does that improve on the account in *Dialectic*?

RB: It shows how to get to the level of being such an agent, and also that as an agent of absolute reason you are not working alone, you are working with everything else on the cosmic envelope. In particular, there is an unrecognised substratum of social life that is a manifestation of the fact that every person has an element or a level in which they are intrinsically divine.

MH: Something like that is already presupposed in *Dialectic*: that people as such are free, for example.

RB: That is right, but it is implicitly there. In meta-Reality it is overtly stated and explicit. That is what the philosophy of meta-Reality does: it makes what was implicit explicit and elaborates it. There is no theorisation in *Dialectic* of the non-dual and no explicit theorisation of the transcendentally real self.

The idea that truth is more basic than reality stems from the fact that the simple subject–object distinction or the basic premise of realism that there is something existing independently of one's consciousness actually breaks down. At the level of non-duality there is not another, there is not something that is existentially intransitive, you are at one with whatever it is that you are identifying with. So you do not have realism; realism does not apply at that level, but truth does. But I would not normally put it like this, that truth is more basic, because of course if you abstract from the moment of non-duality there is a real distinction. Suppose I am in a non-dual relation with this water; if I abstract from that there is a distinction, the water is there and I am here. Reality is not dissolved within our non-dual consciousness, but there are aspects of reality that cannot adequately be thought in a realistic way. That is really what I am saying. When I was coming to understand the importance of non-duality I felt it a nice irony that there is a level of social being at which the whole premise of my previous work, existential realism, breaks down. Had I obsessively wanted to stick to my original intuitions I would never have seen it.

MH: Your case for the always already enchanted nature of the world (6R) as I understand it rests importantly on this breakdown of subject–object duality in transcendental identification, the paradigm case of which is direct mind-to-mind, or more generally consciousness-to-consciousness, action, which you suggest is 'a natural corollary of the thesis already established by critical realism of mind as a synchronic emergent power of matter'.[22] Your paradigm of communication is twofold; on the one hand it is direct and unmediated by physical causes and on the other indirect and mediated. As I understand it, you do not deny that, outside of telepathy and related phenomena (if there be such), there is a sense in which communication is usually mediated by physical causes, at least in the zone of relative reality. But you argue that direct communication still occurs in the moment of understanding and that it is primary, and the physical medium is secondary.[23] Thus far I think I am in agreement, and it seems entirely compatible with synchronic emergent powers materialism: if mind can directly affect material things it seems entirely reasonable to hold that it can directly affect other minds.[24] It is the particular significance you attach to this that I have difficulties with. It seems to be pointing in the direction of the universal detachability of consciousness (viewed as 'primary, or as primary as matter' and implicit in everything) from the physical, or as you put it the 'motility and universality' of consciousness, that is, its ability to move spontaneously and independently anywhere.[25] To this I would say in general that the irreducibility of thought and feeling to their physical expression or to bodies is one thing, their independence from them quite another. Moreover, you seem to be positing the possibility of direct consciousness-to-consciousness communication and (cumulative, recursively embeddable) dialectically universalised responsiveness or reciprocity throughout the cosmos,[26] and that at first sight is a fantastic idea, albeit perhaps a logical one on the basis of the general case for connectivity, which includes of course action-at-a-distance theorised by modern physics. It seems to depend ultimately on a notion of consciousness as primary and matter as secondary, such that what beings '*most* essentially'[27] are is implicit (transcendental or supramental) consciousness. Or are you redefining the physical to include what we conventionally take to be non-physical existence and causality, such that everything hinges here ultimately on the solution you offer to the age-old problem of metaphysical idealism versus materialism?

RB: You say that irreducibility is not the same as independence, and that could be a useful starting point. Transcendental identification in consciousness is irreducible but it normally depends on cues, physical cues of the sort that can be theorised by physics, though not as cues; in other words it operates with cues, and when I understand you, the cue is the sound and then the occasion is direct transcendental identification in consciousness.

MH: Why do you say 'cue' rather than 'medium'?

RB: Airwaves carry the sounds and in this sense are a medium, but when you tell me something I am not aware of any medium, I just hear it. What happens is there is a sound, and I immediately hear it, and that is what I am calling a cue. The basic argument is that my understanding you is irreducible to the existence of the cue. That in itself does not prove that it could occur independently of any cue. But at least it establishes the possibility of that. Of course, it also could be wrong: it could be that we never understand anything without a cue of that kind. So that position is perfectly consistent with synchronic emergent powers materialism. Then what one would have to do is formulate some empirically testable hypotheses with a bearing on whether it is possible or not. But there are phenomena that speak against its not being possible, just at its own level. For example, if you hear a couple of people having a blazing argument and you go into the room that they were in, many people find it easy to feel the argument.

MH: After they have gone?

RB: Yes. When you go back home after you have had a bad day at work, you still feel the workplace, you carry it with you.

MH: You need to take a shower or something?

RB: Yes, you carry it in the aura of your physical being, your physical presence, and it is noticeable. There are far stronger arguments for what you call detachability, but detachability is not the right word, because it is there almost always with you and your understanding of what someone else says remains with you after they have said it, such that you can refer back to it. All this requires complex analysis and I have only indicated my minimal position. That is really all I am trying to say. It is up to our arguments and empirically based science whether direct-mind-to-mind contact without cues is possible.

Here we come back to the kind of considerations we touched on last time when I suggested that the fact that you cannot reduce feelings and minds to physical corporeality makes it possible that they have a post-existence of some sort; and also that we might have the potentiality to connect up with a previous life, where the pre-existence is still arguably physical and the psychic being is purely potential – it would not be an actual conveyer between the past and the present. Another possibility is that the feelings and mind you actually have in your life will not exist after your death but will in some way connect up with a future existence that might or might not be physical. These are purely notional possibilities. You might ask why should I even contemplate these possibilities in this context? It is because your ground-state has a peculiar status as part of the cosmic envelope: it is both outside space–time and inside space–time.

MH: You talk of it as eternal.

RB: And so that is one consideration: there is a kind of a bivalence of the cosmic envelope. And I actually think this is a feature of it, that it is both. And the way we might understand this is by analogy with a surface: you cannot see the side that is outside space–time. So that is one consideration, the bivalence of the ground-state. Another consideration is the interconnectedness of the cosmos. You say that you find it difficult to get your head around this?

MH: Well, the notion that we can have immediate effects throughout the cosmos that, moreover, are recursively embeddable.

RB: What I would say is, OK, it might only have an infinitesimally small effect, an effect that cannot be measured with our existing instruments, but to say it has a small effect does not mean it has no effect. So I am not arguing about the magnitude of the effects. Actually the magnitude of human effects, the magnitude of our intentional actions on the physical world have been enormous, but it is still circumscribed –

MH: We live on this tiny speck of a planet, almost a null-point in the great scheme of things.

RB: If we blow our planet up it will have a discernible effect on neighbouring planets and possibly the solar system. It is the kind of thing we are quite capable of doing.

MH: As I read you, you are saying that what we do, our state of consciousness, can affect the deep evolutionary processes of the cosmos, that is, the whole process of universal self-realisation and god-realisation.[28] This is where I have problems.

RB: And my response to that is to say, all right, I admit for the most part it would be a very small effect. But consider the sort of effects our conscious intentionality is having on the world. These might be restricted to the solar system or something like that, but they are still very big effects in my book. All I am saying is it can potentially have an effect throughout the multiverse. It might be that there are far off states of the universe and configurations of particles or subparticles in fundamental physics that we can never know about, but I think there are good strong transcendental arguments for the unity of the cosmos and, given that, it is at least potentially the case that we can have an effect anywhere in the cosmos. This could be like a butterfly effect. But of course the beings of the cosmos are very differentiated. The argument is then that, while it might only be remotely possible that we can have an effect elsewhere in the cosmos at a physical level, it is much more likely that we will have an effect on other beings like us. Again, what are the mechanisms of this? Well, this is a very interesting field. Many studies of animal behaviour seem to suggest that there is something akin to 'species learning' in which, once some members of a species learn a new form of behaviour, other (even distant) members of that species manifest, or more readily learn or acquire, that new form of behaviour. There is the well-known case of the blackbirds in England, a few of which discovered that they could get at the content of milk bottles by pecking a hole in the aluminium top, and then, quite quickly, blackbirds everywhere in far distant regions got the hang of this. I do not know what the mechanisms are, but there will be mechanisms and we have to discover them. These are the possibilities opened up. I am quite happy at the end of the day if we have a good explanation of all these phenomena that does not invoke any new media or vehicles; but I think this is very unlikely, because in physics and in science generally we are continually discovering new strata or aspects of reality and new kinds of mechanism and I think it quite possible that new levels of being will be discovered when our science is open-minded enough to consider all this.

MH: How does your solution to the problem of metaphysical idealism versus materialism bear on all this? The most succinct statement of your solution is perhaps:

> consciousness is enfolded in all being . . . but matter is not enfolded in all consciousness. This means that there is an inverse chain or synchronic order of ontological priority in the increasing determinacy with which consciousness enfolds itself in matter; and makes matter a synchronically emergent or derivative power of consciousness, while at the same time allowing that consciousness can be diachronically emergent from matter.[29]

I find this a difficult concept.

RB: What I am thinking of is something like this. All matter has consciousness enfolded within it as a more or less remote possibility, in two senses. It has the possibility, first, of evolving into a conscious state, and second of being known through consciousness – through transcendental identification in consciousness. So in those senses all matter has consciousness enfolded within it. But the converse does not apply. Think of, say, the consciousness of Beethoven when composing a symphony. This consciousness does not have matter enfolded in it in the way that matter has consciousness within it. You might say that music presupposes material instruments and so on. That is fine, but it only takes you so far, because you can hum the music, you can remember it and Beethoven did not even hear it late in his life – he ceased to hear it. Or think of e = mc². You can have consciousness of that which does not have matter enfolded within it in any way. We can make sense of this in the following kind of way. We have a view of matter evolving through time–space into a point where it becomes conscious and we have paradigms of consciousness without matter enfolded within it. But having evolved from matter, consciousness does not need to go back to matter. It is not the case that all consciousness has matter enfolded within it: some consciousness might have, but much of what we call high consciousness does not. It might be asked why we have this asymmetry. You can make sense of this by thinking of an evolution where matter becomes more and more self-aware and when it gets to a certain point of self-awareness you do not actually need to go back to the level of brute, inanimate matter. Of course, there would always be the possibility of a degradation of evolution back to that level; if you got rid of consciousness on earth there would still be matter.

MH: With implicit consciousness enfolded within it.

RB: We would have to see. But it is arguable that, at a certain threshold of evolution, you have consciousness without matter: consciousness that is no longer tied to matter.

MH: Why don't we have a dualism here then, if mind can become independent of matter?

RB: To have a monism does not mean that the monism is undifferentiated. What you would have is different modes of consciousness or different modes of what you might want to call being or, as you suggested in conversation earlier, different modes of energy – and I am perfectly happy to say that. I am perfectly happy to think of the most fundamental element in the universe as consciousness with bits of root matter enfolded within it – if you want to call that energy, or matter-consciousness, that's fine.

MH: Don't you say that ultimately reality *is* consciousness, at least in so far as, considered synchronically, matter is the product of a logically prior but notional moment of involution of consciousness?[30]

RB: I am trying not to say that. Let us just call it the cosmic envelope. Consciousness and self-awareness can be thought of as powers or potentialities of beings on that envelope, of some beings anyway, looked at in a very broad historical perspective. You can make sense of evolution then. As I say somewhere, initially the universe emerged out of nothing. Something came out of nothing, then as evolution proceeds we unfold more and more possibilities until, at the end of the day, we get everything in everything.

MH: You seem to go along with traditional cosmologies in seeing the emergence of the cosmos as an act of consciousness, of a creator or god who 'self-creates himself out of the void'.[31] Your notional 'involution of consciousness' corresponds to the descent of consciousness in traditional cosmologies.

RB: We do not really have anything different in Big Bang theory, which posits an explosion out of nothing and eventually an implosion into nothing.

MH: The theory of generalised co-presence, whereby the alethic truth of everything is enfolded as potential within everything else, arguably entrains a solution to the problem of knowledge that critical realism perhaps had not quite resolved: how is it possible to bridge the gap between the transitive and intransitive dimension, to fallibly discover the truth of things? We can come to know truths of the world (including moral truths) ultimately because the world was formed by the same powers that constituted and are enfolded within us, such that in making new discoveries (or actually learning anything) we 'recall' what is already within us as implicit potential, thereby achieving a point of identity or union with what we have discovered. Alethia is thus literally 'the undoing of oblivion' in an important sense, that of Platonic anamnesis: 'truth . . . is most basically the revelation of identity (in the identity consciousness of another being)'.[32] And education is 'the bringing out of what is already in'.[33] Learning and discovery always involves a moment of the suspension of thought (unthought) – of supramental consciousness at the level of ground-states – in which the implicit emerges or is explicated. What are your thoughts on this today? Do we have an element of Platonic idealist realism here as well as anamnesis?

RB: No, I do not think so. This is realism about universals and realism about singulars and realism about all the other things, but it is not a specifically Platonic one. Otherwise I agree with what you have said, although I do not entirely agree with the idea that we need the meta-Real solution to the problem of knowledge, as you put it, because I think that the solution given in transcendental realism is quite adequate. For there is no way we can overcome the fact – this is the language I used at the time – that we are not immediately at the level of the world we study in experimental, or more generally in critical, science. All we can do is to attempt to fashion language in such a way that it expresses as adequately as possible what is independent of us. That is obviously a dualistic formulation, but I think it is quite adequate for empirical science. Even looked at from the point of view of meta-Reality, the transitive dimension of knowledge has its own modalities and its own rhythm which is independent of intransitive reality, even including the intransitive reality of non-duality and the ground-state. Dualistically reflected knowledge will always be with us. When I was going into meta-Reality, I saw it not so much in terms of the problem of knowledge but as allowing us to make sense of a level of experience and understanding in which we become increasingly skilled and accomplished agents, such that the realm of what we can spontaneously know and spontaneously do increases. Meta-Reality points to moments – and this ties in with the philosophy of truth – in which a dualistic subject–object way of looking at the world needs to be complemented. So if there was a problem of knowledge that was not really solved in *A Realist Theory of Science* it is the problem, if it is a problem, at that level, of how you get to a new concept given that you cannot do it by induction or deduction. This is what meta-Reality answers. What it does in relation to subject–object dualism is to point to a level in our experience in which we transcend that dualism easily on the basis of our cognitive accomplishments. So we seem to be in agreement.

MH: Yes, that is what I had in mind. It theorises the subjective condition for learning in a way that your earlier work did not, a condition that I believe we have seen at work in practice in the ability of Sue Kelly to understand your concepts in a basic sort of way.[34] I move on now to your critique of the discursive intellect. Meta-Reality, and especially its thematisation of transcendence as constitutive of creativity or transcendental emergence, entrains a 'radical transcendentalisation of the dialectical critique of analytical reasoning', which you refer to as the critique of the discursive intellect as distinct from the intuitive intellect, 'where "intellect" is just the faculty of discrimination and choice'.[35] The discursive intellect, which includes dialectical as well as analytical thought, is sentential, instrumental, calculative, sequential, and analogical; the intuitive intellect is iconic, unconditional, spontaneous, simultaneous and holistic, and is at least equally important. All creative discovery depends on a synthesis of the discursive and intuitive, 'left' and 'right' brain, a synthesis that is underpinned by supramental consciousness at the level of the ground-state and that depends on five 'others' to thought – consciousness (awareness), intuition or unthought (direct inference – 'I get it'), direct perception, being (of which thought is only a small part), and emptiness or suchness or just being/doing – and your true scientist (or any creative human being) is a 'practical mystic' engaged in acts at or close to the ground-state and simultaneously committed, on scientific grounds, to this-worldly transformative practice to effect (universal) self-realisation or enlightenment. If we just rely on the discursive intellect we mis-identify our self as our ego, 'the wonders of consciousness [as] the reifications of language',[36] creativity as the powers of mind and the ideologies of mind, the immediacy of the now as the clock time created by our minds, and so on. I find this all very convincing, but include it for possible comment because it leads into the next question.

RB: I agree with all that I think.

MH: You say that time is 'a creation of the mind',[37] specifically the modern mind. You do not of course mean that we create time–space and evolutionary process, but clock time and time angst – these (while the former is convenient) mis-categorise the true nature of tense and process, which they consequently occlude. It is only if we 'draw back the curtains of the mind', that is, shed clock time and time angst and the illusion that they are natural, that it becomes possible to live fully 'in the now' rather than in the 'demi-present' of demi-reality.[38] In this context you suggest that a sense of past, present and future is an emergent product of modernity – it did not exist before – whereas in *Dialectic* you argued for the reality and irreducibility of tense. Are you now saying that you got it wrong in *Dialectic* or that what was new in modernity was *awareness* (in the transitive dimension) of tense (in the intransitive dimension) that had been real all along? If as I take it the latter, how does this square with your statement that it is in our essential nature 'to overcome *the illusion* of past and future'?[39] This only makes sense, as you say, from the perspective of eternity – only if our essence is 'an eternal being outside space and time', that is, what you call our (concretely singularised) ground-state or spirit (*jivatman*) as distinct from our soul or psychic being that is formed by the ground-state in its evolution within relative reality (geo-history).[40] If our eternal self changes, past and future would presumably everywhere be real. Are some ultimata unchanging? Or does everything change, as you sometimes seem to imply; for example, 'there is no reason why the absolute cannot encompass an ever deepening process of expansion'.[41] Is the cosmic envelope – absolute reality – inside or outside space–time, or both (immanent/transcendent) and how? (You have touched on this already – you say both – but I include it here for possible further comment.)

RB: I think you are absolutely right in saying that what was new in modernity was awareness of tense that had been real all along. Also new was the illusion of clock time, and illusions are real and causally aefficacious. Critical realism and meta-Reality, with its conception of the multi-tiered stratification of reality, has an enormous advantage over alternative metaphysical approaches here in that it can situate illusion – the smog of the demi-real – as a real causally aefficacious emergent stratum within reality. So clock time is a real emergent illusion within relative reality, and that is one thing. On the other hand, tense and process are real and non-illusory features of relative reality, but when looked at from the perspective of absolute reality, of eternity, they too are illusory. This relates to the issue of whether the cosmic envelope – absolute reality – is inside or outside space and time, or both; and as you know I want to say it is both. This is difficult to make entirely consistent with common sense except by analogy, so I compare it to a surface of which we can only see one side. When we look at the side we can see it is within space and time. But looked at from another point of view – what we would see if we saw the other side – it is outside. You quote me as saying there is no reason why the absolute cannot encompass an ever deepening process of expansion. This is how it is, and I think that transfinite mathematics shows the possibility of greater and lesser infinities; mathematics has gotten round to thinking of infinity as a concept within which you can have various gradations – you can certainly have deepening. What we have to be able to do is both to think (and act) within time and a tensed world and to unthink. Much of the philosophy of meta-Reality is designed to be a propaedeutic to a practical exposition of how we might better live in a eudaimonistic, simple society. In such a society we would be able to remove ourselves from time angst and just enjoy the bliss of something; it might be some music, or it might be anything – that, as the Zens claim, we can go into anything and enjoy it. We have to involute our life importantly in this way.

MH: Your notion of generalised synchronous reciprocity and co-presence, which includes a notion of the intentionality of ground-states, that is, their conatus to the telos of self-realisation, combined with the view that beings with minds and feeling can survive forever even if their physical basis is destroyed, leads you to espouse a view that might be called 'spiritual inevitabilism'. By this I mean the view that sooner or later universal self-realisation will inevitably occur, even if planet Earth is destroyed.[42] (I note that this is not 'triumphalism', which refers to the exorbitation of specifically human powers, in particular cognitive ones. Spiritual inevitabilism presupposes the rejection of cognitive triumphalism.) I take it you are not being determinist in an actualistic sense here – the inexorability is in the tendency which, since it is robust, must win out over the very long term; there is war between peace and war, love and hate (between non-duality and the structures of dualism or demi-reality) for relative reality that is not really a war because in the long run peace must triumph through the peaceful dissolution of war, which unilaterally depends on it. That seems all very logical, and it makes the whole show all the more sublime; and I can accept, as you memorably say, that 'it is not that there are the starry heavens above and the moral law within, as Kant would have it; rather, the true basis of your virtuous existence is the fact that the starry heavens are within you, and you are within them'.[43] But how crucial to it all are the notions of reverberating reciprocity and enduring psychic beings with minds and feelings that pre- and post-exist embodied personalities? If crucial, most secular critical realists will part company with you here, and to that extent you would not have 'a spirituality within the bounds of secularism, consistent with all faiths and no faith', a transcendence of the dualism of the sacred and profane.[44] Paradoxically, the price of this guarantee/inexorability seems to be the postponement of the full realisation of eudaimonia, which is but the end of pre-history and the beginning of history proper on Earth, to a remote epoch: 'When the whole of creation is self-realised, when it reflects back its own divinity, then and only then will there be peace'.[45]

RB: I do not think they really are crucial. If I could just break down the question
into two parts. Is universal self-realisation inevitable? And does this mean
that we have to postpone the idea of eudaimonia until the moment when literally we have universal self-realisation? First, it is very important to stress that
it is not inevitable for us as corporeal beings on our planet. Even – indeed,
especially – from the point of view of being in our ground-state, what we first
have to do is to try to ensure the survival of our planet. We cannot have any
other practical perspective, we are ineluctably tied to the physical. Alongside
the tendency of the non-dual to win out over the demi-real is the tendency of
the particular form that the demi-real takes to destroy its physical basis. The
second is at present occurring at a much faster rate than the first, which is not
to say that things could not be reversed, but that is the way it is. If you are in
your ground-state the best way of speeding up the counteracting tendency will
also necessarily involve trying to halt the negative tendency to the destruc-
tion of physical life, because this physical life is tied to things of intrinsic value
and has its own ground-states. We cannot want to destroy the basis of physical
life. On the contrary, it has to be strengthened, and meta-Reality conceives
itself as an agent in this task. The inevitability at issue is the inevitability only
of a tendency.

MH: But regardless of what happens to us as corporeal beings, as a species, the
process of cosmic unfolding will go on.

RB: Yes, that is right. But it would be scant compensation to us as embodied
beings. Does this involve postponing eudaimonia until universal self-
realisation is achieved? No. We need eudaimonia now; we need to get rid of
the demi-real to have a better existence in the world of duality. It is a necessary step on the long path to universal self-realisation. When I say that only
when everything is self-realised will there be peace, I do not mean that
there cannot be eudaimonia short of that, because when we have a eudaimonistic society it will still be within the world of duality; there will still be
challenges and conflicting points of view and orientations, but they will be
resolvable, and the more people are at their ground-state the easier it will be
to resolve them. When there is universal self-realisation, on the other hand,
we would be in a form of existence which you could say is post-mental, in
which thought itself had been transcended and all the challenges of thinking
being had given way to being being itself at a self-realised level. No one can say
that evolution would come to a stop. We might discover whole new challenging domains. But perhaps the very concepts of challenge and resolution would
no longer have applicability. Universal self-realisation is the limit situation
and eudaimonia is a practical concept designed to apply in the world as we
know it.

MH: Alex Callinicos's recent *The Resources of Critique* has as its central theme the
issue of how transcendence, defined as our ability 'to go beyond the limit set

by existing practices and beliefs and produce something new', is possible today. His answer, at this moment of transition 'in which one political subject has died and a new one has yet to emerge', is to hold on to the standpoint formulated by Marx in 1843 and developed by Lukàcs: that of the proletariat as the universal class.[46] You see transcendence rather as a universal *human* capacity to go beyond existing states of consciousness that informs our every act and is grounded ultimately in the deep creativity of the cosmos. Are these two positions reconcilable?

RB: I would say that they are reconcilable only on three conditions. First, if you have a non-actualist definition of class, that is, if you do not identify class positions immediately with particular human beings. Second, if you allow for the totality of master–slave-type relations, and accept that you have to work on all the other master–slave-type relations and inequities at the level of social structure besides class. Third, and most importantly, if you also understand the project as one involving work on all four levels of four-planar social being. That is to depart from the letter of Lukàcs's formulation, I think, but not from its spirit, which is something dialectical critical realism and meta-Reality take up.

MH: You end *Reflections on meta-Reality* with a quote from Jelaluddin Rumi:

> Every forest branch moves differently
> in the breeze, but as they sway
> they connect at the roots

Taken as a metaphor for the cosmos this, along with much else in the philosophy of meta-Reality, is very much in keeping with deep ecology. Most of the main meta-Reality concepts are at least implicitly present in deep ecology, including anti-anthropism and a concept of the intrinsic value of being, and an emphasis on self-realisation as a cumulative process, a conception that like yours is significantly indebted to East. Thus Arne Næss holds, like you, that the higher the self-realisation attained by anyone, the broader and deeper the identification with others and the more its further increase depends upon the self-realisation of others; and that the complete self-realisation of anyone depends on that of all. The related Gaia Hypothesis holds that the earth is alive – a living system – and that we are a part of it. Would you say meta-Reality is a vitalistic philosophy, not in the sense that the life force (consciousness, intentionality, energy) it postulates as animating and cohering the cosmos is necessarily different from the energy modern physics theorises but in the sense that it just is the ultimate form of that energy, reducible neither to 'matter' nor 'spirit' as understood in western philosophy but analogous to the *ch'i* or *qi* (vital force) postulated by Confucianism, which you invoke a number of times?[47] I take it that you see yourself here, as always, not as going against the best modern science but on the contrary as taking its implications seriously, especially quantum physics and the life sciences?

RB: I would not exactly call it a vitalistic philosophy, but I think it does have analogies with Taoism and Confucianism. I think that MinGyu[48] gives a very Taoist interpretation of Confucianism by the way. I do not know whether Tu Wei-Ming, the scholar he refers to, would be regarded as an orthodox Confucian or not, but it is obviously a very Taoist interpretation and it has much in common with many Buddhist conceptions as well. I think meta-Reality goes a little bit deeper than the philosophy of *ch'i*, but certainly there are very interesting analogies and overlaps. Perhaps what Taoism lacks is a really clear conception of stratification. As for the relation between meta-Reality and deep ecology, this is something I am currently working on;[49] but as a general orientation I would say that deep ecology is strong in the domains of 3L, 5A and 6R, less so in those of 1M, 2E and 4D, of stratification and a geo-historical negating praxis.

MH: Your message in the meta-Reality books is in the end a very 'simple' one, both at the personal and social level and at the level of practical reason. 'The fool', you remind us, 'is the Shakespearean wise guy, and the idiot is the enlightened one.'[50] Master–slave-type societies are 'ontologically extravagant', particularly capitalism; 'we should be striving toward a society that is both ontologically simple and ontologically honest'.[51] 'We do not have to construct an alternative order, the system which is despoiling us entirely depends on what we already have. All we have to do is recognise that we already have and are this order.' To realise eudaimonia we 'just' have to be who we really are, and that's it – the dominating and occluding order 'will collapse without resistance'. And 'then the rest is up to the workings of a universe and cosmic envelope connecting all our ground-states which no-one can attempt to second guess'.[52] It is indeed a simple, if profound, message; some will say too simple. But one thing that strikes me is that, as is your wont, it is ahead of its time – you push to their utmost logical conclusion wider intellectual currents that are eschewing commandist notions of seizing and using state power to construct a new order in favour of relying on the organised creativity of the oppressed, which you construe as the whole of humanity.[53]

RB: I think we do have to simplify our life radically. What we have now, capitalism and everything associated with it, is the spectre of a bad infinite, a bad infinite that will come to an end. Logically, its end is of course when there is nothing left to commodify, but unfortunately long before that happens our planet will have come to an end, because it cannot take much – if any – more, and human beings will have ceased to exist.

MH: But it could not commodify everything – in terms of meta-Reality, everything pertaining to the ground-state.[54]

RB: That is right, and that is a very important point. It cannot commodify, or ever touch, the meta-Real world that it presupposes; that world is a real limit to alienation. It could of course reduce its scope and recognition, but meta-Reality would still be necessary to it. If you imagine some horrendous dictator giving an order to destroy everything, that order would still have to be carried out and that would depend on a vein of trust.

9 Where do we go from here?

Applied critical realism and beyond (2002–)

MH: Before broaching the issue of where we go from here, I would like to ask about your personal trajectory since the publication of *Meta-Reality* in 2002, culminating in your recent appointment as World Scholar at the Institute of Education, London. In your notes for this book, you described these years as a period of 'return to the concrete and consolidation'. I am aware that, besides the visits to India you mentioned last time, you also made a number of trips to Europe, North America and Australia to promote critical realism and meta-Reality. You also established a Foundation for Meta-Reality. Can you tell us a little about these activities and their rationale?

RB: First I should say a little bit about what I have been doing intellectually over the intervening years. All the recent activity I am going to describe has been done under the sign of economic necessity. Had I been able to carry on my pre-existing practice, at least initially I would probably have continued to work systematically on the three projected meta-Reality volumes that we mentioned last time, but this was not possible. Much of my actual time after 2002 was spent in Scandinavia, where interest in basic or first-level critical realism is very strong. And of course, in so far as I was in the market selling my labour-power and I wanted to do something that was connected with critical realism and meta-Reality, the most feasible option for me was to talk and write about first-wave critical realism. When I arrived in Sweden people such as Göran Therborn told me that to all intents and purposes critical realism was hegemonic there. I am not so sure about that, but it is at least widely known.

I can best indicate the rationale of the work I have been doing by locating it within a topology of ways of developing the argument of *A Realist Theory of Science* that were in principle open to me. One way, obviously, was the way I followed in the 1970s, which was to consider the transapplicability of the argument, or rather its results, to the domain of the social sciences, which I did in *The Possibility of Naturalism*. Another way was to go into the matter of the experimental physical sciences in much greater detail. That path has not actually been taken up very much by any critical realist to my knowledge. As the main thrust of *A Realist Theory of Science* is to understand science as concerned with the movement from events to explanatory structures, another path in principle open to me was to look in much more detail at the first term in this kind of dialectic, that is the nature of events as complex, as constituted in open systems. This is basically the province of applied or concrete critical realism. There are of course critical realist studies of particular concrete phenomena and subjects in open systems, but we do not have anything like a logic of the concrete as such.

The path I actually followed after *The Possibility of Naturalism* in the 1980s and 1990s was two-fold. First, the deepening of the ontology from the first level of critical realism to the other six levels of the ontological–axiological chain (MELDARA). That was undoubtedly the main thrust. Second, there was a subsidiary thrust into the conditions of the possibility of false or ideological forms, and this was the metacritical development.

After 2002 I turned to the logic of the concrete. This took me into the whole field of applied critical realism because I was now working with scientists, social scientists, philosophers and professionals of various kinds (such as social workers or teachers) who were concerned with concrete research projects and practices and wanted to apply critical realism. There is a book project I have in hand, which is not very far written, called *Applied Critical Realism*; it would be a research manual. The beginnings of something like a logic of the concrete is contained in my forthcoming book with Berth Danermark on interdisciplinarity and health.[1] So that is one thing I have been doing.

A second area moved very much into view in the period after 9/11. This was the problem of cultural and moral incommensurability. I think to some extent we can think of what I called the fifth phase of the development of modernity, western bourgeois triumphalism, inaugurated in 1989 with the collapse of the Soviet Bloc, as falling into two sub-phases: an intense phase of globalisation under the dominance of market fundamentalism, followed by a second phase around about the time of 9/11 characterised by the clash and proliferation of fundamentalisms: the clash of market fundamentalism in alliance with Christian and perhaps also Jewish fundamentalism, on the one hand, with Islamic fundamentalism on the other, coupled with, and overlaid by, the breaking out of myriad local and petty fundamentalisms, chauvinisms and absolutisms. This is the period of the Bush–Blair 'war on terror'. Recently (August 2008) there are signs that we might be about to enter a new sub-phase, marked by a partial return to a multi-polar world (in which the emerging BRIC [Brazil, Russia, India, China] countries provide a partial counter-weight to US hegemony), increasing crises of international law and co-operation and the accentuated urgency of economic and ecological challenges. However the main features of the second sub-phase persist.

(September 2009[2]). The financial crisis of September 2008 onwards and the current economic recession has been created most fundamentally by a triple disembedding: of money from the real economy; of the real economy from society; and of society from its spiritual infrastructure (or meta-Real basis). This has occurred in the context of the manifestation of symptoms of growing alienation and stress at all four planes of social being; and a growing increase in inequality in many of the advanced western countries, in which income no longer bears any relation to merit, effort or need, a fact widely apprehended and inducing a normative crisis, a crisis of legitimacy in the economic order and the social relations it presupposes, a crisis of social justice. The crises at the level of social structure and our transactions with nature have been coupled in the UK with a breakdown in trust in the governing classes (the parliamentary expenses scandal). In the USA, in the week of the Pittsburgh G-20 meeting, Obama is besieged by raucous critics from the right and the traditional working-class left, who have lost faith in the project of globalisation at the very time when U.S. governmental action is most needed to take the measures which are required now – at the Copenhagen climate change conference in December 2009 (towards which some of us critical realists are making our own intervention[3]) – if ecological catastrophe is to be avoided.

What is required in the short and transitional run includes (1) re-regulation of finance and the economy; (2) the reconstitution of a public sphere nurturing an extended and deepened democracy in which the quality of information and the depth of discussion becomes as important as, and a condition for, voting; (3) the defence and rebuilding of a public sector and a welfare state with a renovated public sphere in which informed and reasoned decisions can once more take place over collective, including economic, decisions (i.e. over social welfare and objective functions); and (4) a state which is unafraid to intervene in the market to implement social choices and at the same time opens itself up to the participation of an informed public. In the not-so-long run, we require the silent revolution of the meta-Real against the demi-real.

In all this, ideas, and a fortiori intellectuals (the more organic the better), have a great potential role to play in concrete utopian projects at all levels – about alternative productions, distributions, rates of growth and life-styles or ways of living. A multi-polar world externally and internally (i.e. within a nation state) gives us greater scope than we have had for some time and new opportunity to begin to implement our concrete utopian visions, at least in some measure, wherever we are.

In this context, the thesis of cultural incommensurability, that civilisations cannot talk to each other, re-visits the thesis of paradigm incommensurability floated by Kuhn and Feyerabend in the 1960s on a moral plane. If you assume that force is ultimately the only way to resolve these issues, as is still widely assumed on all sides, including most recently by David Miliband,[4] then you will not really have the possibility of any non-violent response. I did a great deal of work on the problem of moral incommensurability, the results of which will be published in a book provisionally called *Understanding, Peace and Security*. This took me back into consideration of issues of non-violence and I would very much like to give a fuller account – I have given talks on it – of Gandhi's *satyagraha*, his theory of non-violence, which is also a theory of social change. It is not a theory of compliance or acquiescence to oppression, but a theory about how to deal with it. And of course he was the figurehead in an arguably very successful campaign to get the British out of India. I would like very much at some point to do a hermeneutic study of Gandhi. It might be very interesting to put this alongside other figures outside of traditional western philosophy in a book of hermeneutic studies of thinkers such as Kant and Marx. That is a project that is still to come.

In *Understanding, Peace and Security* I formulate two axioms – of universal solidarity and what I call axial rationality – which I think are very strong. They provide the metatheoretical underpinnings to attempts to transcend incommensurability in practice. But of course this leads immediately into the philosophy of meta-Reality, so a third thing I have been doing in recent years is attempting to refocus the themes, or some of the themes and theses, of meta-Reality; and I would like to put this work together into a short book. First, and in particular, I have resumed my interest in the problem of modernity. I have extended the concept back in time, such that I now view western modernity as a particular capitalist and European form of development of civilisational structures that are far older. That takes one back to the axial revolutions of the first millennium BCE that we talked about last time, then sideways to Indigenous societies, because they have been carrying on more or less successfully sustaining themselves the whole time. I am also looking at the particular forms that modernity took, especially as they have been theorised around motifs such as Eurocentricity, and at alternative modernities, or more generally alternative routes from the level of axiality that would be a necessary condition of human being in the future. Second, at a personal level there is an interest in the great classical religions, and I already have a project that will be a follow-up on *From East to West* called *Beyond East to West*. This will be a secular restatement of spirituality – of the argument that spirituality is a presupposition of emancipatory projects in general, that it is not the same as and does not depend upon religiosity, although for those who want religion that is always an option. Third, I have refocused meta-Reality on the esoteric sociology of everyday life: the way in which reciprocity, solidarity, tolerance, forgiveness, mutual understanding and even features such as reflexivity are actually there as part of the humus and matrix of social life, a hidden or at least unrecognised substratum that is a tremendous resource for the struggle against oppression. Once we begin to see this unnoticed substratum everywhere, it can be tied in with the reconciliatory aims of the *Understanding, Peace and Security* project by looking at the way in which something like the golden rule is accepted as important in every society, because it is a necessary condition for social bonding, and we are a social species. Actually, the golden rule needs to be amended to take into account the great gain of modernity, recognition of individuality, because we are not all the same, we are concretely singular individuals, so you need to do unto the other, not so much as you would, but as they would be done by, that is, according to their specificities and differences. But it is a very good start.

A fourth development, following on from this, is a renewed and deepened interest in education associated with my taking up a position in October 2007 as World Scholar at the Institute of Education in the University of London. The project of education has to be understood in principle as a life-long one concerned with enhancing, critiquing, refining and transforming the componential springs or bases of human action. There is nothing that happens at any of the planes of our social being that is not mediated through intentional action. The components of action are set out diagramatically in Figure 2.29 in *Dialectic*.[5] They include beliefs, feelings, values and norms, wants, and needs and capabilities for expression and for performative efficiency, supplemented by skills and facilities (access to resources), and it is the task of education to enhance them. Education is thus not only life-long but also as wide and broad as the intentional activities one engages in, and it can be as deep, furthermore, as the levels of rationality I sketched out in *Scientific Realism and Human Emancipation*.[6] Moreover, it needs to be deep if we are going to consciously, rationally change society. Following on from this, finally, there is of course my renewed interest in the problems of actually existing socialism. These are the areas in which I have been working.

MH: Do you want to comment on the setting up of the Foundation for Meta-Reality?

RB: The motivation behind it was basically the same as in the case of the other critical realist organisations and institutions, which I have already commented on. But there were two additional motives. First, I felt that meta-Reality was in danger of getting lost or emasculated in the official structures of critical realism itself, because as you know there was a great deal of hostility to it. I also felt, in the second place, that academics were not likely to be the main supporters and beneficiaries of this philosophy, and I wanted the Foundation to provide a basis for talking to non-academics about it. Of course, in exactly the same way there is a need to involve non-academics in the activities and organisations of first-level critical realism and dialectical critical realism, as they experience it as helping and empowering their practice.

MH: Last time I asked you whether meta-Reality was necessary for carrying through the anti-anthropic intent of your system. Part of your answer was that there was in fact no intent; anti-anthropism was rather a consequence of your search for truth, and in particular I take it of your determination to question the 'very widespread assumption of western thought . . . that basically we do not really have any grounds for anything in life. Any grounds for belief.'[7] If by some kind of clairvoyance you could have known at the outset, that is, in the late 1960s or early 1970s, where your quest would take you, what if anything would have surprised you? During your journey, did you ever feel that you might have to give up on some of the earlier stuff; that you had reached a point at which you might have to leave some or much of what you had achieved behind? Were there – are there – moments of crisis and radical doubt?

RB: I think in a peculiar way I would have been surprised to know that I was going to be a philosopher for the rest of my life. I did not foresee that. I would also have been surprised to learn that I would be as constrained by economic necessity to the extent that I have been. This has to do with the social conditions of the time: there was a feeling that such things would take care of themselves, everyone would be looked after. I and many of my friends had a feeling, an optimism and a naive confidence, that given that we did have talent there would not really be a problem about reproducing our material being; in other words, we would not have a problem getting reasonable jobs. And of course when someone is young, as Buddha pointed out, they also do not feel that they are going to be subjected to physical ill-health. Because of my struggle against parental restrictions in childhood and adolescence, I was aware of the level of risk involved in trying to realise your dharma in some sense, but in the late 1960s and early 1970s any problem of economic survival seemed inconceivable.

MH: In retrospect one can see that you did not play the game to maximise your career prospects. But had you played it, you probably would not have been able to write books such as *Dialectic*.

RB: It would have taken me a great deal longer. In some ways, the struggle to come into my dharma in my early years is mirrored in the struggle I have had for the last five or six years to be able to be in my dharma doing what I want to do. Of course, what I have been doing makes perfect sense in retrospect, there is a rationale, but it is not what I would have chosen. This is a continuing struggle.

MH: Is that the sum total of surprises – that you are a philosopher and afflicted by economic necessity?

RB: A third surprise is the problem I have recently had with my feet, occasioned by a neuropathy of unknown origin and manifest in a syndrome known as Charcot's disease, which has recently resulted in the amputation of my right foot and in my being constrained by physical necessity of a sort we do not imagine to be possible when we are young. There may of course be more surprises to come. But of course, at quite an early age I had a critique of historicism that meant that I knew I could not predict what I was going to be or do, so I do not think it would have totally surprised me that there were going to be so many dialectical twists and turns in both my life and the development of the system.

MH: Including spirituality?

RB: I might not have been able to see it at some stages, and I might have disliked it at others, but I do not think it would have been a total surprise. I certainly never gave up my awareness of the transcendent and my enjoyment of what I would now call non-dual experiences in life. I do not think I would have been surprised by it.

MH: What about the last part of the question: were there any moments of crisis and radical doubt in your intellectual development?

RB: Certainly from time to time I had a crisis turning on whether my environment would support and sustain me, because obviously whether you can survive and flourish depends not only on you yourself and whatever innate self-confidence you might have but on your environment. In Hegelian terms, I experienced moments of concern that I might suffer the fate of the Beautiful Soul in the sense that my ideas were too removed from conventional academic under-standing. Of course, the method of immanent critique is supposed to take account of that, but what it does not in itself specify is how hard or soft you should be, and I have from time to time gone to one extreme or the other: I have tended to be either too challenging to the environment, perhaps *From East to West* was a case of this; or not challenging enough, which is probably my natural disposition. I am very conscious of there being a delicate line. The method of immanent critique is a matter not only of balance in relation to the totality of one's life but also of discrimination and judgement about what people can take. *A Realist Theory of Science* did prove to be palatable in main-stream analytical philosophy in the sense that people read it and liked it. But then many just left it, not doing anything more with it. Nowadays, in turning my attention to the realm of education studies, I have tended mainly to listen to what people say – this is the first stage of immanent critique. But I am aware that at some point people need to be challenged, to have me say look, that is not right, your view of education as a process whereby knowledge is transmit-ted by a teacher leaves out all the questions raised by meta-Reality about what is already enfolded within, the process of its unfolding, the dialectic of learn-ing, and so on. The danger is that people will like the ideas but not do anything much with them. The whole process is a delicate one. It is a sensitive hermeneutic process involving people, getting their attention, talking to them, being open to learning from them – and of course you always need to do that for an immanent critique – but also getting them to see the transforma-tive possibilities inherent in what you are saying so that they can see how they need what you are proposing for their praxis. This presupposes that they have a domain of freedom; I suppose all academics do to a certain extent, but if they are very busy on research projects or subject to a strict timetable they might well feel they do not have the time or freedom to attend to the opportunities that the critique is offering them. For these kinds of reasons I am currently involved in a project to set up a Centre for Critical Realism and Education Studies so that a culture can be grown, a culture of critical realists involved in education.

So that is one enduring area of concern. There have been of course many more transient ones. Thus I was concerned whether I would ever get my

DPhil, whether I would ever lick the problem of dialectic, whether the meta-Reality books would ever be acceptable to my existing constituency. I think these are mundane crises that befall any intellectual or any writer.

MH: The method of immanent critique does of course have its advantages. If you can locate and remedy absences in the best that is going, you can be sure that you have done as well as can be, that you occupy the intellectual high-ground. I was going to ask you if, after the better part of a lifetime deploying it, you think it has any downside, but you have just answered that really, at least in part. How would you respond to the suggestion one sometimes hears that, in the dialectical and more particularly the spiritual turn, you have moved from a philosophical practice of underlabouring for science via immanent and transcendental critique to one in which philosophy is master-science?

RB: Immanent critique, as you know, is just the first stage of critique; it always has to be followed up by omissive critique and then explanatory critique. There is always a danger that you will forget this and become so involved in the immanent practice itself that you drown in it. So that is a further possible downside. That is the problem with what the Trotskyists used to call 'deep entryism': that you go in, join the Labour Party, prove your trustworthiness, become an MP and eventually a very conservative Prime Minister – and your socialism sinks without trace. It can be averted if you keep in mind that the follow-up to immanent is omissive and then explanatory critique – that there will be something wrong with the practice, something that can be explained in terms of its social context. I was never in danger of forgetting that in most of my work, except momentarily when reading Hegel and, as I have recounted, to some extent during the investigative phase of the spiritual turn. This is of course the result of a very soft approach in which the immanence outweighs the critical element, but then the converse is also a danger: being impatient, not going into the practice fully and coming out with too hard and premature judgements. This is the sort of shrill, ungrounded criticism that normally passes for critique. Ideally critique involves a perfect intellectual balance, and I think in one or two places in my books I have achieved that.

   As for the objection that my later work is in the tradition of philosophy as master-science rather than as underlabourer for the sciences, what this betrays is a lack of appreciation of how much can in fact be said by relatively a priori arguments. They are of course only relatively a priori because you are taking on board some data in your premises, but there are two essential things you have to remember here. The first is that transcendental and dialectical arguments are continuous with explanatory-retroductive arguments, and the second is categorial realism. The form of the transcendental argument is exactly the same as a substantive explanatory-retroductive argument in science – and it has exactly the same status. What distinguishes the philosophical deployment of this argument-form is the fact that you are talking about the most abstract features of the domain of reality, whereas when you are advancing explanatory-retroductive substantive arguments in science you are talking about more concrete features. In philosophy we talk about substance, whereas a chemist would talk about iron or copper, which are substances and which instantiate what the philosophy, if true, is saying about substance. The other thing the objection overlooks is categorial realism. This is indispensable for critical realism because otherwise you have a two-world, split ontology. Critical realism avoids such a split by upholding a stratified and differentiated monism that applies to the form of arguments as well, and of course the whole project is to underlabour for emancipatory practices among which I include science. I have always been concerned to elaborate a general conceptual schema for the sciences.

MH: Yes, I think people who make the objection misconstrue underlabouring negatively as doing a bit of conceptual tidying up or removing debris for the sciences when in fact you have always been concerned with the more positive side of this, that is, with delineating the general contours of the world at an abstract level.

RB: What *A Realist Theory of Science* says is shocking: that we have got science wrong in our philosophy – what science discloses is something fantastic, a very rich and deep world, and the nature of the disclosing, science itself, is an exciting and arduous process of transformation and revolution that has been overlooked in philosophy.

MH: Last time we agreed that the developmental logic of your thought has undergone three main phases: critical realism, dialectical critical realism, and the philosophy of meta-Reality. Would you want to say that any of these were more crucial or fundamental than the others? If we descend to the next level of specificity and take your books, Ted Benton, for example, thinks *A Realist Theory of Science* is your most important book,[8] whereas I would be inclined to say that *Dialectic* is, while recognising that it was possible only on the basis of your previous work and is itself unfinished business. What do you think? With the benefit of hindsight, what would you say were your most crucial and far-reaching insights and breakthroughs? I have been struck during these interviews by the way in which you keep coming back to depth-stratification as a fundamental lack in other positions, so perhaps you feel that that is the most far-reaching? On the other hand, from an emancipatory point of view the theory of explanatory critique could be seen to be your most radical breakthrough since it is pretty axiomatic in the scientific community that values are science-free.

RB: The three great errors of western philosophy are the epistemic fallacy, ontological monovalence, and what I call primal squeeze on the Platonic–Aristotelian fault-line. The answer to primal squeeze is of course the alethic depth-stratification of the world, which includes beliefs. So it is a very

204 Where do we go from here?, 2002–

important theme and can be very useful in pointing up a fundamentally correct intuition premised on lack of stratification. Thus for example when Shankara talked about what I call demi-reality as an illusion, he did not clarify that illusion is real, as real as steel; it is not just the absolute that is real. You need the stratification of reality to situate this by transposing the realm of illusion into the realm of demi-reality and seeing that as embedded within the realm of duality, itself reposing on the realm of non-duality. But important as it is, I would not say basic, first-level or -wave critical realism is more fundamental than the dialectical or spiritual moments or waves. I think what you have in terms of the main phases of my thought is an asymmetry between presuppositions and implications. You could argue that meta-Reality is the most fundamental because it actually presupposes the other two, but it would be equally logical to say that the transcendental realism of *A Realist Theory of Science* is the most fundamental because it is a necessary condition for the others. So there is a kind of asymmetry of presuppositions and implications. You cannot really say that any one is more important than the other.

I would say the same of the major themes and theses of each of the main phases. They are all fundamental. Here is a bare list. In that part of basic critical realism which is transcendental realism: the revindication of ontology together with the method of transcendental arguments; the stratification you have within it; and then the fact that you have emergence. In critical naturalism: the situation of intentional causality and therefore synchronic emergent powers materialism as the mechanism by which mind acts on the world; the transformational model of social activity; and the critique of Hume's law. These are fundamental to the project of social science and rational self-emancipation. In dialectical critical realism, in relation to the first aim I set myself, the dialectical deepening of critical realism: the extraction of the *rational kernel* of Hegelian dialectic as the general form or logic of progressive change; the isolation of the *mystical shell*, which is ontological monovalence or the elimination of absence – which is fundamental to the logic of freedom, because to understand praxis properly you have to see how all praxis is an absenting of an absence; what I called the *golden nugget* or the co-presence of absence and presence; and the *platinum plate* or the way in which philosophical mistakes can point to the social absurdities and errors that underlie them. Then, in relation to the second aim, the dialectics of freedom: the deepening of the logic of emancipation to include the dialectic of desire to freedom and eudaimonia. And then, third, the totalising critique of western philosophy. I have perhaps not stressed enough that this metacritique isolates the general form of irrealism, and that it points the way directly to the philosophy of identity in meta-Reality. In meta-Reality, splits and alienations are resolved and embedded within a rich, differentiated, and developing monistic structure. Then you have the moments of this new philosophy of identity – the ground-state, the cosmic envelope and the themes of non-duality, co-presence and so on.

So that is really what I want to say. All these theses and themes are fundamentally important. You cannot say that one is more important than another.

From one point of view the move to establish or vindicate ontology is the most important, from another the view of ground-states lying on the cosmic envelope and the dynamics I have recently been working on of how you get reconciliation between human beings through ground-state to ground-state interaction is the most important, because this is the way we must move forward.

MH: You say that the metacritique of irrealism in the second wave points the way directly to the concept of the ground-state and the philosophy of meta-Reality. Would you say the same of your thematisation of absence and the logic of freedom? What is the connection there?

RB: Yes. Human freedom is, and depends upon, the absenting of absences (constraints) and it is attained when we are flourishing in a eudaimonistic society. For this, we must be at one with our ground-state; without that, there is a constraint upon our well-being and flourishing imposed from within.

MH: I turn now to the question of where we go from here. The question of the political implications of critical realism, if any, recently surfaced – as it does from time to time – on the Critical Realism List, and was discussed at some length. Some feel that critical realism is above politics, or at any rate indifferent in its implications as between left and right; others feel that critical realism has no political implications but that dialectical critical realism does; others that it is a philosophy of the left. How would you summarise this matter? Would you describe yourself as a philosopher of the left?

RB: This is a very interesting question. What I would like to say is that in one sense I agree with the claim that critical realism is above politics, and in another sense I clearly am a philosopher of the left. The sense in which critical realism is above politics is a *synchronic* one. It is above politics in that ex ante, before it does its work, it does not take sides but typically seeks to show how apparently contradictory philosophical positions leave out a crucial feature of the domain – and this actually holds true of many human conflicts – and then of course ex post, after the philosophical work of critical realism, you have a more inclusive totality. And so critical realism attempts to usher in a more inclusive conceptual totality that can inform transformative praxis and make it more rational, *ceteris paribus*, in open systems. In transcending oppositions in this way it does of course have practical implications. This is the way it seeks to be a practically aefficacious philosophy. *Diachronically*, however, one has to say that, adopting the standpoint I have sketched, which is roughly that of dialectical critical realism, developmentally and genealogically critical realism is a philosophy of the left in so far as it favours more inclusive totalities and what it is doing is isolating absences that include social inequities and imbalances that exist in social life, and it is this that powers the system.

Of course, what I have said so far does not really get us very far if you have two bodies of armed human beings confronting each other, for example.

However, meta-Reality suggests a technique for resolving oppositions. To take the case of armed conflict, what the critical realist peace worker would basically try to do is to get the warring parties to sit down with each other in their ground-states and talk to each other; and on the basis of that hermeneutic they would, at least in the ideal case, come to see that they had a common interest in tackling relevant common problems and constraints – it might be a common bully or a structure of master–slave relations or a natural constraint. The value of the hermeneutic encounter and the exchange of positions is that, when you are talking with someone in this way, you cannot in general any longer be afraid of them, and if you are to go on in transcendental identification with them, empathetically talking to them, you cannot at the same time beat them up (you would be beating up what is now experienced as part of yourself). Just being in a situation in which you have to talk to someone means that you have to empathise with them a little, and so you begin to see their point of view. Of course, it is easier to get the two parties to move to common ground that allows them to see how a practical reconciliation could be achieved if you are armed with an explanatory critical theory. This will give them a clear conception of the ground of their opposition and their mutual interest in removing it. Very often it will also involve a crucial moment of concrete utopianism in which the parties, having perhaps concluded that there is no way they can do anything about the ground now, imagine a possible future. They will then need a third thing, which is a theory of transition – how you actually get to it. All of this might allow some good strategic action oriented to the removal of the ground and the construction of the concretely utopianly imagined and envisioned realm. Now you cannot actually get this hermeneutic off the ground unless you get them both in or moving towards their ground-states. They are then in a state of maximal negentropy, maximally alert and maximally flexible – and many peace negotiations go astray because the parties are just re-stating well-rehearsed positions. An instance of something like this in practice was the Truth and Reconciliation Commission established by Nelson Mandela in South Africa after the ending of Apartheid (the full experience of which has to be looked into).

MH: Arguably what it fundamentally achieved was a reconciliation to the existing class structure, the alethic untruth of which is currently becoming apparent.

RB: Yes, rather than the isolation under explanatory critical theory of the ground that had to be removed. But you see, at the end of the day capitalism is not kept in business by anything other than people, including the soldiers, and when they walk away, then it will go, just as actually existing socialism in the Soviet Union went. Change is ineluctable.

MH: Even considered diachronically, then, although it comes out of the tradition of the left, there is a sense in which critical realism wants to go beyond left and right. That is the overall trajectory: transcending the big oppositions.

RB: When it stops moving towards that goal, the left becomes ostracised and part of the problem.

MH: The philosophy of meta-Reality gives an unequivocal metatheoretical answer to the question of what is to be done: 'What we have to do is, as Krishna did in the *Bhagavad Gita*, resolve the problem of action by an expanded conception of the self. The Leninist question "what is to be done?" has to be resolved by asking the transcendental question "who am I?" or "what is the self?"'[9] What follows more concretely from this in terms of what is to be done, in particular in relation to the Leninist answer?

RB: From the point of view of meta-Reality one wants a practice oriented to universal self-realisation at all levels of four-planar social being, including levels that do not explicitly thematise themselves as political. The practice of actually existing socialism, as we have discussed, was fixated on one level, namely the level of social structure and even so did not really attempt to carry out the socialist vision of that level, which was to transfer power to the immediate producers in the labour process. That was never done; instead, one master–slave economy and society was replaced with another. The Leninist project has to be radicalised to include all levels of social being. At the plane of the embodied personality, this immediately sets you on a path to self-realisation in which you are engaged in practice at all the other planes of social being. And necessarily so because, as you become less egoistical and less full of heteronomous emotions and prejudices, you come to see that your own freedom depends on the freedom of everyone else and your practice comes to be oriented to the abolition of master–slave relations everywhere, including master–slave relations you have internalised and master–slave relations you have imposed on nature. So what is to be done involves breaking with the one-dimensionality of traditional projects for socialism.

The only way I can conceive the good society for humans being achieved is through the freeing up of our agency by the abolition of heteronomous elements that impede it wherever it is. If you can transform relations at the workplace, that is what you must do. If you cannot do this, then you must improve relations in your family, and of course you might have to take tactical decisions. Gandhi, for example, was notoriously bad with his family and many of his friends. This was a necessity, he felt, for the sake of the role he could play in the struggle for Indian freedom. Very few people today would accept that kind of justification, and that is probably a good thing, because we want to aim as high as we can. Moreover, this vision does not deny that there might be difficult decisions that you have to take in the realm of necessity. So while political change requires a concerted orientation to, and attack on, all planes of social being, the dominant moment is going to be that of our transformed transformative praxis, and that amounts to engaged self-realisation oriented to the project of universal self-realisation.

MH: In *From Science to Emancipation* you explicitly link the question of what is to be done, and the necessary change in our conception of our selves, to

> 'the politics of disenchantment', the politics of Nietzsche and Weber and the politics of social democracy . . . which has so profoundly influenced the politics of the left. We need to produce a different conception of ourselves in the world. The revolution will be nothing less than this: the transformation of our understanding of ourselves and of the whole world in which we live, our situation in the cosmos.[10]

It could be, then, that one of the ways forward at the level of philosophy is a closer engagement with Nietzsche. Of course, at one level, in terms of political implications, as in other ways, there could not be a greater contrast. In a definitive recent study, the Italian Hegelian scholar, Dominico Losurdo,[11] has shown pretty convincingly that, contrary to the fashionable view that he was above politics, Nietzsche was through and through a philosopher of the right, the great modern antagonist of Rousseau, Marx and generalised human emancipation. Thus Nietzsche's consistent basic concern was to nip the modern revolutionary tradition in the bud, whereas yours has been to rejuvenate and enrich it. Nietzsche's perspective is that of the unmediated domination of a revitalised master-class, yours is the transcendence of master–slavery in all its forms. Where Nietzsche thematises will to power and egoism unbridled by altruism, you thematise moral alethia and the pulse of freedom. Yet arguably, precisely because Nietzsche is such a great champion of the master-classes, he has much to teach us from an emancipatory point of view: the impossibility of founding a eudaimonian politics on resentment, for example, and the need to move beyond slavery and any kind of overmanliness as such, as well as diagnostic clues to the real basis of the current round of the 'imperialism of human rights', which he exposes as a sham.

RB: It is important to have an understanding and a good critique of Nietzsche and Nietzscheanism. The first thing I would like to say is that what has been called the hermeneutics of suspicion is extremely valuable and is an important part of critical realist emancipatory axiology, because what it draws attention to are precisely the heteronomous elements in human life: the power and aefficacy of what has not been resolved. This links in to my second point, which is a critical one: that Nietzsche and Nietzscheanism is a philosophy based on the repression, denial and forgetting of what has not been included in the totality; it is a philosophy of split in which some values and some human beings are privileged over other human beings, issuing in a politics of split. The whole thrust of Nietzscheanism is to forget what you must forget, which of course in our world is that the masters exist in virtue of the slaves and their activity. Freud has shown that the strategy of forgetting is untenable. The conscious exists in virtue of the unconscious, you cannot just forget about the unconscious. What you have to do is redress the imbalance, the asymmetry, between the top component and the bottom component. If you forget about it, you are excluding it from the totality of your concerns and will pay the price of this omission. The strategy of forgetting is however typically the standpoint or position of oppressing masters; it is what the neo-conservatives around Bush did: they forgot about the culture and traditions of Iraq, and the vibrant Iraqi human beings – all became just part of the project.

MH: The neo-conservatives are incarnations of the Nietzschean philosophy.

RB: Absolutely. So the Achilles' heel of Nietzscheanism is that it draws attention to heteronomy, and then the impossible answer is forget about it – do not bother about it, rise above it. Of course, this is the very dualistic standpoint of radical split and master–slave society. So what we have to do is situate both the Nietzschean problem and the Nietzschean answer within the structures of dialectical critical realism and meta-Reality, within a moving conceptual formation that will incorporate the repressed and resolve this aporia. What Nietzscheanism overlooks or neglects is not only that what has been forgotten, denied or repressed is (1) actually part of a totality with, and (2) bound eventually to be causally aefficacious on, the unforgotten, affirmed part, but also – and this is my third point – the dialectics of co-presence, namely, that (3) what is excluded is just the unrecognised or undeveloped part of yourself. Such exclusion is the basis of all oppositions according to the philosophy of meta-Reality. The person you are fighting with is just bringing out or developing aspects of yourself that you have not acknowledged. That is at the deepest level. Of course, at more superficial levels you can apply other modes of criticism and understanding, but at the end of the day that is what the repressed is. The repressed is what you yourself have not developed. And when you have developed it – this is the thrust of Freud – there is then no need to repress it at all because it will now be part of your moral economy in sublated or sublimated form. It is of course very difficult actually to achieve a society that incorporates all the oppressed such that there are no longer any master–slave-type distinctions and oppressions, but that is the only position that is tenable. Sooner or later this process of sublating and radically incorporating will yield joy, you will experience those bits of yourself that you have left out as enjoyable and rewarding and wonder why you did not think about and acknowledge this before.

MH: So in fundamental ways your philosophy could be viewed as a response to Nietzsche: if you think in terms of thesis, antithesis, synthesis you have something like Hegel/Marx, Nietzsche, Bhaskar. But I take it you did not consciously intend this; you do not engage with Nietzsche in detail, it is mostly implicit.

RB: I am not sure whether I will have time to get round to it but of course it might be that this way of looking at my work is the best way, in which case I will have to make time. There is no doubt that Nietzsche together with Heidegger, who combines Nietzsche and hermeneutics, are the most influential philosophers in the vogue part of the academy at any rate, because they are the thinkers the poststructuralists are mainly indebted to.

MH: I think it was Gary MacLennan who first described the critical realist project as a 'long march' through the academy, and it strikes me as in some ways pretty apt. It is not just a matter of 'winning the intellectual high ground' for eudaimonia, as you have put it,[12] but of getting the dialectics of emancipation going in the sense of a proliferating array of progressive research programmes organically articulated with wider social movements. The weakness of this strategy seems to me the structural positioning of your typical academic as prone to insecurity and careerism. Standing in the way is thus one of the main sources of error in western philosophy on your own account, fear of change. What is to be done?

RB: I think you are absolutely right about the insecurity and careerism of the typical academic. This is a long-standing structural feature of intellectuals. Throughout the written history of civilisations, at any rate, they have been a dependent stratum, and today the academy is very implicated in the structures of government, globalisation, market fundamentalism and so on. They are thus even more vulnerable than they have been historically. The only way you can overcome this is to cultivate a sense of solidarity within the academy. The critical realist workshop in Cambridge, the new Institute of Advanced Studies in Lancaster, and the critical realist book series with Routledge indicate some ways forward. Then you have the autonomous institutions of critical realism: the Centre for Critical Realism (CCR), the developing International Centre for Critical Realism and Education/Education Studies (CCRES), the International Association for Critical Realism (IACR) together with its journal (*Journal of Critical Realism*), and within IACR you have regional bodies such as the Australasian Association for Critical Realism and the Nordic Network of Critical Realism, and also developing national bodies such as the Danish Network of Critical Realism and new thematically oriented groupings such as the Critical Realism in Action Group in the UK.

MH: There might well soon be a Latin American Association arising out of the 2009 IACR conference in Rio.

RB: There are signs that things are happening in North America too, partly as a result of the Philadelphia conference in 2007, and something like this has been on the cards in India for some time too. A European-wide network could also be in the offing. Also encouraging are recent developments in Italy, France and Germany, which for a long time were difficult constituencies for critical realism to gain a foothold in because they have their own, very strong national traditions. In Italy there is a great deal of critical realist activity, including translations of books such as *The Possibility of Naturalism* and an

Italian critical realist reader. There is also a project for a French reader and in Berlin this academic year there has been a weekly seminar in critical realism. We already have relatively better reception in Iberia and in Greece, together with the growth of critical realism within the Nordic areas. That leaves eastern Europe, but there are things happening there too. I was recently asked to go and do interviews in Moscow, and Jamie Morgan stepped into my shoes when I could not find the time. There is also quite a strong critical realist presence in Turkey.

MH: Japan is perhaps another. There are institutions subscribing to the journal.

RB: That's right, and there are Japanese translations now of *A Realist Theory of Science* and *The Possibility of Naturalism*. There is also a Korean translation of one of my books. The philosophy of meta-Reality, as the work of Seo MinGyu suggests, holds out the prospect of a reappraisal of Taoism and Confucianism that might attract interest in China. And then of course there is considerable interest in South Asia, especially India, and southern Africa. So this is the way forward in the academy.

MH: What about outside the academy – where do we go there?

RB: There is no general answer, but if you take specific cases then you can see a way forward. You have to look at this problem in a concretely singular way. In some countries there are strong traditions of self-education and self-improvement that can be tapped into, for example in America and then of course India. Again, many research projects have a proleptically organic form that necessitates involvement with people outside the academy. You cannot really do a project on health workers or social workers without talking to them and that gives rise to the possibility of setting up discussion groups and workshops. In Sweden, as a consequence, there are I think very few social workers who do not know something about critical realism. I have been to Umeå a couple of times, where there is an excellent critical realist presence in the academy, but many of these are not conventional academics – they include for instance organic intellectuals with strong roots in the social work community. I call such persons 'organic critical realists'. Sweden is of course a special case, but one will have particularities in each context. In the case of Australia, for example, there is much critical realist work being done in education studies that often involves organic links to communities. One of the first areas in which critical realism caught on was in management and organisational studies and management science, so there is interest in critical realism even in the business community. If you think of business as an enemy, that is fine, but do remember there are critical realists in the business schools. It is obviously a long struggle to make critical realism part of the common sense of the age, but it is important to remember, as we have discussed, that critical realism is already implicit in everyday life, and this is a tremendous resource.

MH: Considered as an intellectual tradition, critical realism is by any standard pretty impressive, as you have indicated. In little more than thirty years it has become a genuinely international movement, underlabouring for a rich array of research programmes across the social sciences and increasingly in the humanities, with growing interest in some of the non-human sciences. Yet this is not without seeming paradox. In particular, one notes that its impact in philosophy has been much less marked than in social theory and the social sciences, though this is changing, and that, in the main intellectual vehicles of left and left-liberal opinion, such as (in the UK) *Radical Philosophy, New left Review*, or *London Review of Books*, philosophers such as Alain Badiou, Giles Deleuze and Slavoj Žižek, who cannot match you in terms of impact across the academy as distinct from some sections within it, are far more in vogue than yourself.[13] What is your take on this apparent paradox?

RB: I am quite happy for you to give your reasons for it and ask me to comment on them.

MH: I would adduce three main reasons. (1) Because of its emphasis in an age of judgemental relativism and actualism on scientific knowledge as necessary for emancipation, first-level critical realism (hence, for some, your whole project) is wrongly regarded as scientistic or even positivist in some quarters. (2) Most left philosophy ultimately operates in a fundamental sense within the tradition of western philosophy and within the paradigm of the bourgeois enlightenment. Your totalising metacritique of both, issuing ultimately in the spiritual turn, is experienced as threatening in an academy not much given to dialectic and where the default position is atheism. (3) Relatedly, your philosophy is, perhaps uniquely, uncompromisingly revolutionary and anti-capitalist. Quite a few critical realists, let alone mainstream scholars, reject explanatory critique (the move from facts to values), not to mention the emancipatory axiology of the dialectical turn and 'the universal silent revolution'[14] of the spiritual one. It strikes me that, to be more in vogue while capitalism (notwithstanding that it is now in deep crisis) still seems to most the only game in town, you would need to be operating on the terrain of modernism and postmodernism, that is, fundamentally within the problematic of the philosophical discourse of modernity rather than diagnosing its problematicity as crucially linked to our power$_2$-stricken condition and transcending it from within in an attempt to move to a new paradigm of enlightenment. In sum: science, dialectic and spirituality, and revolutionism, both philosophical and practical.

   If I had to choose between the three, I would pick the first. Notwithstanding the important qualifications about fallibilism and epistemic relativity, you have been above all on about alethic truth and its indispensability for human emancipation. That is what the left and left-liberal avant garde, in an age of spin and institutionalised lying for which they help to provide a rationale, finds so unpalatable. Thus whereas Žižek, for example, emphatically endorses Hegel's subjective anthropic and actualist view that there is nothing behind the 'curtain' of appearances that veils reality other than what the subject who goes behind it to look puts there herself, such that there are no 'objective social fact[s]',[15] you demonstrate that this view entails the anomaly of a second self-consciousness appearing 'out of the blue' in the dialectic of master and slave, which only the alethic truth of our common humanity as a natural kind and of the priority of dialectics of solidarity, trust and love over those of recognition can resolve.[16] Eric Hazan, commenting on the scene in France today, has put the general point well:

> It makes little sense to demand transparency: the appointment of committees of inquiry, mediators, observers, high authorities of all kinds; what we need to demand is the truth. But that would run against one of the basic postulates of the postmodern thinking that guides the champions of 'pragmatism' and inspires their speeches, in which the word 'concretely' appears in every other sentence. According to this postulate, truth is a relative notion, a matter of interpretations between which it is impossible to decide, each of them casting a distorted reflection on the others.[17]

'What we need to demand is the truth.' That, for me, is your fundamental message, and what I most deeply appreciate in your work. It is one that is out of kilter with its age, for central to all the main tendencies of the philosophy of late modernity is the displacement of the metaphysics of truth by the question of language and meaning.[18]

RB: I think I agree with the three main reasons you give. What is really important to remember about the stress on science is that I do not see science as being opposed to humanity; there is not a contrast between science and the realm of humanity, culture, and history, nor in particular is there another contrast between science and emancipation. Science properly understood, which is the crucial thing, is an agent of emancipation, and what I think we have to stress here is that for critical realism science is always specific to its subject-matter. Positivism's standard received view of science is doubly wrong in the field of the human world, because it is not an account of what natural science does, let alone of what social science or any other form of science does. Undoubtedly the fact that critical realism starts from science lends itself to the charge of scientism, so let me just reiterate why I started there. I started from science because it was the most prestigious intellectual practice and I was concerned about problems of poverty and so on in the Third World. It was obvious to me that we needed to understand, first, what the problem was, then to correct it. So it was a pragmatic interest in science that initially led me to formulate the critical realist project. It is true that science has yielded some extraordinarily impressive cognitive structures, and that Marx, Freud and other agents of liberation could see themselves as scientists. That is all on the positive side. What we have to understand is that, if you have a subject-matter that you want to study scientifically, you are in principle free to argue the case for any method, providing it is grounded in some way in the nature of your subject-matter. There are certain moves that one might see as essential to science given such a wide brief. One is the attempt to move from the already known, given, superficial or obvious to its explanation; another is that what you discover must be of potential utility for the project of human emancipation. Those are virtually the only constraints. So I really cannot understand objections to critical realism on the grounds that it is scientistic, and of course critical realism is very critical of the abusive practices of science.

MH: These objections come from people who reject or are hostile to science – in theory, although not often in practice.

RB: There are of course, as I have mentioned, those who think that critical realism is not scientific enough, for example in its theory of emergence. But that theory is posited precisely on a critique of reductionist science.

The second thing you mention is dialectic and spirituality. Now a big opposition is normally posited here between the emphasis on self and emphasis on society, but again I think what I have done in the theory of universal self-realisation is break this opposition down. The way to be a good social agent is to be in touch with and informed by your ground-state; you cannot then be oblivious to structural sin and ecological degradation, you must be an active agent involved in remedying them. Revolutionism, specifically anti-capitalism, has been opposed by many to spirituality. But you cannot ground capitalism in any religion that I know of. It systematically promotes gross sins, whether personal sins such as greed and avarice, or social sins such as the exploitation of your fellow human beings and insensitivity to their suffering. There is nothing in common between capitalism and spirituality. Just as we have a social spirituality, so we have more specifically an anti-capitalist one; an anticapitalist spirituality that does not neglect the self: in other words the onus is on you to make yourself a better person and a better agent of social change. This entails working on yourself, which means getting rid of your jealousies and prejudices. And actually I would add being in favour of emancipation to your trio of science, dialectic and spirituality, and revolutionism. There is a bit of us that does not like emancipation, that wants to remain stuck in master–slavery, and so is very concerned to flatten the emancipatory impulse. This is definitely one of the malign effects of Nietzscheanism. That is, if you talk about emancipation rather than supremacy then you are on the side of the slaves, in a context in which human beings have internalised master–slave relations. So in looking at your philosophy they will identify with the master in the dialectic of master and slave, and not like its outcome; they will take the side of the master without realising that the element of authentic mastery in their own personal lives is minimal.

MH: Nietzsche was right, they are pathetic.

RB: That is the value of understanding Nietzsche, although not of adopting a Nietzschean approach to life. So this is what I call a flattening. And that goes on in the academy as well, because any philosophy that is really going to make a difference is avoided like death. So I would say the fourth thing is the emancipatory impulse; that is the reason why critical realism is not in vogue – although it is attracting a lot of attention from those who really want to know.

MH: Emancipation entails revolution.

RB: Of course it does. I would add that, in so far as there is a touchstone, that must be truth. Truth is not something we make, it is something we discover and so the alethic conception of truth is very important, and arguably perhaps – I am agreeing with you – the single most important moment.

MH: It's implicit in the others – presupposed.

RB: It is. Unless you are committed to the truth you will be undermined: reality will get back at you. You might not live to see it as an embodied physical being, but you will not be well judged by posterity.

Endnotes

1 Childhood and adolescence

1 Bhaskar 2000: 4 et passim.
2 Gujranwala has since developed into a city of more than a million inhabitants, the fifth largest in Pakistan.
3 Wikipedia, 'Theosophy', http://en.wikipedia.org/wiki/Theosophy. See also especially Blavatsky 1995.
4 In orthodox Hinduism there were so many incarnations of Vishnu, who can be loosely related to God the Son in the Christian trinity. [RB].
5 'Heathen' or 'pagan' was a commonly used descriptor throughout the British Empire (and also in Western Europe and North America) for any person not of European descent who practised a non-Christian religion. Something of the opprobrium it conveyed, together with its far-flung pervasiveness, was brought home to me [MH] during a recent visit to the town cemetery in Gympie, Queensland, Australia, where my parents are buried: the cemetery is segregated not only on both class ('private' and 'public') and Euro-denominational (Church of England, Methodist, Roman Catholic, etc.) lines but also has a special ('public') 'Pagan' section containing the remains of Aboriginal Australians, South Sea Islanders, Chinese, South Asians and so on.
6 'It is alarming and nauseating to see Mr. Gandhi, a seditious Middle Temple lawyer, now posing as a fakir of a type well known in the East, striding half naked up the steps of the vice-regal palace, while he is still organising and conducting a campaign of civil disobedience, to parlay on equal terms with the representative of the Emperor-King' (Winston Churchill commenting in the House of Commons on Gandhi's meeting with the Viceroy of India in 1931, quoted in Ashe 1968: 37).

2 Oxford days

1 Bhaskar 2002c: 299.
2 Bhaskar [1975] 2008: 11.
3 Harré 1970.
4 Cf. Bhaskar [1975] 2008: 164, n. 39. Contrary to a common view that Harré was, with Bhaskar, co-founder of critical realism, it thus seems probable that, to the extent that he was, for a time, a transcendental realist, Harré was far more influenced by Bhaskar than vice versa. He had been reading Bhaskar's manuscripts since the second half of 1970. *A Realist Theory of Science* was completed in its present form as a thesis in the first term of 1974 and published as a book in December 1974. The book in which Harré's (transient) realism is perhaps most full-blooded (Rom Harré and E. H. Madden (1975) *Causal Powers: A Theory of Natural Necessity*) appeared in the following year.
5 For an account of one aspect of this, see Pratten 2009, esp. 200–5.

6 The development of the philosophical system of critical realism and meta-Reality falls into three main stages: critical realism (transcendental realism and critical naturalism), dialectical critical realism and the philosophy of meta-Reality. 'First-level' or 'basic' (or 'first-wave' or 'original') critical realism refers to the first of these stages, not just to 1M in the MELDARA schema. [RB].

7 Cf. note 4, above.

8 Since published as Harré 2009.

9 Bhaskar 2002c: 200.

10 'Great spirits have always found violent opposition from mediocrities. The latter cannot understand it when a man does not thoughtlessly submit to hereditary prejudices but honestly and courageously uses his intelligence' (*The New York Times*, March 19, 1940). Rejection of a highly creative academic thesis is thus by no means a fate unique to Bhaskar (although rejection of two such theses which both became famous books in their own right doubtless belongs in *The Guinness Book of Records*). When in 1925 Walter Benjamin's *The Origins of German Tragic Drama* was rejected by the University of Frankfurt as a *Habilitationschrift*, his professors adopted the strategy of the examiners of Bhaskar's first thesis (ignore it and hope it will go away), declaring that they were unable to find anything in the thesis relating to the topic (the philosophy of art). See Brodersen 1996: 146–50.

11 In so far as the anti-cringer shares this inability, anti-cringer and cringer are, in Bhaskar's later terminology, tacitly complicit dialectical antagonists whose opposition is ultimately phoney. Cringing/anti-cringing has its counterpart within the critical realist movement in the inability of some to acknowledge the philosophical stature of Bhaskar in a mature way, issuing in a tendency to puff their own work at the expense of his; or to recognise that metatheory necessarily and appropriately proceeds at a high level of abstraction, issuing in the inverse elitism of those who hold that it should be written in 'plain English'.

3 Beyond empiricism and transcendental idealism

1 Hilary Wainwright (1949–) is the founding editor of *Red Pepper*. She read PPE at St Anne's College, Oxford, graduating in 1970. She gained a BPhil in Sociology from St Antony's College, Oxford in 1973 (http://en.wikipedia. org/wiki/Hilary_ Wainwright).

2 Bhaskar [1975] 2008: 47.

3 Bunge 1977 and 1979.

4 Callinicos 2006: 159.

5 E.g. Bhaskar 2002a: 14.

6 Bhaskar [1975] 2008: 37.

7 Ibid.: 250.

8 Ibid.: 195; cf. 180–1.

9 Porpora 2007: 425.

10 Groff 2004: ch. 5.

11 Bhaskar [1975] 2008: 21.

12 Bhaskar 2002d: 67–93, 83–4.

13 Bhaskar [1993] 2008: 335 and Bhaskar 2000: 24 n. 4.

14 See Tyfield 2007a, and also 'The debate about transcendental arguments in critical realism', presentation to the seminar launch of *Dictionary of Critical Realism*, Institute of Education, London, 17 March 2007. See also Agar 2006 and David Tyfield's 2008 review of this book.

15 Westphal 2004. See the 2005 review essay of Westphal's book by Jamie Morgan.

16 Bhaskar [1993] 2008: 224f.

17 Paul Eluard, cited in White [1966] 1969: epigraph.

18 It is important not to confuse 'categorical' here with 'categorial', as in 'categorial realism'. Categorial realism refers to the existence of the categories (causality, law, etc.) independently of the categorising mind or community. Categorical as opposed to dispositional properties are those which constitute or inhere in a thing itself rather than its behaviour. [RB]
19 Groff 2009: 269–70.
20 Bhaskar [1975] 2008: 259.
21 Ibid.: 260.
22 Ibid.: 196.
23 Ibid.: 262.
24 Farnell forthcoming 2010.
25 Proleptically, this points the way to the concrete universal and stands to the emergence of 3L as emergence itself stands to that of 2E. [RB]

4 The critical realist embrace

1 Bhaskar [1979] 1998: 48.
2 Ibid.: 137.
3 Ibid.: 173.
4 See Hartwig, 'Duality and dualism', in Hartwig (ed.) 2007: 149–50.
5 Bhaskar [1993] 2008: 154–60.
6 Archer 2000: 87.
7 Jessop 2005: 47.
8 In *Dialectic* and subsequently, Bhaskar usually employs 'social cube' to refer to a sub-cube of four-planar social being comprising power$_2$, discursive/communicative and normative/moral relations, intersecting in ideology. See Hartwig, 'Human nature' and 'Social cube', in Hartwig (ed.) 2007: 243–4 and 420–1.
9 Bhaskar [1979] 1998: 97–8.
10 Bhaskar, 2000: 86.
11 Bhaskar [1979] 1998: 90, 101f.
12 Dean 2007. We are grateful to Kathryn Dean for permission to cite this paper. The quotes are from Bhaskar [1979] 1998: 103, 105.
13 World Health Organisation 1980.
14 Bhaskar [1979] 1998: 100; see also 29, 35, 81, 112.
15 Bhaskar [1986] 2009: 129.
16 Bhaskar 1994: 103.
17 Dean 2007: 15f.
18 Bhaskar [1979] 1998: 113–14.
19 Jenny Cobner typed the current manuscript from a recording. The exclamation marks are hers.

5 'Prolegomenon to a natural history of the human species'

1 Jameson 1984.
2 For a trenchant (immanent and explanatory) critique of the 'postmarxist' strand of postmodernism/poststructuralism in the last two decades of the twentieth century from a perspective that has strong affinities with critical realism, that of structural Marxism, see Boucher 2008.
3 Bhaskar 1989: 1.
4 Will 1980 and 1986.
5 Collier 1977.
6 For evidence that it is currently coming back into fashion, together with an indication of the striking fit between Freudian thought and critical realism, see Kran forthcoming 2010.

7 Cohen 1978 and Timpanaro 1976.
8 Bhaskar [1986] 2009: 'Preface'.
9 An earlier, incomplete, version of this Table appears in Hartwig, 'Introduction' to Bhaskar [1986] 2009: xiii.
10 Bhaskar [1986] 2009: 16.
11 Ibid.: 18–19.
12 Ibid.: 12.
13 Bhaskar [1979] 1998: 173.
14 See also Hartwig, 'Ecological asymmetry', in Hartwig (ed.) 2007: 152.
15 Bhaskar [1986] 2009: 104.
16 Ibid.: 149.
17 Ibid.: 215.
18 The concept 'rhythm' (in *Dialectic*, 'rhythmic') is deployed in the sense of 'a space-time flow' (see ibid.: 213, 220).
19 Ibid.: 181.
20 E.g. Bhaskar, 'General introduction', in Archer, Collier, Lawson and Norrie (eds) 1998: xvii–xix; Bhaskar and Collier, 'Introduction: explanatory critiques', in ibid.: 385–94.
21 Bhaskar 1989: 187.
22 E.g. Hammersley 2002.
23 Bhaskar [1986] 2009: 142.
24 Ibid.: 201.
25 For an excellent recent account, see Glyn 2006.
26 Bhaskar [1986] 2009: 182. See also Bhaskar [1979] 1998: 60 n. 84, 177 and Bhaskar 1989: 6.
27 Bhaskar [1986] 2009: 207, 209, original emphasis.
28 Bill Bowring, 'Legal studies', in Hartwig (ed.) 2007: 278.
29 Bhaskar 1989: 7.
30 Assiter and Noonan 2007: 179.
31 Ibid.: 189.
32 Hartwig, 'Concrete utopianism', in Hartwig (ed.) 2007: 74–5.
33 Bhaskar 1989: 6.
34 Collier 2008: 279.
35 Bhaskar [1986] 2009: 307–8.
36 The idea of a Tina formation is already present in all but name in Bhaskar [1979] 1998: 19–20, 122.
37 See Bhaskar 1989: chs 3, 8.
38 Bhaskar [1986] 2009: 308.
39 Bhaskar 2002b: 84–5.
40 Bhaskar 1989: 10.
41 Bhaskar [1986] 2009: 250.
42 Ibid.: 25, 291.
43 Ibid.: 292.

6 The axiology of freedom

1 See Bhaskar [1993] 2008: 7n.
2 'When I started out people who had been influenced by my work found themselves frequently marginalised in academic life. They had extreme difficulty in getting critical realist papers published, and I found myself acting as a sort of one person support mechanism for people influenced by my work. It was helped a little by the publication of books by Ted Benton, Russell Keat, John Urry and others – and it began to develop an academic reputation. Nevertheless, there was still a feeling of isolation and fragmentation. Then four of us got together – myself, Ted Benton, Andrew Collier and William Outhwaite – in the early 1980s, and we would begin by discussing important theses

in philosophy and end up by discussing what was wrong with the state of politics or whatever. Out of that was born the *Realism and the Human Sciences* conferences movement. From 1983, we had annual conferences, characterised by friendliness and intellectual stimulation, solidarity and great enjoyment. Not really marked by careerism, position taking, fractious argument, but a real sense of comradeship and an idea of the exploration of truth' (Roy Bhaskar, interviewed by Christopher Norris, *The Philosopher's Magazine* 8 [1999]; reproduced at http://www.raggedclaws.com/criticalrealism/ archive/ rbhaskar_rbi.html). The *Realism and the Human Sciences* conferences continued until 1994. They were the precursors of the International Association for Critical Realism conferences, sponsored initially by the Centre for Critical Realism, that have been held annually since 1997.

3 E.g. Creaven 2007: 37.
4 E.g. Joseph 2002: 13.
5 See Bhaskar [1993] 2008: 47n.
6 See e.g. Davies [2006] 2007: 91–3.
7 E.g. Creaven 2007: 63.
8 Bhaskar [1993] 2008: 377.
9 See ibid.: 344.
10 Ibid.: 49.
11 Arthur 2002: 63 (paraphrasing Hegel's *Encyclopedia Logic*, §63).
12 Collier 2002: 88–114, 162. See also Collier 2008.
13 Hartwig, 'Ont/de-ont', in Hartwig (ed.) 2007: 333. As Tobin Nellhaus has pointed out on the Critical Realism List, the entry is mistaken in postulating an etymological connection between the Bhaskarian concept 'de-ont' (a negative being) and '*deon*' (one of the two Greek roots for 'deontology'). The 'de-' in 'de-ont' is the Latin preposition in its meaning of 'away from', not the Greek conjunctive particle 'de'.
14 Hartwig, 'Alethia', in ibid.: 24.
15 Bhaskar [1993] 2008: 200.
16 Ruth Groff, 'Truth', in Hartwig (ed.) 2007: 487, and Groff 2004: 85.
17 Hegel [1969] 1997: 755–7, original emphasis.
18 Groff 2004: 82–3.
19 Callinicos 2006 devotes a number of pages (173–9) to the critical realist conception of truth without mentioning alethic truth.
20 Bhaskar [1993] 2008: 371.
21 Ibid.: 362. See also Bhaskar 1994: 133, 220, 243.
22 See especially Bhaskar 2000: 37, 56.
23 E.g. Collier 2008.
24 Creaven 2007: 69.
25 Jamie Morgan 2007: 117–25, 121 ('Change is not motivated because actual explanatory mechanisms are not set out which promulgate emancipation'); Alan Norrie 2005: 107. Norrie has since abandoned this view.
26 Callinicos 2006: 158.
27 Callinicos, in Bhaskar and Callinicos 2003: 95.
28 Heikki Patomäki 2001: 158.
29 Callinicos 2006: 159 ('It would seem better to strip away the transcendental superstructure that obscures what is interesting and original in Bhaskar's work and offer it simply as a philosophical presentation of the world as revealed to us by the sciences.')
30 Creaven 2007: 50.
31 Bhaskar [1993] 2008: 333.
32 Bhaskar 1994: 209.
33 Collier 2007: 110–16.
34 Collier 2007: 'Power$_{1,5}$', 114; Morgan 2007: 121; Creaven 2007: 51–2, 59.
35 E.g. Creaven 2007: 53–5.
36 Bhaskar 1994: 154.

37 Norrie forthcoming 2009. We are grateful to Alan Norrie for letting us see a draft of this work.
38 Creaven 2007: 5, 37, 325f.
39 Radha D'Souza, 'Colonialism, neo-colonialism, post-colonialism', in Hartwig (ed.) 2007: 69–70.
40 Bhaskar 1994: 236.
41 Bhaskar [1993] 2008: 104.
42 Mervyn Hartwig, 'Problem', in Hartwig (ed.) 2007: 381–4, 381. The quote from Popper is taken from Morgan 2004: 334. The second quote is from Bhaskar 1994: 9.
43 Bhaskar argues that the problems of philosophy have their source ultimately in the generative separation (alienation) that inaugurates and underpins master–slave society and their 'real resolution' only in its transcendence via transformative praxis. It follows that, if philosophers really want to resolve 'their problems', they should devote their energies to the eudaimonian project. See the discussion in Bhaskar 1994, 'Appendix: explaining philosophies', especially §3, 'On the problems of philosophy and their real resolution', which invokes Marx's eleventh thesis on Feuerbach.
44 Bhaskar [1986] 2009: 13.
45 Bhaskar 1991.
46 The preface to *Plato Etc.* adds a further projected volume to this list: *Critical History of Western Philosophy*. *Dialectic, Plato Etc., Hume, Kant, Hegel, Marx* and *Dialectical Social Theory* were conceived of as a quartet devoted to carrying through 'an anti-Parmenidean revolution, reversing 2500 years of philosophical thought' (Bhaskar 1994: xi). *Philosophical Ideologies* developed the metacritique₂ of irrealism sketched in the Appendix to *Plato Etc.* And it was intended that *Critical History of Western Philosophy* should flesh out the critical history outlined in the last two chapters of the same book.

7 The spiritual turn

1 Cf. Bhaskar 2002c: xi: 'In genealogical terms, elaboration of this moment of non-duality occurred to me by reflection [on] the way in which there was a non-algorithmic moment in any scientific revolution, discovery or even ordinary learning, that is a moment of pure creativity which could not be derived from induction or deduction or any mechanical formula.'
2 See especially p. 76, where 'the driving impulse of the book' is said to be 'love for, and desire to be one with, the divine'.
3 Archer, Collier and Porpora 2004.
4 The propositions and debate are recorded in Bhaskar 2002c: 145–64.
5 Bhaskar 2000: 40–50
6 Bhaskar first deployed the concept of 'structural sin' in *From East to West* (2000). 37.
7 Pope John Paul II, *Solicitudo Rei Socialis [On Social Concern]*, 1987.
8 The interviews were conducted in a hotel dining area.
9 Something of my initial hostility is recorded in Hartwig 2001: 139–65, which, however, may also be viewed as transitional towards my current, far more positive assessment.
10 Callinicos 2006: 158.
11 Bhaskar 2000: 103, n. 10.
12 See Mervyn Hartwig, 'Epistemological dialectic', in Hartwig (ed.) 2007: 176.
13 Seo 2008: 5–28. In *From Science to Emancipation* (p. ix), Bhaskar brackets transcendental dialectical critical realism with critical realism in a context that sharply differentiates critical realism 'in all its forms' from the philosophy of meta-Reality.
14 Collier 2001: 22. Collier does however argue that reincarnation (like resurrection) is compatible with critical realism.
15 Bhaskar 2002a: 364.
16 Bhaskar [1979] 1998: 98.
17 Potter 2006: 93.

18 Bhaskar 2000: 134.
19 Ibid.: 6, n. 5.
20 Mervyn Hartwig, 'Demi-reality', in Hartwig (ed.) 2007: 113.
21 Bhaskar 1994: 123n.
22 Bhaskar [1993] 2008: 64, 73n, 115, 194, 198, 274, 310.
23 Bhaskar 2002d: 68.
24 Hamilton 2007: 92.

8 The philosophy of unity-in-difference

 1 *The Philosophy of Meta-Reality, Volume 2, Between East and West: Comparative Religion and Spirituality in an Age of Global Crisis; The Philosophy of Meta-Reality, Volume 3, Re-enchanting Reality: A Critique of Modernity and Modernisation; The Philosophy of Meta-Reality, Volume 4, Work In: A Manual; Fathoming the Depths of Reality: Savita Singh in Conversation with Roy Bhaskar.*
 2 Seo MinGyu 2008.
 3 See Mervyn Hartwig, 'Introduction' to Bhaskar [1986] 2009.
 4 Bhaskar 2002a: 152–3.
 5 E.g. the deep ecology movement, the proliferating organisations for which the journals *Kosmos* (http://www.kosmosjournal.org/) and *Integral Review* (http://integral-review. org/) provide a focus and the work of Michael Lerner and associates in America, leading to the formation of the Network of Spiritual Progressives in 2005 (www.spiritualpro-gressives.org/). Terry Eagleton's *The Meaning of Life* (2007) is a sign of the times, and the 'new atheism' is in important ways an alarmed response to a resurgent spirituality, albeit focused largely on the fundamentalist right. For accounts of its resurgence, see Benedikter 2006; Berger (ed.) 1999; Job forthcoming 2009; and Heelas and Woodhead 2005. For the renewal of interest in the transcendent with the waning of modernity, see McGrath 2008: ch. 2. For the recent '(re)turn to religion' in philosophy, see e.g. Bradley 2004; Roberts 2008; Davis, Milbank and Žižek (eds) 2005; and Žižek and Milbank 2009. Eagleton 2009, esp. ch. 4, offers a broad contextualisation of resurgent spirituality that chimes in important ways with a critical realist approach.
 6 Mervyn Hartwig, 'Preface', in Hartwig (ed.) 2007: xvi; Seo MinGyu 2008.
 7 Collier, 'Emancipation, social and spiritual', in Archer, Collier and Porpora 2004: 173.
 8 Philip Tew, 'Literary theory', in Hartwig (ed.) 2007: 281.
 9 Bohm 1980. Like Bhaskar, Bohm holds that consciousness is enfolded in all matter in varying degrees of unfoldment. His concept of 'sustained incoherence' arguably antici-pates the theory of the Tina form and demi-real.
10 Bhaskar 2002a: 127.
11 Callinicos 1994. The burden of Callinicos's view on this issue is repeated by Creaven 2007: 42–3.
12 Bhaskar 2002c: xiv; 2002a: xi f., 315f.
13 Bhaskar 2002b: 267ff.
14 Bhaskar 2002a: xiv, xvf.
15 Morgan 2003: 115–46.
16 Ibid.: 117, 135. Morgan correctly sees that Bhaskar's 'characteristic mode of philosophising' is one of immanent critique that departs from premises 'shared by dis-puting positions in some discourse', but overlooks that Archimedes sought a non-immanent vantage point from which to move the world with his fantastic lever.
17 Ibid.: 140.
18 'Imagining ourselves in the environment and simulating identification with aspects of it helps us to negotiate it but does not necessarily indicate that the totality itself has any particular characteristic that facilitates or is necessary to that process' (ibid.: 142).
19 Bhaskar, 2002b: 239 and 2002a: xlviii.

20 Bhaskar 2002a: xxiii–xxiv. Cf. p. 51: 'truth … is a more basic concept than reality'.
21 Ibid.: xx.
22 Ibid.: 318.
23 Bhaskar 2002b: 245.
24 Bhaskar 2002a: xl.
25 Ibid.: xxvii, 153, 156.
26 E.g. ibid.: xlix, 114–15; Bhaskar 2002b: 249, 273–4.
27 Bhaskar 2002a: 87, emphasis added.
28 See especially ibid.: 144, 324–5.
29 Ibid.: 70.
30 See e.g. ibid.: 21, 70.
31 Ibid.: 110.
32 Ibid.: xv n.
33 Ibid.: 117.
34 See ch. 4, 89–90, above. Cf. Bhaskar 2002d: 79–80; and the view of Marcel Proust (whose work aimed to provide readers with 'the means of reading within themselves') that the family servant Françoise 'had an intuitive understanding of my task', 'in a way that all unpretentious people who live alongside us do' (Proust [1927] 2003: 343). In thematising the subjective conditions for learning, meta-Reality arguably achieves at the level of philosophy what Proust achieves at the level of art, while moving beyond the Proustian irrealism that asserts that 'it is only coarse and inaccurate perception which places everything in the object, when everything is in the mind' (ibid.: 221), but simultaneously champions the reality of domains – of the meta-Real ('the essence of things'), of the transcendentally real self, of the past-in-the present, in short of truth as such – that are irreducible to the human mind.
35 Bhaskar 2002a: 122, 135.
36 Ibid.: xvii.
37 Ibid.: 101.
38 Ibid.: xvi, 104.
39 Ibid.: 104, emphasis added.
40 Bhaskar 2002b: 217.
41 Ibid.: 227.
42 Bhaskar 2000: 45; 2002a: liii, 184, 332, 361–2; 2002c: 277.
43 Bhaskar 2002a: 351.
44 Bhaskar 2002b: 93; cf. 273–4.
45 Ibid.: 262.
46 Callinicos 2006: 1, 248f., 257.
47 Bhaskar 2002a: 19n, 90, 187.
48 Seo 2008.
49 See Bhaskar, Frank, Høyer, Næss and Parker (eds) forthcoming 2010.
50 Bhaskar 2002a: xlvi.
51 Bhaskar 2002c: 193.
52 Bhaskar 2002a: li–lii.
53 See e.g. Holloway 2002.
54 Cf. Suzuki 2005.

9 Where do we go from here?

1 Bhaskar and Danermark forthcoming 2009.
2 The comments in this and the next two paragraphs were made in September 2009.
3 Bhaskar, Frank, Høyer, Næss and Parker forthcoming 2010.
4 Foreign Secretary, UK, 2007–.
5 Bhaskar [1993] 2008: 166.

6 Bhaskar [1986] 2009: 180f.
7 Bhaskar 2002c: 13.
8 Ted Benton, 'Foreword', in Frauley and Pearce (eds) 2007: x.
9 Bhaskar 2002c: 43.
10 Ibid.: 201.
11 *Losurdo* 2002. See the review essay by Jan Rehmann (2007).
12 Bhaskar 1989: 1.
13 Thus even Christopher Norris, who is philosophically close to critical realism, can write a whole, in many ways superb, book about Badiou without mentioning Bhaskar or critical realism (which disappears into a melting pot called 'realism'), albeit otherwise ranging across the panoply of contemporary philosophical tendencies. See Norris 2009. Both the affinities and disaffinities between the two systems of thought, which (claim to) revindicate ontology in different ways, could prove illuminating. These include matters as fundamental as the identification of fundamental ontology with the findings of mathematics (Badiou) and its derivation by the method of transcendental critique (Bhaskar); an ontology of infinite multiplicity (Badiou) and a richly differentiated depth-ontology of causal powers (Bhaskar); the distinction between 'being' and 'event' (Badiou) and the 'intransitive' and 'transitive dimensions' (Bhaskar); the 'void' (Badiou) and 'absence' (Bhaskar); ontological and alethic truth (Bhaskar's names for possibly similar notions in Badiou); truth-procedure (Badiou) and epistemological dialectic (Bhaskar); and 'indiscernment' (Badiou) and 'unthought' (Bhaskar). Although Norris evidently thinks otherwise, Bhaskar's *Dialectic* is a book of at least comparable scope and ambition to Badiou's *magnum opus* (*Being and Event* [1988] 2006). Moreover, Bhaskar, but not to date Badiou, thereafter breaks through to another 'breakthrough' – the philosophy of meta-Reality. (Badiou's *Being and Event* and its sequel, *Logiques des mondes* [2006] have been hailed, first by their author and most recently by Žižek, as making an 'ontological breakthrough' [Žižek and Milbank 2009: 90f.].)
14 Bhaskar 2002a: xlix–l, 72.
15 Žižek 2007. John Milbank, the 'radical orthodox' theologian and sparring partner of Žižek in *The Monstrosity of Christ*, agrees, and to that extent reveals himself to be, not so much a thoroughgoing opponent of Žižek's militant atheism, as a complicit dialectical antagonist. He has recently revealingly summarised his disagreement with critical realism as follows. 'The mistakes of Bhaskar and his followers are: (1) To imagine that there are identifiable "laws" more ultimate than the contingency of flux and event. (2) To fail to see that these "laws" are no more than the projections of human instrumental reason and its encountered limits on to an imagined "reality". (3) To fail to see also that the social is in no sense a "reality" over against us, since it is *us*, and therefore entirely coterminous with our endlessly revisable interpretations: the social world both *is* an act of interpretation, and also endlessly subject to reinterpretations which *really* alter how it "is" or how it occurs in time. Thus "Realism" spatialises the real, in such a way that the reality of occurrence (time, history) is obliterated. (4) Still to lust after a false marriage of socialism and scientific objectifying reason.' Milbank 2009: 228 n. 3, original emphasis. Socialism's true marriage, for Milbank, is with Toryism (see his 'Red Toryism is the best hope of a new progressive politics', letter to *The Guardian*, 22 May 2008).
16 Bhaskar [1993] 2008: 327.
17 Hazan 2007: 83.
18 Badiou [1997] 2006. Unlike Bhaskar's, however, Badiou's metaphysics is a (self-avowed) first philosophy that in effect substitutes a mathematical version of the epistemic fallacy for the linguistic fallacy. See especially Badiou, 'Ontology is mathematics', 2004: 1–93.

Bibliography

Agar, Jolyon. 2006. *Rethinking Marxism: From Kant and Hegel to Marx and Engels*. London: Routledge.

Archer, Margaret S. 2000. *Being Human: The Problem of Agency*. Cambridge: Cambridge University Press.

Archer, Margaret S., Andrew Collier, Tony Lawson and Alan Norrie (eds). 1998. *Critical Realism: Essential Readings*. London: Routledge.

Archer, Margaret S., Andrew Collier and Douglas V. Porpora. 2004. *Transcendence: Critical Realism and God*. London: Routledge.

Arthur, Christopher J. 2002. *The New Dialectic and Marx's Capital*. Leiden: Brill.

Ashe, Geoffrey. 1968. *Gandhi: A Study in Revolution*. Heinemann: London.

Assiter, Alison and Jeff Noonan. 2007. 'Human needs: a realist perspective'. *Journal of Critical Realism* 6(2): 173–98.

Badiou, Alain. [1988] 2006. *Being and Event*. London: Continuum.

Badiou, Alain. [1997] 2006. 'The desire for philosophy and the contemporary world'. http://www.lacan.com/badesire.html.

Badiou, Alain. 2004. *Theoretical Writings*, ed. and trans. R. Brassier and A. Toscano. London: Continuum.

Badiou, Alain. 2006. *Logiques des mondes*. Paris: Editions du Seuil.

Benedikter, Roland. 2006. 'Postmodern spirituality: a dialogue in five parts'. *Integral Review*, May. http://www.integralworld.net/benedikter.html.

Berger, Peter L. (ed.). 1999. *The Desecularisation of the World: Resurgent Religion and World Politics*. Michigan: Eerdmans.

Bhaskar, Roy. [1975] 2008. *A Realist Theory of Science*, with an introduction by Mervyn Hartwig. London: Routledge.

Bhaskar, Roy. [1979] 1998. *The Possibility of Naturalism: A Philosophical Critique of the Contemporary Human Sciences*. London: Routledge.

Bhaskar, Roy. [1986] 2009. *Scientific Realism and Human Emancipation*, with an introduction by Mervyn Hartwig. London: Routledge.

Bhaskar, Roy. 1989. *Reclaiming Reality: A Critical Introduction to Contemporary Philosophy*. London: Verso.

Bhaskar, Roy. 1991. *Philosophy and the Idea of Freedom*. Oxford, and Cambridge, MA: Blackwell.

Bhaskar, Roy. [1993] 2008. *Dialectic: The Pulse of Freedom*, with an introduction by Mervyn Hartwig. London: Routledge.

Bhaskar, Roy. [1994] 2009. *Plato Etc.: The Problems of Philosophy and their Resolution*, with an introduction by Mervyn Hartwig. London: Verso.

Bhaskar, Roy. 2000. *From East to West: Odyssey of a Soul*. London: Routledge.

Bhaskar, Roy. 2002a. *The Philosophy of Meta-Reality*, Volume 1, Meta-Reality: Creativity, Love and Freedom. New Delhi, Thousand Oaks, London: Sage.

Bhaskar, Roy. 2002b. *Reflections on meta-Reality: Transcendence, Emancipation and Everyday Life*. New Delhi, Thousand Oaks, London: Sage.

Bhaskar, Roy. 2002c. *From Science to Emancipation: Alienation and the Actuality of Enlightenment*. New Delhi, Thousand Oaks, London: Sage.

Bhaskar, Roy. 2002d. 'The philosophy of meta-Reality, part 2: agency, perfectibility, novelty', interview by Mervyn Hartwig. *Journal of Critical Realism* 1(1): 67–93.

Bhaskar, Roy and Alex Callinicos. 2003. 'Marxism and critical realism: a debate'. *Journal of Critical Realism* 1(2): 88–114.

Bhaskar, Roy and Berth Danermark. 2009. *Interdisciplinarity and Well-Being: A Study in Applied Critical Realism*. London: Routledge.

Bhaskar, Roy, Cheryl Frank, Karl Georg Høyer, Petter Næss and Jenneth Parker (eds). 2010. *Interdisciplinarity and Climate Change: Transforming Knowledge and Practice for our Global Future*. London: Routledge.

Blavatsky, Helena. 1995. *The Key to Theosophy: Being a Clear Exposition, in the Form of Question and Answer, of the Ethics, Science, and Philosophy for the Study of which the Theosophical Society has been Founded*. Pasadena, CA: Theosophical University Press.

Bohm, David. 1980. *Wholeness and the Implicate Order*. London: Routledge.

Boucher, Geoff. 2008. *The Charmed Circle of Ideology: A Critique of Laclau and Mouffe, Butler and Žižek*. Melbourne: Re.Press. Open Access: http://www.re-press.org/book-files/OA_Version_9780980544046_Charmed_Circle_of_Ideology.pdf.

Bradley, Arthur. 2004. *Negative Theology and Modern French Philosophy*. London: Routledge.

Brodersen, Momme. 1996. *Walter Benjamin: A Biography*, trans. Malcolm R. Green and Ingrida Ligers. London: Verso.

Bunge, Mario. 1977 and 1979. *Treatise on Basic Philosophy*, Volume III: Ontology: The Furniture of the World; Volume IV: Ontology: A World of Systems. Dordrecht: Reidel.

Callinicos, Alex. 1994. 'Critical realism and beyond: Roy Bhaskar's dialectic'. Working Paper 7. Department of Politics, University of York.

Callinicos, Alex. 2006. *The Resources of Critique*. Cambridge: Polity.

Cohen, G. A. 1978. *Karl Marx's Theory of History: A Defence*. Oxford: Clarendon.

Collier, Andrew. 2001. 'The soul and Roy Bhaskar's thought'. *Alethia* 4(2): 19–23.

Collier, Andrew. 2002. 'Dialectic in Marxism and critical realism'. In Andrew Brown, Steve Fleetwood and John M. Roberts (eds) *Critical Realism and Marxism*. London: Routledge.

Collier, Andrew. 2007. 'Power$_{1.5}$ and the weakness of liberalism'. *Journal of Critical Realism* 6(1): 110–16.

Collier, Andrew. 2008. 'Philosophy and politics: an interview with Andrew Collier, part I', interview by Gideon Calder. *Journal of Critical Realism* 7(2): 276–96.

Creaven, Sean. 2007. *Emergentist Marxism: Dialectical Philosophy and Social Theory*. London: Routledge.

Davies, Paul. [2006] 2007. *The Goldilocks Enigma*. London: Penguin.

Davis, Creston, John Milbank and Slavoj Žižek (eds). 2005. *Theology and the Political: The New Debate*. Durham, NC: Duke University Press.

Dean, Kathryn. 2007. '"Mind" and its matters: an explanatory critique of the mind-body problem'. Unpublished manuscript, London.

Eagleton, Terry. 2007. *The Meaning of Life*. OUP: Oxford.

Eagleton, Terry. 2009. *Reason, Faith and Revolution: Reflections on the God Debate*. New Haven, CT: Yale University Press.

Farnell, Brenda. 2010. *On the Move: Dynamic Embodiment for Social Theory*. London: Routledge, forthcoming.

Frauley, Jon and Frank Pearce (eds). 2007. *Critical Realism and the Social Sciences: Heterodox Elaborations*. Toronto: University of Toronto Press.

Glyn, Andrew. 2006. *Capitalism Unleashed*. Oxford: OUP.

Groff, Ruth. 2004. *Critical Realism, Post-Positivism and the Possibility of Knowledge*. London: Routledge.

Groff, Ruth. 2009. 'Editorial: introduction to the special issue [on causal powers]'. *Journal of Critical Realism* 8(3): 267–76.

Hamilton, Clive. 2007. 'Building on Kyoto'. *New left Review* 45: 91–103.

Hammersley, Martyn. 2002. 'Research as emancipatory: the case of Bhaskar's critical realism', *Journal of Critical Realism* 1(1): 33–48.

Harré, Rom. 2009. 'Saving critical realism'. *Journal for the Theory of Social Behaviour* 39(2): 129–43.

Harré, Rom and E. H. Madden. 1975. *Causal Powers: A Theory of Natural Necessity*. Oxford: Basil Blackwell.

Hartwig, Mervyn. 2001. 'New left, new age, new paradigm? Roy Bhaskar's *From East to West*'. *Journal for the Theory of Social Behaviour* 31(2): 139–65.

Hartwig, Mervyn (ed.). 2007. *Dictionary of Critical Realism*. London: Routledge.

Hazan, Eric. 2007. 'Under new management'. *New left Review* 48: 59–83.

Heelas, Paul and Linda Woodhead with Benjamin Seel, Bronislaw Szerszynski and Karin Tusting. 2005. *The Spiritual Revolution: Why Religion is Giving Way to Spirituality*. Oxford: Blackwell.

Hegel, G. W. F. 1969/1997. *Science of Logic*, trans. A. V. Miller. New York: Humanities.

Holloway, John. 2002. *Change the World without Taking Power: The Meaning of Revolution Today*. London: Pluto.

Jameson, Fredric. 1984. 'Postmodernism, or the cultural logic of late capitalism'. *New left Review* 146: 53–92.

Jessop, Bob. 2005. 'Critical realism and the strategic-relational approach'. *New Formations* 56: 40–53.

Job, Sebastian. 2009. 'Rise of a global God-image? Spiritual internationalists, the international left, and the idea of human progress'. *Third World Quarterly* 30(1): 205–26.

Joseph, Jonathan. 2002. *Hegemony: A Realist Analysis*. London: Routledge.

Kran, Anne Pernille. 2010. 'Comparing causality in Freudian reasoning and critical realism'. *Journal of Critical Realism* 9(1), forthcoming.

Losurdo, Dominic. 2002. *Nietzsche, il ribelle aristocratico. Biografia intellettuale e bilancio critico*. Torino: Bollati Boringhieri.

McGrath, Alister E. 2008. *The Open Secret: A New Vision of Natural Theology*. London: Blackwell.

Milbank, John. 2008. 'Red Toryism is the best hope of a new progressive politics', letter to *The Guardian*, 22 May.

Milbank, John. 2009. *Being Reconciled: Ontology and Pardon*. London: Routledge.

Morgan, Jamie. 2003. 'What is meta-Reality? Alternative interpretations of the argument'. *Journal of Critical Realism* 1(2): 115–46.

Morgan, Jamie. 2004. 'The nature of a transcendental argument: toward a critique of *Dialectic: The Pulse of Freedom*'. *Journal of Critical Realism* 3(2): 305–40.

Morgan, Jamie. 2005. 'An alternative argument for transcendental realism based on an immanent critique of Kant', review of *Kant's Transcendental Proof of Realism*, by Kenneth R. Westphal. *Journal of Critical Realism* 4(2): 435–60.

Morgan, Jamie. 2007. 'The merits of enumeration: powers of power and the political'. *Journal of Critical Realism* 6(1): 117–25.

Norrie, Alan. 2005. 'Theorising "spectrality": ontology and ethics in Derrida and Bhaskar'. *New Formations* 56: 96–108.

Norrie, Alan. 2009. *Dialectic and Difference: Dialectical Critical Realism and the Grounds of Justice*. London: Routledge.

Norris, Christopher. 2009. *Badiou's 'Being and Event'*. London: Continuum.

Patomäki, Heikki. 2001. *After International Relations: Critical Realism and the (Re)Construction of World Politics*. London: Routledge.

Potter, Garry. 2006. 'Re-opening the wound: against God and Bhaskar'. *Journal of Critical Realism* 5(1): 92–109.

Pratten, Stephen. 2009. 'Critical realism and causality: tracing the Aristotelian legacy'. *Journal for the Theory of Social Behaviour* 39(2): 189–218.

Proust, Marcel. [1927] 2003. *Finding Time Again (In Search of Lost Time 6)*. London: Penguin.

Rehmann, Jan. 2007. 'Nietzsche, the aristocratic rebel'. *Historical Materialism* 15(2): 173–93.

Roberts, John. 2008. 'The "returns to religion": messianism, Christianity and the revolutionary tradition. Part I: "Wakefulness to the future", Part II: The Pauline Tradition'. *Historical Materialism* 16(2): 59–84 and 16(3): 77–103.

Seo MinGyu. 2008. 'Bhaskar's philosophy as anti-anthropism: a comparative study of Eastern and Western thought'. *Journal of Critical Realism* 7(1): 5–28.

Timpanaro, Sebastian. 1976. *On Materialism*. London: New left Books.

Tyfield, David. 2007a. 'Chasing fairies or serious ontological business? Tracking down the transcendental argument'. In C. Lawson, J. Latsis and N. Martins (eds) *Contributions to Social Ontology*. London: Routledge.

Tyfield, David. 2007b. 'The debate about transcendental arguments in critical realism'. Presentation to the seminar launch of Dictionary of Critical Realism, Institute of Education, London, 17 March. http://criticalrealism.wikispaces.com/Critical+Realism+Media.

Tyfield, David. 2008. 'Review' of J. Agar, *Rethinking Marxism: from Kant and Hegel to Marx and Engels* (London: Routledge, 2006). *Journal of Critical Realism* 7(2): 330–7.

Westphal, Kenneth R. 2004. *Kant's Transcendental Proof of Realism*. Cambridge: Cambridge University Press.

White, Patrick. [1966] 1969. *The Solid Mandala*. Harmondsworth: Penguin.

Wikipedia, 'Theosophy'. http://en.wikipedia.org/wiki/Theosophy.

Wikipedia, 'Wainwright, Hilary'. http://en.wikipedia.org/wiki/Hilary_Wainwright.

Will, David. 1980. 'Psychoanalysis as a human science'. *British Journal of Medical Psychology* 53: 201–11.

Will, David. 1986. 'Psychoanalysis and the new philosophy of science'. *International Review of PsychoAnalysis* 13: 163–73.

World Health Organisation. 1980. *International Classification of Impairments, Disabilities and Handicaps*. Geneva: World Health Organisation.

Žižek, Slavoj. 2007. 'On Alain Badiou and *Logiques des mondes*'. http://www.lacan.com/zizbadman.

Žižek, Slavoj and John Milbank. 2009. *The Monstrosity of Christ: Paradox or Dialectic?* ed. Creston Davis. Cambridge, MA: MIT Press.

Index

234   *Index*

Made in the USA
Coppell, TX
12 November 2022

86226532R10138